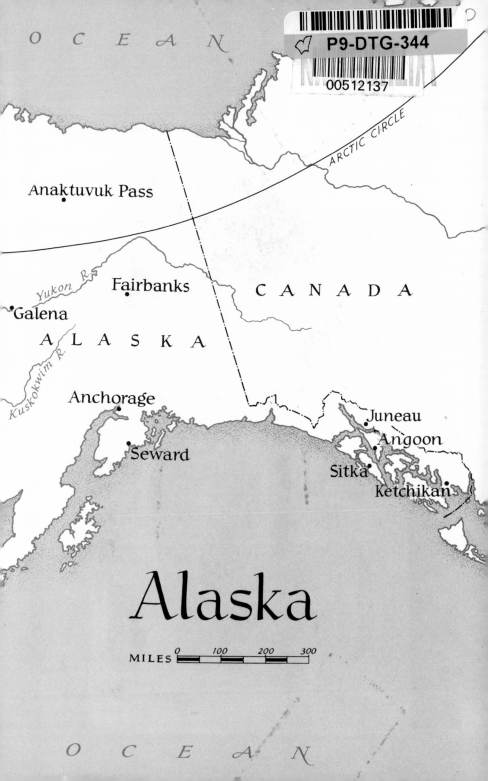

O C E A N

ARCTIC CIRCLE

Anaktuvuk Pass

Yukon R.

Fairbanks

C A N A D A

Galena

A L A S K A

Kuskokwim R.

Anchorage

Juneau

Angoon

Seward

Sitka

Ketchikan

# Alaska

MILES  0    100    200    300

O C E A N

# AND THE LAND PROVIDES

# And the Land

## ALASKAN NATIVES

**ANCHOR PRESS / DOUBLEDAY**

# Provides

## IN A YEAR OF TRANSITION

## by LAEL MORGAN

**Doubleday & Company, Inc., Garden City, New York
1974**

Library of Congress Cataloging in Publication Data

Morgan, Lael.
    And the land provides.

    1. Eskimos—Alaska.   2. Indians of North America—
Alaska.   3. Aleuts.   I. Title.
E99.E7M82      970.4'98
ISBN: 0-385-00081-2
Library of Congress Catalog Card Number 73–20523

# Preface

ALASKAN NATIVES IN A YEAR OF
TRANSITION

Back in 1965 a man representing a pulp mill in southeastern Alaska spoke to the Juneau Chamber of Commerce to tell us what was wrong with the Indians. His company had chosen the area, he explained, not only for the lush forest but because it had a lot of unemployed Tlíngits. It looked like a good labor market and had worked out well in the beginning. All the Indians signed on and proved to be excellent workers.

"But in two or three months, when those Tlingits had a little more money than they needed, they quit. Went off to hunt and fish," he reported, still struck with the incredibility of it all. "And then, three or four months later, when they were broke, they came back and wanted to go to work for us again!

"Now, what we've got to teach these people is that they have to work an eight-hour day, a five-day week and a fifty-week year."

As a reporter for the local paper, I took it all down and I sympathized with the speaker. Industry is hard to come by in Alaska and hard to run. But it also occurred to me to wonder who had the right philosophy—the pulp mill speaker or the Indians?

A few months later I quit my job—spent a season camping and hunting—and decided right was on the side of the Indians. I believe it even more today in the light of our national struggle with the four-day work week and the dilemmas of utilizing leisure time, but my interest has traveled well beyond the realm of the southeastern pulp mill.

Alaska had about 43,000 aboriginal people when I first moved to Anchorage in 1959 but it was very hard to meet them.

Most of the jobs and the white people were located in three major cities (Anchorage, Fairbanks, and Juneau), while most of the natives lived by subsistence hunting and fishing in remote areas with no highways. I couldn't afford the fare to tour their villages and it was even more prohibitive for jobless natives to get to the cities. When necessary, the Public Health Service sent them into town for medical treatment or a village raised enough cash to dispatch its best dog-sled musher to compete in city races. We occasionally encountered sophisticated Eskimos or Indians in business or at cocktail parties but they were so well educated they didn't seem much different from the whites, and the dead-enders, who wound up in city bars and passed out on city sidewalks, weren't representative.

Like most newcomers to the state, I didn't have much cause to think about the natives until I got roped into doing some publicity for a heart clinic in Anchorage. It was run in conjunction with the United States Public Health Service which sent native children with heart problems beyond the skills of public health nurses in the bush to be studied by a group of imported specialists. The youngsters were boarded in private homes in Anchorage for the duration of treatment and my assignment was to photograph them.

They were the most beautiful, well-behaved children I'd ever seen. Most of them were quite young, thousands of miles from home, with no understanding of English; but they seldom cried or acted cranky. Some of the babies arrived wrapped only in newspapers because, I was told, they rode inside their mothers' parkas until they were two or three years old and usually needed no clothing of their own. My favorite child, in his early talking stage, had lived mainly on seal meat and whale blubber and was intrigued with the fried chicken his foster parents fed him. He spoke mostly in Eskimo but anything that was good was "fried chicken" in his vocabulary and I wondered how he'd adjust to his wildlife diet again.

I learned that he came from a culture where children are highly prized and that he had a mother who loved him. I was also told that the maximum average age he could hope to at-

tain was twenty-seven under the health conditions that existed
in his area and that the birth and death rate of Alaskan natives
was higher than anywhere else in the world including India.

Later, when I became aware that Alaska didn't have enough
expertise or even enough working citizens to run the state
properly, I thought again of the native people and wondered
why they weren't more active citizens. Outsiders were often
malcontents, complaining about the weather and unhappy with
the remoteness of the place. The natives, on the other hand,
liked the country. Why in hell didn't they help run it?

In the spring of 1965 I visited Ruth and Cameron Edmond-
son, old friends who had moved to Port Graham, a small settlement of Aleuts on the south-central Alaskan coast. The Edmondsons were the only whites in the village with the exception
of the school teacher and a weathered old trader. They were
well accepted and I was welcomed as one of their family.

It was fun living among the Aleuts. Their English was halting
but there was nothing wrong with their thought process and
they had a keen sense of humor. With an Aleut accent, my
name came out "Lethal Bargain" instead of Lael Morgan and
the Edmondsons insisted it was an astute assessment of my
personality, not a mispronunciation. The Aleuts did, indeed,
size me up in short order but the results were compassion, not
ridicule.

I was broke at the time and after a few weeks with the Edmondsons, I moved to nearby Seldovia to work in a crab cannery where, because the season was late in starting, I found myself stranded with only ten dollars and a book called *Edible
Wild Plants of Alaska.* One day some Port Graham Aleuts un-
expectedly came to visit just as I was bringing in some edible
wild greens. I offered them coffee. They noticed it was the last
of the can and made tactful inquiries. I was apparently the first
really broke white person they'd ever met and it created a
bond. One young girl, who kept in touch later, never wrote me
without enclosing blank stationery for my answer, assuming, I
guess, that I'd never reverse my finances. But they were careful

not to embarrass me with their sympathy. They knew the in-
dignity of poverty all too well.

Just before I'd moved to Port Graham, two of its youngsters
had died for want of food. One, a hungry toddler, had wandered along the beach, eaten a rotten salmon and died of food
poisoning. Another was apparently neglected when his mother
went on a drinking bout. The accounts left considerably more
mark on my consciousness than had the mortality statistics of
the heart clinic. I also got a close look at our native education
system and was appalled.

The Port Graham teacher had not realized (even after running a school there three years) that the children spoke Aleut
in the home. She simply assumed that, because they didn't
speak English well, they were stupid and treated them accordingly.

"If I came up to you and tried to talk to you on a street in
Seattle, I guess you'd run," speculated Walter Meganack, Port
Graham chief. "But I'm not so dumb."

He wasn't and neither were his youngsters, but they didn't
have much chance of proving it under the going system. Anyone who did manage to make it through the village grammar
school was forced to leave home to attend high school in a
larger city. Few bridged the cultural gap and those who did
found themselves woefully ill prepared scholastically.

After the crab season closed I got a job as a reporter in
Juneau and one of my first assignments was to photograph native children who stopped there en route from their Arctic
homes to Indian schools outside the state. They were being
sent out, I understood, because there were no education facilities in their villages, but some of them were so young and so
sad that I was haunted by the pictures I got.

Juneau at the time was two towns. There was Juneau proper
in the hills where state employees and the Chamber of Commerce types settled and there was the tattered old Indian village on the tide flats where most of the natives resided. It
wasn't segregation exactly. There were no signs, ordinances, or
men with white sheets. In fact, Juneau had one of the few

really integrated school systems in the state. But somehow
things seemed to get sifted down to native and white and the
natives always ended up in the flats.

A year later, in 1966, I moved north to work for the Fairbanks *News-Miner* and got a close look at the justice a native
could expect from our court system. Fairbanks attracted a lot
of Eskimos and Indian visitors who often tangled with the law
when touring the bright lights. The majority of these natives
spoke little English and were bewildered by their arrests.
There were no interpreters and very little attempt was made to
explain citizen's rights to them.

Once I heard a compassionate arresting officer testify that
he'd picked up a young native girl for drunkenness when the
temperature was 50° below zero simply to keep her from freezing to death.

"Her speech was slurred, her vision was blurred, there was
frost in her hair but her attitude was generally good," he reported.

"She goes to jail," the judge decided and I got so upset I
switched from police reporting to covering the legislature.

That was a good year, 1967, the year of the "Young Turks"
and militants, when native leaders emerged throughout the
state, demanding equal rights and pushing to get a foothold.
They said their Alaskan land had been taken from them without compensation or treaty and they still laid claim to it.

In the bush there was little talk of land claims, for the people
were still too busy dealing with the problems of survival.

"If I don't get a rabbit today, my family will not eat," an
Eskimo told me one morning. Hand to mouth it was, almost
everywhere in the bush. Yet somehow they kept it together,
backed their native leaders who (with hardly more financial
resources than the rabbit hunters had) lobbied Congress.

Late in 1968 I decided I had gotten too involved with the
native problems and that I had nothing on which to gauge
Alaska's situation. I'd never seen a race riot or a student demonstration and I needed perspective, so I left Alaska. The job I
landed with the Los Angeles *Times* proved ideal. Through it

I met Margaret Mead, Angela Davis, Mrs. Richard Nixon, Southern California Birchers, Mexican farm migrants, Middle American housewives, and bona fide freaks.

Then, in 1971, it became obvious there would be no trans-Alaska oil pipeline until the land claims were settled and so oil men formed a weird alliance with the natives. The fight for settlement was coming to a head and I wanted to be in Alaska for the final rounds. I wrote Howard Rock, the Eskimo editor of Alaska's only native newspaper, *Tundra Times*, for whom I'd often freelanced, and he hired me for the summer.

The day I arrived in Alaska I found Rock being interviewed by Ford Foundation men who were considering making an education grant to Alaskan natives.

"Just who is the native leader that we should contact?" they asked him. "Someone who can tell us what the native people want in the way of education."

Patiently Rock explained there was no single native leader nor a single criterion for native needs. That the Northern Eskimos wanted one thing and the interior people wanted another and that the Athabascans and Aleuts and Tlingits lived in separate worlds. But the Foundation people never seemed to grasp this and I knew we still had a long way to go to educate the public.

We got some good stories that season. Native legislators had formed the "Ice Bloc," a coalition with white rural legislators, and walked away with a chunk of the state budget that left urban opposition in shock. The Bureau of Indian Affairs sponsored an Eskimo dance class in their Kotzebue school and the Kotzebue church opposed it (unsuccessfully) on the grounds it fostered shamanism. State and federal housing officials discovered that the Eskimos in Nome for whom they'd built a low-income housing project were too poor to pay the minimum rent and went in search of a "better class of poor" until *Tundra Times* printed the story and the matter was reconsidered.

The city of Fairbanks was inspired by Indian leaders to remove its "No Loitering" signs which, in an analysis of arrest records, appeared to have applied only to natives. And the tiny

Eskimo village of Kivalina sued the State of Alaska and forced it to provide a high school education at home for youngsters who failed to survive the shuffle of schools outside.

By August 1971 I was sure the land claims would be settled. It looked so good that a few white friends of ten years' standing began acting cool to me or charging outright that I was helping "give away our lands" to the natives. Others, including a number of natives who'd never been interested before, suddenly realized there might be money in the land claims and scrambled to align themselves with "the cause." The politics of the settlement became so unpleasant that I headed back to California, but the more I thought about 1972, the more interested I became. It would be the turning point, the year of transition for the native people. After that, Alaska would never be the same, and who would record the change? The best native writer-photographer I knew had been drafted and was overseas. *Tundra Times* kept Rock and his one-man staff busy seven days a week. Besides, most natives were bound to encounter hostility from people of other cultures (and even from different native groups—Indians still tread lightly in Eskimo territory and vice versa). But because I'd started covering native issues before most white reporters were interested, natives in many areas had come to trust me. They would help, I was sure, in trying to capture a comprehensive picture of transition.

From touring Indian reservations outside the state, I knew that Alaska's poorest native people were in better shape—mentally and physically—than the majority of "stateside" Indians. Generally, Alaskan Indians didn't live on reservations and had less government control. Perhaps my assessment of how they'd managed would help other minority people. But what about expertise? I had no training as a sociologist or anthropologist. Each year I spent covering native issues I found myself with more questions and fewer answers.

Finally, I recalled an encounter I had had with a cheerfully drunken Indian on the Fort Apache Reservation, in Whiteriver, Arizona. I'd been waiting two days to meet the busy tribal

chairman and, to fill in time, had interviewed his business manager who was white. As I came from his office, the drunk wavered forth, planted the toes of his shoes squarely on the top of
my shoes, looked me in the eye, and asked, "If you want to
know what an Indian thinks, why don't you ask an Indian?"

The approach could be as simple as that. Using it as a basis
for my argument, I wrote the Alicia Patterson Foundation for
a fellowship to chronicle the transition of the Alaskan natives
from a subsistence to a money economy. While I was waiting
for the decision of the Patterson judges, one of them, Pyke
Johnson of Doubleday, called to say he would be interested in
a book along the lines of my proposal and I started collecting
my arctic gear.

The Patterson Foundation secured funding for the venture
through the Rockefeller Foundation. There would be no salary
but they would pay expenses. My obligation to them was to
write monthly newsletters which would be available free to
newspapers and researchers.

Congress also co-operated, voting that same month (December 1971) for a land claims settlement on Alaskan natives of
$465 million in federal funds, $500 million in state mineral
rights, and 40 million acres of land. And so I found myself at
the beginning of 1972 in the Brooks Range, 125 miles north of
the Arctic Circle, in the Eskimo settlement of Anaktuvuk Pass.
My assignment was to stay with the people, eating what they
ate, living as they lived, to try to capture their point of view—
which is where this book begins.

# Contents

# Introduction

During the ice ages when the seas lowered, a tough breed of Mongoloid hunters—veterans of the harsh Siberian winters—are believed to have crossed from Asia to Alaska on a narrow bridge of land. Some may also have come by boat through the Bering Strait, for the widest expanse of open sea at one point between the continents is less than twenty-five miles, with convenient islands to serve as way stations to the New World.

The earliest traces of Alaskan settlement unearthed by scientists have been dated back about eleven thousand years, but beyond that there is little agreement as to when or how the nomads established themselves in the savage, virgin country. The Alaskan terrain varies from winter-darkened steppes in the frozen north to nearly impenetrable mountain ranges in the interior, to lush rain forests along the southeastern coasts. Alaskan natives speak five distinctly different languages with hundreds of variations. Their traditions and cultures differ widely and their past is as misty as the clouds that hang perpetually from the lofty mountains and the ice fogs that drift about the frozen tundra.

Alaskan legends, passed down from generation to generation for thousands of years without benefit of written language, tell of the ice ages and the flood. Man did not always walk upright, they say. Once mammoth creatures roamed the forests. The whale originated from an animal similar to the deer and the deer of old were hornless, flesh-eating creatures.

As far back as the legends go, the Eskimos of the north were enemies of the Indians of the interior. In the southwest, along the Kuskokwim River, the Eskimos assimilated their rivals, while the Indians established strongholds along the Yukon, rimming Cook Inlet, and to the south. But the larger war was always with the climate, which ranks as one of the harshest in the world, and over it the Alaskans triumphed, adapting to it more admirably than any other people have to theirs.

The Eskimos of the Arctic, the Inupiat, developed ingenious fur clothing so impervious to cold that modern science could improve but little upon it. They invented sun glasses to protect them from snow blindness and learned to kindle fire by sparking iron pyrites with quartz. On the coast they devised methods of hunting off the treacherous ice floes which enabled them to take bowhead whales of fifty to sixty tons. They discovered they could kill the powerful polar bear by feeding him lethally bent pieces of whale bone encased in balls of blubber and, inland, they pursued the fleet, fickle caribou with snares and bows and arrows.

They built sod houses so snug they needed only the heat of stone seal-oil lamps to make them habitable in the dead of winter. They believed in good and evil spirits and laid their dead to rest ceremoniously on platforms above the ground. They also learned to tell time by the sun and the stars, established twelve months to the year and could count into the hundreds.

Their Eskimo cousins of the southwest, the Yupik people, were less skilled as hunters for there were no mammoth whales or polar bear to challenge them and the climate was not as severe as that of the high Arctic. But because living was easier and they were less nomadic than their northern neighbors, they developed a more sophisticated sociocultural structure evolving around a central kashgee—men's living quarters—in every village.

The Yupik Eskimos wore colorful bird-skin parkas and fish-skin boots as well as fur clothing, and they ornamented themselves with belts of caribou teeth and bone or ivory labrets, or plugs, which they wore in holes cut under the bottom lip. The Yupiks' religion was strong, under the leadership of shamans. Their numerical system went only to ten and they were regarded by many as the most backward Alaskans, but they were the only native people to devise their own written language after the coming of the white man.

Further southwest, on a chain of 144 islands, lived the Aleuts whose culture was alien to that of the Eskimo although their language is thought to have come from the same roots. The Aleuts took their living from the sea, paddling marvelously engineered skin boats thousands of miles over perpetually stormy waters to capture sea animals, with bone- and stone-tipped darts and harpoons. They could navigate by the stars, tell time, and count. They perfected cleverly sewn waterproof garments from the intestines of sea mammals and also fashioned clothing of fur, bird skins, and woven grasses.

They believed in many spirits and sometimes mummified their dead. They developed an intricate knowledge of medicine which included suturing and the use of certain plants as cures. They learned to make fire with sulfur and quartz, but because they were extraordinarily tough, they lived in heatless houses and often traveled through winter snows without shoes.

They organized loosely structured governments headed by a toyon, or chief, on each island and warred constantly with one another.

The Athabascan Indians, who populated the interior of Alaska to the shores of Cook Inlet, were restless hunters, constantly following the game, with only a minimum of tribal organization. They wore clothing of deerskins and parkas of marten and beaver. In summer they traveled by birchbark canoes and in winter in light birchwood sleds pulled by dogs or on cleverly crafted snowshoes.

They hunted with bows and arrows and snares and lived occasionally in underground houses but more often in skin tents. Their religion consisted mostly of songs and speeches addressed to the birds and beasts and imaginary creatures, when they sought assistance in performing cures of the sick. In some areas they left the dead where they fell and in others the bodies were cremated.

The Athabascan language was intricate with many variations and, strangely, of the same stock as the language of the

Navajos who lived in the southwestern United States. The Athabascans were the minority people in Alaska, but they grew in strength and were much feared as fighters.

The most sophisticated Alaskan natives were the Tlingit Indians of the southeast who, because of bountiful fish and game and a relatively mild climate, had considerable leisure time to develop a strong tribal system and some extraordinary skills.

Their nation was divided into two main clans and numerous smaller ones, ruled by strong chiefs and shamans. One third of their population was made up of slaves taken through warfare. Their weapons, which included copper knives, were superior to those of other Alaskans and they were merciless warriors.

The Tlingits lived in ornamented wooden tribal houses in well-ordered villages and traveled in fast-moving wooden canoes which could accommodate up to fifty warriors. They learned to spin and weave the wool of the mountain goat, to carve wood and stone, and work copper, and to create remarkably fine music.

The southeasterners judged a man's worth by accumulated wealth, and their chiefs were forever trying to outdo one another in staging elaborate celebrations. They also ornamented their persons with symbols of wealth including large wooden, ivory, or metal labrets worn through cuts in the bottom lip and metal and shell jewelry.

Before the coming of the white man, the population of Alaska is estimated to have been about 66,900, with 20,000 Eskimos in the northwest and interior and 12,000 in the southwest and Bristol Bay region; 16,000 Aleuts; 6,900 Athabascans; and 12,000 Tlingits.

Despite the vast distances that separated these people, there was growing commerce between them as well as trade with Siberia. Iron was becoming known to them through the Siberian natives who traded with the Russians, and their cultures were advancing.

"Left alone, the natives of Alaska might have unfolded into

as bright a civilization as that of Europe," speculated Hubert Howe Bancroft, a historian who in the 1800s studied the remnants of Alaska's culture. "They were already well advanced, and still rapidly advancing towards it when they were so unmercifully stricken down."

It was Vitus Bering, a Dane on a mission of exploration for Russia, who put Alaska on the maps of the world in 1741. It was an era when powerful nations were discovering and subduing pagans in the name of Christianity and for profit, and Russia, a late starter, was anxious to make up for lost time. Peter the Great personally had put together the first Bering mission in 1725, completing final plans only a few days before his death.

"Now that the country is in no danger from enemies, we should strive to win her glory along the lines of arts and science," he charged the leader of the party. And if gold was discovered in the process, so much the better!

Bering failed to sight the American mainland on that trip. In June 1741 he sailed with two ships and seventy-seven men from the Kamchatka peninsula, on the Siberian coast. Alexei Chirikov, the captain of his second ship, was the first to sight land, spotting the mountainous, forested coast near Cape Addington in southeastern Alaska on July 15. Three days later he sent eleven armed men ashore in Tlingit country for water and, after waiting five days for their return, dispatched four more including a calker and carpenter equipped for boat repair. These men, too, disappeared. Later two canoes of natives made a cautious reconnaissance of the Russian ship but could not be persuaded to come aboard and Chirikov, convinced disaster had fallen his landing parties, sailed home.

Bering first sighted the 18,000-foot peak of Mount St. Elias a day after Chirikov's discovery and sent men ashore on nearby Kayak Island to secure water. Exploration was brief for the crew was beginning to succumb to scurvy and Bering was justifiably anxious about the weather, but Georg Steller, a German naturalist accompanying Bering, did have time to make history's first written record of an Alaskan settlement.

"I had not gone more than a verst along the beach before I ran across signs of people and their doings," he reported. "Under a tree I found an old piece of log hollowed out in the shape of a trough, in which, a couple of hours before, the savages, for lack of pots and vessels, had cooked their meat by means of red-hot stones, just as the Kamchadals [Siberian natives] did formerly. The bones, some of them with bits of meat and showing signs of having been roasted at the fire, were scattered about where the eaters had been sitting . . . There were also strewn about the remains of yukola, or pieces of dried fish, which, as in Kamchatka, has to serve the purpose of bread at all meals. There were also great number of very large scallops over eight inches across, and also blue mussels similar to those found in Kamchatka, and, no doubt, eaten raw as the custom is there . . . I discovered further beside the tree, on which there were still live coals, a wooden apparatus for making fire, of the same nature as those used in Kamchatka . . . From all this I think I may conclude that the inhabitants of this American coast are of the same origin as the Kamchadals, with whom they agree completely in such peculiar customs and utensils."

Without further exploration, Bering headed home but storms delayed him and he was forced to land again for water. In the process, his ship was wrecked and Bering, with thirty of his crew, died before the vessel could be rebuilt to sail for Russia. The survivors reached home in fair shape, however, with a collection of lush, rich sea-otter pelts from the New World that would assure Bering fame.

From the return of Bering's ship in 1742 until the late 1780s, hordes of buccaneering Russian enterprisers plundered Alaskan territory, forcing the natives to pay fur tribute to them or enslaving them.

"Fortunately for the Indians of the north, it was contrary to the interests of the white people to kill them in order to obtain the skins of their animals; for, with a few trinklets, they could procure what otherwise would require long and severe labor to obtain," historian Bancroft noted in 1874. "The policy, therefore, of the great fur trading companies has been to cherish the Indians as their best hunters, to live in peace with them, to heal their ancient feuds, and to withhold from them intoxicating liquors."

But there are many records of whole island populations of Aleuts being wiped out by Russian traders and later of the annihilation of Tlingit clans that challenged the Russian right to settlement. Other nations, too, participated in the rape of the country. The English, Spanish, French, and Americans all sent trading expeditions and, although records are scanty, it appears that the epidemics of smallpox, diphtheria, influenza, measles, and syphilis the visitors left in their wake, took a devastating toll of the native population.

Towards the end of its stewardship of Alaska, the Russian Government apparently had pangs of conscience about the appalling condition of their Alaskan savages and sent increasing numbers of churchmen to the rescue. Among the brightest and most compassionate was Ivan Veniaminov who became fluent in both Aleut and Tlingit and established numerous churches and schools among the native people, but little could be done to improve their lot. The invaders had nearly exhausted their once bountiful supply of game and the Alaskans no longer had control of their own destiny. In 1867, without consulting the original occupants or obtaining title to their land through purchase or conquest treaty, the Russians sold Alaska to the United States for $7,200,000 in a contract that stipulated, "The uncivilized tribes will be subject to such laws and regulations as the United States may, from time to time, adopt in regard to aboriginal tribes of that country."

The Alaska purchase was hotly contested in the United States Congress and was an embarrassment to many who felt the land was overpriced. As a result, American administrators did their best to ignore their new holding for several decades, leaving jurisdiction to small, undermanned Army outposts.

Secretary of State William H. Seward, promoter of the purchase, made an inspection tour in 1869 and reminded the residents of Sitka, which had been the Russian capital, that as long as Alaska had no more than 2,000 whites and as many as 25,000 Indians, a display of military force was needed. Major John Tidball, one of the first commanders in the area, reported that the Indians were savages and that they possessed the same villainous traits of character found among the warring Indians in the United States. But even after the Army withdrew the bulk of its Alaskan troops to put down an uprising of Nez Percé Indians in Idaho, fears of Alaskan Indian warfare proved groundless. The natives, it seemed, were too busy fighting for their existence against the exploiters of Alaska's natural resources.

Along the Arctic coast large fleets of whaling ships were slaughtering sea mammals and caribou, the chief food of the Eskimos. Commercial fishermen, pioneering a vast canning industry, were already depleting the waters of southeastern Alaska, and a gold stampede, started in Juneau in 1880, made further inroads into native territory. To complicate matters, many discouraged Indians and Eskimos took enthusiastically to drink—becoming expert in the manufacture of alcohol despite numerous government bans—and those who survived the temptation were felled by new epidemics of smallpox, diphtheria, and tuberculosis.

Yet despite the degradation of the Alaskans who came up against white exploiters, there remained much in them to be admired. Vincent Colyer, special Indian commissioner to Alaska during this period, reported to Washington, "I do not hesitate to say that if three fourths of them [Alaskan Indians] were landed in New York as coming from Europe, they would be selected as among the most intelligent of the many worthy immigrants who daily arrive in that port."

And, precarious though it was, there was something intriguing about the traditional lifestyle to which the natives clung desperately.

"The individual savages have been educated with a fair degree of success," Bancroft observed. "But, with a degree of far greater certainty, no sooner is the white man freed from the social restraint of civilized companionship, than he immediately tends toward barbarism; and not infrequently becomes so fascinated with his new life as to prefer it to any other."

Missionaries, affronted by the seemingly loose moral values of the natives, moved to convert them to the greater virtues of Christianity and educators sought to Americanize them by banning native languages and customs.

In 1885 Sheldon Jackson, a Presbyterian missionary and dedicated educator, called a meeting of all interested church groups and divided up the territory, the Baptists getting Kodiak and Cook Inlet, Episcopalians working the Yukon and lower Arctic coast, the Methodists moving into the Aleutian chain, the Moravians taking the Kuskokwim region, the Congregationalists settling in the area of Cape Prince of Wales, and the Presbyterians taking southeastern and the northern Arctic coasts.

The action, which came after fruitless attempts on Jackson's part to get the United States Government to take an interest in educating the natives, proved beneficial in many areas where the missionaries were true humanitarians or at least good medical men. But acculturation was their watchword and their proselytizing made vigorous assaults on native tradition.

What saved some of the old ways was the same thing that had been the natives' enemy of old—the harshness of the country. No matter how much the outsiders ridiculed their native cultures, the Alaskans saw that by maintaining them they could survive in the country well beyond the endurance of the average newcomer. And because of this knowledge they developed a cagey distrust of the system of limited reservations in which the government from time to time attempted to corral them. Chief Alexander of Tolovana, an Athabascan leader who attended a hearing on reservations held by the federal government in 1915, clearly outlined the native view to United States District Judge James Wickersham, presiding:

"You told me that you were our people's friend, and you did not like to see us get into any kind of mischief. You stated to me that anything we want we shall talk to you about now.

Therefore, the people now being present, I say that I feel the same way as I felt at that time, and I tell you that we are people that are always on the go, and I believe if we are put in one place we shall die off like rabbits. I tell you also that if you wanted to do anything good for us, you must select somebody for us who was truthful and not untruthful.

"I ask you not to let the white people come near us. Let us live our own lives in the customs we know. If we were on government ground we could not keep the white people away."

About 1929 some of the more sophisticated native villages, especially in the southeast, began to incorporate as cities. In 1934 Congress passed the Indian Reorganization Act providing economic assistance to Indian tribes so that they could charter corporations. And, in 1935 the Tlingit-Haida Jurisdictional Act gave Indians the right to sue. One year later the Tlingit people filed suit against the United States Government for $80 million in lost timberland, but the case was shuttled about the courts for three decades before settlement.

During World War II, when the federal government left the Alaska coastline undefended against possible Japanese attack, Alaskan Eskimos united and became a fully chartered branch of the Territorial National Guard, patrolling the borders and earning the respect of many white citizens. In 1925 a Tlingit, William Paul, Sr., had been elected to the territorial legislature, and by the end of World War II several other native leaders had served as elected officials. Then in 1945 the legislature passed a nondiscrimination act—the first under the United States flag—removing officially all the "We-do-not-cater-to-native-trade" signs from Alaskan eating places and hotels.

Yet Alaskan natives remained among the world's poorest people, with severe health and educational problems, and they still had little control over their lives.

The turning point came in 1958 when the Atomic Energy Commission developed a plan to excavate a harbor with nuclear explosives off Alaska's northwest Arctic coast. They failed to take into account the eight hundred Eskimos who lived in the harbor area and only belatedly offered to move them to city housing projects. To defend their heritage, Eskimo leaders from twenty villages, backed by the Association of American Indian Affairs, held an unprecedented meeting called "Inupiat Paitot"—the People's Heritage.

Until this time there had been little communication between native communities and even less between natives and whites. Major Alaskan newspapers seldom carried news of Indians and Eskimos and showed little concern for the problems of native people. Inupiat Paitot resulted in the founding of the crusading, statewide native newspaper *Tundra Times*, published by Howard Rock, and through it a statewide native movement gained a powerful voice.

Through efforts of the newspaper the AEC harbor-blasting program was canceled. Rock and the co-founder of *Tundra Times*, Tom Snapp, a white man, did much to bring to light the discrimination problem in Alaska, and in 1962 they began to push for settlement of the native land claims.

Also in 1962 five oil companies filed leases with the native towns of Nenana and Minto. The state government got wind of this oil activity and started making tentative land selections under the provisions of the Alaska Statehood Act that allowed the state to acquire land from the federal government. But nobody paid any attention to the native claims on the area, which had accumulated over the years.

Rock and Snapp helped the natives file their suit, going so far as buying the land maps and helping to plot boundaries. More native suits followed until the whole state was blanketed by them and the Secretary of Interior invoked a land freeze.

In 1966 the first united group of young, alert Alaskan natives entered politics. There had been successful individual native politicians before them—Tlingit Frank Peratrovich and William Beltz, an Eskimo, had both served terms as president of the Alaska Senate, but they had not had the benefit of a strong native coalition. Now even remote villages became politically aware, and the natives—now numbering about 50,000 and making up one fifth of the Alaskan population—began to take their vote seriously. In 1968 it counted heavily in electing Mike Gravel to the United States Senate and subsequently native politicians formed a strong legislative bloc in Juneau.

Adding momentum to the movement were two articulate young leaders in the state legislature. Athabascan John Sackett, a member of the Republican majority, landed a seat on the influential House Finance Committee and Eskimo Willie Hensley, a Democrat, buckled down to a House apprenticeship that would later help him win a seat in the Senate.

It was Hensley who pressed for the land claims suit against the federal government which had never purchased aboriginal title from the natives. Reading from one of his college research papers, Hensley introduced the issue at a meeting of the Juneau Democratic Club in a cramped hotel basement. Before his first legislative session was over, he had mustered enough support to push through a bill promising a state royalty to Indians and Eskimos if the federal government would settle their claims.

The spring of 1967 a statewide coalition of natives organized to push a federal settlement through Congress. Outsiders predicted that the Alaskan Federation of Natives would not survive because survival required close co-operation among aborigines who had warred for centuries. The natives buried their differences, however, and overcame the barriers of diversified languages and cultures to gain a federal settlement of $1 billion and 40 million acres of land in 1971. Administration of the settlement has been delegated to the natives themselves and a new era of self-determination now lies ahead.

# Anaktuvuk Pass

## THE LAST OF THE INDEPENDENTS

*The people of Anaktuvuk Pass were the last of Alaska's independent Eskimos. For centuries they followed the track of the migratory caribou through the Brooks Range far north of the Arctic Circle. They were proud to call themselves "Inupiat," the Real People. They lived wholly by hunting, surviving the earth's fiercest cold in tents of caribou skins and splendid fur clothing designed by their forefathers.*

*By the end of the nineteenth century, whale hunters had killed off the game, forcing the Eskimos to abandon the mountains and camp with coastal cousins. There they discovered the white man and the civilization he was introducing, but the Anaktuvuk people remained aloof. When the caribou herds grew strong enough in the late 1930s, a small nucleus of families moved back into the mountains and more joined them as the game increased.*

*Long after other Eskimos had settled into white man's ways, the Anaktuvuk people enjoyed a free, nomadic life. To the east their Canadian counterparts grew dependent on the traders, dulled their hunting skills, and starved by the hundreds. The Inupiat knew hard times, too, but their traditions sustained them.*

*Then, in 1961, they decided a school must be built at Anaktuvuk Pass—the influence of the white man had*

*at last penetrated the mountains. There was no arguing.*
*It was obvious that the next generation would need a*
*white man's education, but no one dreamed then how*
*high the cost would be.*

*The state of Alaska built Anaktuvuk a fine school*
*and federal funds were provided to run it. But there*
*was one catch. The Inupiat had to give up their no-*
*madic lifestyle before their youngsters could attend.*
*Children could not be excused from classes to follow*
*the caribou herds and the parents could not abandon*
*their children. To live the Inupiat must hunt, and to*
*hunt they must travel. But the school held them fast.*

The last day of January 1972 I moved in with the Inupiat in
their now-permanent settlement at Anaktuvuk. The population totaled 112, with 108 Eskimos, one white man married to a
native, two white teachers, and me. I was accepted tentatively
because I worked as a feature writer for Alaska's native newspaper, *Tundra Times*, but no one seemed ready to believe that
a single white woman really intended to stay there a month in
the dead of the Arctic winter.

The plane was scheduled to arrive at Anaktuvuk twice
weekly, weather permitting. I'd taken it that morning—a small,
heatless Otter that struggled the five hundred unpopulated
miles from Fairbanks to scale the Brooks Range just as an
apricot sun touched the mountains' keen-edged peaks. Rough
winds toyed with us but the pilot held his course, finally
letting us down into the pass and flying parallel, almost level,
with four enormous gray wolves running on a frozen gray
river.

There were six other passengers, all Eskimo. One was Riley
Morry, a friend of a friend with whom I had corresponded
about finding a place to live in the village. He was pleasant but

*A sod house backed by the Brooks Range on a winter morning.*

he kept to his own people, and I knew I would have to make my own way among strangers.

We landed on a snow-decked gravel strip, rattling to a stop in front of a small crowd of Eskimos. The men and boys wore mostly modern winter gear but the women and girls were dressed in long, brightly colored cotton parkas with fur linings and ruffs; and everybody wore mukluks, the traditional fur boots.

My fellow passengers received an enthusiastic welcome. They'd attended an important regional meeting of natives in Barrow, been detoured via Fairbanks when their charter pilot got drunk, and were four days overdue. Now they hustled off the plane, carrying the paper bags that served them as brief-cases, and shook hands all round.

I mustered last, completely losing my breath in the force of the wind. I had taken off my mittens to get a better grip on my camera cases, but saw immediately it was a mistake. My hands were cramped with cold before I could get them covered again. It was probably no more than 20 degrees below zero but the wind brought the chill factor to 40 below. Miserable and unsure of myself, I waited by the plane. Finally Riley Morry remembered me, untangled himself from his family, and fetched my landlord.

David Mekiana was the most Eskimo-looking of Eskimos—stocky, about my height (five feet six), with a broad, pleasant face. I took him to be as simple as the English he greeted me in. I was wrong but I didn't have much on which to gauge that first impression. Blindly I followed him through the drifts. The village was obscured by snow-laden winds and I prayed it wasn't far.

Mekiana was apologizing over the howling of the storm for the house he was renting me. It was small and not as clean as it ought to be, he said, but he did have the stove on.

Mention of the stove was heartening. My hands seemed frozen to my baggage and my face had lost its feeling. Finally a plywood house appeared among the snow mounds and we

*Meeting the plane.*

*My "hotel" in Anaktuvuk Pass. In foreground is caribou fur trimmed outhouse.*

found its welcome warmth. It was small—one room—but no apologies were necessary.

The Eskimo had agreed on a $30 rent, according to my letter from Morry, but seeing I was satisfied with his house, he now suggested $145. I wondered if I was losing something in translation. My thinking was muddled and my bargaining power was weak, but I decided to stay with the written agreement as I understood it even though I had neglected to bring the letter. I couldn't afford to appear rich and gullible, so I talked him back to $30, offered to pay an extra $20 if he would lend me a kerosene lamp and provide me with ice for drinking water and a bucket to melt it in, and we were both happy to be done with the matter.

Mekiana himself lived in an old sod house, he told me. He'd bought this second, plywood, house last year and everyone in the village wondered what he would do with it. All last summer he had labored to improve it, without a single offer of assistance from his relatives or anyone else. They'd thought he was crazy, he confided. Then, cautiously, he tried out the phrase "hotel business" and seemed relieved when I considered it reasonable.

Mekiana's "hotel" was eleven feet by thirteen and had once housed a family of five. It was constructed of plywood and tin, insulated with Lord-knows-what and weather stripped with caribou fur. The interior, of which the landlord was particularly proud, boasted "mahagaa" (mahogany) paneling which had cost more to ship in than to buy.

Inventory included a cot from Sears, Roebuck that had once been an upper bunk, a kerosene heater with four inches between the top of the burner and its metal grid into which I could just squeeze a frying pan, a waste box and broom, a wooden Blazo box for a chair, a food box with a cover and a broken hinge, a table with another Blazo box on top for storage, a clothesline, and a "honeybucket" toilet fashioned from a Chevron Pearl kerosene can with a graceful whittled willow handle for carrying. (The bucket was to be emptied in a fifty-five-gallon oil drum planted conveniently in my entry-way.)

With me I had brought a sleeping bag, two changes of clothing, a mess kit, and $58-worth of groceries which had cost an additional $30 to ship air freight. And I was to unpack them under careful scrutiny. David left about 3 P.M. to be replaced by my young neighbors, Lena and Louise Paneak, who welcomed me with a ball of unwrapped bubble gum. Louise was a four-year-old beauty, all dimples and red cheeks. Her older sister was a match but much graver and quite reserved for seven.

As soon as school let out, more youngsters descended on me and a group of eight- and nine-year-olds took over. For our first event, they announced in excellent English, we would all take off our clothes. I guess it was a scouting expedition to check my philosophy. Anyway, when I said that wasn't on today's agenda, they immediately settled in to entertain me with Eskimo dancing and then sat, as if I were conducting Sunday school, and sang sweetly for an hour. Everyone took turns using my honeybucket, too, informing me it was a very good one. The girls tried it first, with the boys discreetly study-ing the mahogany paneling of the far wall. Then the boys lined up behind a shield of coats.

Finally, after suppertime came and went without a break, I hit upon the only polite way I could think of to clear the house. I went to visit someone else.

Nancy Ahgook, an intense-eyed youngster with a severe Dutch cut, took me with a company of young friends, to meet her mother, Lela, the postmistress. Their home—living room, dining room, kitchen, bedroom, and post office—was all one room, but well ordered and clean. Lela, whom I judged to be in her early thirties, was a fine-boned woman who smiled easily and spoke careful English. We didn't have much to say to each other, but she seemed surprised and the children scan-dalized when I announced after a brief visit that I was going home to bed. It was only 9 P.M. and early by their social

*A shy young neighbor hides behind her caribou-skin mitten.*

*David Mekiana, my landlord.*

standards, but I'd gotten up at 5 A.M. to make the plane and I was weak from lack of food.

At 3 A.M. I awoke to find the stove was cold and my big water bucket freezing fast. I dipped a small bucket from it, figuring it would thaw faster for coffee if and when I got the heat back on, but water froze to the side as I dipped.

Shivering compulsively, I grabbed a bag of carrots and onions, my only fresh vegetables, and shoved them into my sleeping bag. Then I pulled on my insulated underwear and a sweater and crawled in to snuggle up with the vegetables, pulling the drawstring of the bag tight around my face with only a small breathing hole left open. I calculated my chances of waking up alive were fair. The manufacturer claimed my sleeping bag had been successfully tested by Mount McKinley climbers.

When I awoke at ten dawn had just arrived and the sky was the color of weak tea. It was about 20 degrees below zero outside and there was wind to fight. Desperately I blundered around the wrong sod house for a while, then located my landlord in one adjacent.

"Out of fuel, maybe," he speculated. Yesterday he'd assured me I had enough for three days. Well, no matter. Raymond Paneak, treasurer of the Brooks Range Fuel Co-op, was the man to see. I had met Paneak one balmy summer day four years earlier when I landed at Anaktuvuk briefly on a bush flight to somewhere else. He'd just been chosen one of the first native trainees for the VISTA volunteer program and was living in a tent outside the village as most Anaktuvuk people do in summer. I had no idea where his house was, but David motioned vaguely in the direction of the airport and after a brisk five minute walk I found it.

No one answered my knock on the outer door so I opened it and proceeded through a series of entrance sheds and storage rooms. Finally I found the main room and Paneak with his shy young wife and two children eating breakfast of scrambled eggs and bacon. He didn't remember me, but he was cordial in fluent English. He said they were planning to drop the price of

fuel at the end of the month, but currently it was $74 for a
fifty-five-gallon drum. That was about seven times the usual
price, but it sounded good to me. At the beginning of the winter they'd had to charge $115 a barrel, he added.

As I was leaving he offered me a cup of coffee. I hadn't
thought of food or drink in so long I at first refused. Eskimo
fashion, he ignored my foolishness and stated the offer again as
if for the first time.

"It is bad in a city not to know anyone and the same here,"
he added gently.

The business of survival kept me well occupied for the next
week, even though my stove went back on. There had been
fuel in the tank but not enough to fight its way through the ten
feet of copper tubing David had coiled behind the stove on
installation for want of a copper cutter. Even with a full tank,
the fire burned fitfully and I didn't trust it.

I was even more dubious about the out-of-doors. For some
years I had lived in Fairbanks, often walking half a mile to
work at 40° below. But that was city living where help was
readily available. This tundra was new to me.

Keith Arnold, an old friend, had presented me with *Cold
Weather Operations Survival,* a book he had done for the
Alaska Oil and Gas Association. It was waterproof, wouldn't
rip or burn, he assured me proudly. Great—I would read it at
60 degrees below while I was freezing for want of kindling, I
told him. And while I was waiting for my hotel to warm up, I
cracked it.

It was not a cheerful book. The chill-factor page warned that
at 25 degrees below with a fifteen-mile-an-hour wind, flesh
may freeze within one minute. At 75 degrees below with a ten-
mile wind, it takes only thirty seconds. For treatment of super-
ficial frostbite in the field it suggested "Cover cheeks with
warm hands until pain returns." There were also graphic descriptions of trench foot and snow blindness which I found too
painful to read.

On the recommendation of a mountain climber from Nepal,

I had purchased a down-filled parka, pants, socks, and mittens along with Canadian felt-lined snowmobile boots. Everything looked clownish, being men's sizes, and my Eskimo editor, Howard Rock, was appalled. I should wear fur, he insisted. I agreed, but pointed out that fur takes time to tailor and more money than I had.

"Well, the Eskimos will worry about you," he assured me. And he lent me his beautiful fur-seal mittens.

Now, gingerly, I set out to test my duffel. Each day I walked increasing distances on the wind-beaten hills around the village. At first I had to keep reminding myself to check for frostbite and bury my nose periodically in the furry backs of my mittens to keep circulation going. Running could freeze a lung. Walking too slowly was chilling, but going fast enough to work up a sweat was even more dangerous because when you stopped, you froze.

If the Eskimos worried about me, they didn't say so and I soon discovered they had no need to. Ungainly as they might be, my fine feathered wrappings kept out the cold and I began to feel at home on the tundra. I felt more at ease with the land, in fact, than with its natives.

The villagers were weary of outsiders and I was hesitant to approach them. Ever since they'd settled, ten years earlier, they'd been targets of unceasing scientific inquiry. There'd been extensive research on their diet, blood types, metabolism. One scientist had gone so far as to try and check their temperatures with a rectal thermometer. Then it was discovered that, because of Russian atomic testing, the Anaktuvuk people had the highest body radiation count in America. The Eskimos lived on caribou and caribou ate lichens and lichens absorbed Soviet fallout. So the Atomic Energy Commission routinely sent a man with a Geiger counter to listen to the Anaktuvuk people click. Skeptics speculated that this was more to monitor Soviet testing than to guard Eskimo health, but whatever the reasons, the Anaktuvuk people had been too closely scrutinized for too long.

They were also leery of cameras because, they complained,

visitors tried to get them looking prehistoric and published pictures of them in compromising positions without their permission. They had no reason to believe that I'd be any different, although some of them had heard of the native-owned newspaper for which I worked. Visiting was obviously the way to make my intentions known but I wasn't sure how to go about it.

To my rescue came Doris Hugo, wife of the Eskimo Presbyterian minister and mother of five. I liked her immediately. She had the self-confidence that came with three years of city living, yet there was a school-girl modesty and freshness about her. Her speaking voice was laced with laughter and she looked like a vibrant madonna.

Mr. Hugo—Zack—was hunting on the farthest-off mountain of our horizon, she said. They had been raised in this area but moved to Fairbanks when he got a job taking care of the animals at the Arctic Health Research Laboratory there. He had liked the work, liked the animals, but she got lonesome for the company of the village and decided to move back home with the children. He couldn't let her come alone—life is too rough in this country for a woman alone with children—so reluctantly he left the animals and came back too.

"Once he went back to visit and all the animals recognized him," she added proudly. "The bear and even the monkey."

She didn't speak much about the church. Zack was minister because paid professionals seldom got out that way to preach. She didn't seem to view herself as a minister's wife. Her husband was first a hunter and she'd come to visit me simply as a neighbor.

She left inviting me to return her call, and I decided that that would be a good way to get acquainted with the social routine. Waiting for what I hoped was a discreetly late hour, I knocked on her door at eleven the next morning. Someone said "Yes" and I entered, coming face to face with a man in Mrs. Hugo's bed. If her husband was hunting, who the devil was this, I wondered, making a hasty retreat. Obviously I had a few things to learn about visiting.

To make matters worse, I had offended my landlord. He had gotten into the habit of dropping in to check my stove, then planting himself by it for lengthy conversations. Despite his ragged English, he was delightful, but I was nervous about spending so much time alone with him, especially late at night. He was a bachelor of about twenty-eight, he'd informed me. And in the same breath he'd warned me, "A lotta single boys here you gotta watch out for." Naturally, he would be one of them.

One night he sat past eleven to tell of a party of white hunters who'd rented the hotel and tried to live as the Eskimos did, sleeping together under caribou fur blankets. He also spoke of renting the place to some anthropologists who sometimes got so tired of being overrun by young visitors that they hung out a "No Trespassing" sign.

Then he launched into a cold-weather saga about fighting with his relatives one winter, then taking a canvas tent and going off by himself into the mountains in the depth of the cold. He was gone so long that they thought he was dead and dispatched the mail plane to find his body. He had hidden from the plane and sneaked home to surprise them.

It was a good story and later I found it was modestly told and true. The adventure had established him in the minds of the villagers as their toughest man, but that night I was feeling too skittish to appreciate it. Tired and anxious about the late hour, I finally told him I was putting out my "No Trespassing" sign, but this was no country for a broad hint. Mekiana was hurt and went home immediately, leaving me to ponder Eskimo diplomacy.

The next morning he stopped by to inquire tersely about the stove. He was going hunting down in the timber—a three-day trip—and his Uncle John would bring ice for me. He asked me to pick up a box of groceries he had ordered on the next plane so his relatives wouldn't get them. Then he left without formalities, bluntly refusing a cup of coffee. The children were still in school and without him the hotel seemed very empty.

Clearly, it was time to try visiting again. David had told

me Simon Paneak had a fur ruff for sale and I decided to inquire. It would be a business visit and certainly I couldn't do
any worse socially than I had already. Simon was the village
patriarch. I had heard him give a demonstration of birdcalls at
the Eskimo "Olympics" during one of his rare visits to Fairbanks, and any book written about Anaktuvuk included him.
It was because of him the village had been established.

In 1947 a biologist, Dr. Laurence Irving, was weathered in
at Chandler Lake in the Anaktuvuk area with Sig Wien, owner
of Wien Airlines. They had discovered Paneak camping with
his family and spent a week with them. Irving, who was studying bird migration, soon enlisted Paneak to do work with him.
They speculated (correctly) that Anaktuvuk Pass might be
the main migration route and Wien began flying in supplies
there. Eventually a rough airstrip was carved out, a white
trader settled in, and a post office was established. Then
Paneak, who had a lot of children to educate, moved into the
settlement permanently with several other families to establish
a school.

His house sat on the outskirts of the village bordering the
airstrip. It was a modern frame building, large by Anaktuvuk
standards but consisting only of a single room with one big
bed and a smaller one. The walls were covered with an exotic
collection of jigsaw puzzles—feeding flamingos, biblical scenes
—which had been taped together on the back. It was a bright,
cheerful home and I felt welcome.

Paneak estimated his age at about seventy or seventy-one.
His nose had grown large with the years, but he had been a
handsome youth and maintained the bearing of a young man.
Although plagued with an ear infection and respiratory problems, he still did a day's work, driving his snowmobile, otherwise called a snow machine, hunting, teaching his grandchildren calisthenics. His wife, Susie, appeared to be in her forties
and their youngest child, Harold, was six. She was his second
wife, he explained. He had eight children all told and too many
grandchildren to count.

My business was welcome. They did have a wolf ruff for sale.

A beauty. Thirty dollars. Susie would back it with the same bright cotton print from which she'd made her parka and I was pleased. The price was fair on both sides and I needed the ruff, for it is impossible to travel far in such cold without a protective halo of fur about the face.

They offered tea. Susie sat sewing quietly. Simon was carving a large wooden face as a frame for a mask she was planning to shape from caribou skin. Usually the villagers made life-sized masks but this one, for a museum, would be about a yard across. Something new, Paneak said.

His English was good, although he hadn't heard the language until he was past twenty and was self-taught. He'd worked for the Arctic Health Research Lab and the University of Alaska since Irving discovered him, and he was considered to have a knowledge of birds that a Ph.D. in biology would envy.

Sitting next to a little oil stove, carving expertly and spitting occasionally into a tin can at his feet, he told of capturing live ptarmigan (an Arctic game bird) by the thousands in nets, then banding them and setting them free. That was a few years ago and not many hunters had turned in the bands. Now nobody seemed interested in bird tracking.

I left by way of the frozen river that rambled in back of the house. The village looked grand, set about with mountains looming six thousand feet, glistening white in the pale morning sun. Not far from Simon's I stumbled across twenty ptarmigan, so tame or dumb that they wouldn't fly until I threatened to step on them. They were ridiculous, pigeon-sized birds, engineered like Al Capp's shmoo in winter white with puffy white feather leggings. Dusting over the snow before me like dandelion silk on the wind, they chuckled to themselves at a private joke I wished I might share. Perhaps they were heading to visit their friend Simon.

In winter it's hard to count the houses in Anaktuvuk Pass, even hard to locate them, for they're caught in continuing drifts, and even the plywood frames are disguised as mounts and hummocks, but I set out to visit them all. I had gained a measure of social self-confidence after negotiating with the Paneaks and after a second stop at Doris Hugo's revealed that the man in her bed was her husband, home from the hunt early because the weather was poor. The villagers, having nothing much to get up for in the cold morning, often sought the warmth of their blankets until noon. After that, they enjoyed having company.

My closest neighbors were the most reticent. Robert Paneak, one of Simon's progeny, had generously offered me the use of his caribou-fur-shrouded outhouse, but otherwise he and his wife, Marie, kept pretty much to themselves. He spent most of his days outside, trying to repair his snowmobile, and she always seemed to be going out when I came to visit. Her teen-aged daughter, Betty, was one of my favorites, for her mind was quick and sensitive, but her father, Marie's first husband, had committed suicide and the girl didn't seem much closer to the Paneaks than I. She had been adopted by Elijah Kakinya, an old trapper, and his wife and visited her mother and step-father sparingly.

Robert Ahgook, village council president and health aide, was also reserved, but well worth the trouble it took to get to know him. Although soft-spoken with little formal education, I found he had an open, inquiring mind and considerable knowledge. Because there are no doctors within hundreds of miles of Anaktuvuk and airplanes are often weathered out, the government had trained Ahgook, with health aides from other remote villages, to serve as a doctor's eyes, ears, and hands. Each day through an experimental satellite radio hook-up with the U. S. Public Health Service doctors in Tanana and Anchorage, he discussed the medical problems of the Eskimos who showed up in his kitchen clinic and then followed the city doctor's instructions. When his cases were serious, he arranged for the patients to be flown to the hospital, but most of the time he was able to handle things himself.

There were no major health problems in Anaktuvuk at the moment, he assured me. None except tapeworm from caribou which was carried via the dogs who often ate the infected lung of the animal. He had caught the first case himself and it had put him in the hospital, but he had discovered that generally Dr. Jones' Patent Medicine could keep the plague under control.

The Riley Morrys, it turned out, had had so much trouble finding a house for themselves in Anaktuvuk, it was a wonder they had had courage to look for me. Riley had gone to California for Bureau of Indian Affairs (BIA) training and had married Betty, a pretty Navajo. For some time the BIA had refused to pay his way home (although they were willing to send him anywhere else in the United States), and the couple had only recently arrived with their sixteen-month-old daughter Kathleen. Housing was so tight they'd finally settled in a small sod house with a temperamental stove on the outskirts of the village. It was hard on Betty, who was often left alone with the baby when Riley traveled. The villagers tried to make her feel welcome and adored her baby who was truly beautiful, but she was a long way from her warm New Mexico home and she was an Indian, not an Eskimo.

The most intriguing house in the village belonged to Riley and Rachel Sikvayugak. It was a big mound of snow-topped sod in the midst of the village. Rachel showed up at my door one night to collect her son, who, with a dozen other youngsters, threatened to camp at the hotel forever. As she stepped in from the dark entryway into the glow of my kerosene lamp, I caught my breath, for her face, framed in the perfection of a red-fox ruff, was the most beautiful I'd ever seen. Her cheekbones were high and perfect and her coloring had the quality of the mellowed paints of the Old Masters.

She and Riley, her handsome match, had five children. Marilyn, five, was the only plump Eskimo in the village and Rachel referred to her fondly as "my fat little daughter." Riley, Jr., a couple of years older, had his father's good looks and dignity. Then there were the young twins, boys. They were smart as foxes but cross-eyed and they couldn't enter any crowded room without someone yelling, "Here come the cross-eyed Eskimos." The family also had a younger daughter, Marlene, who had been adopted by the Zack Hugos, their closest friends. The Sikvayugaks' fortunes had been up and down and I suspected Marlene showed up during one of the rough times. Riley was from Barrow on the north coast, had operated a store there and apparently gone broke. Rachel, who'd been brought up here, decided Anaktuvuk was a better place to raise children so they'd moved down and were doing well as BIA welfare agents. Their house, which also served as an office, was large for a sod structure and boasted wallpaper over the cardboard insulation. It was lighter than most and I would have given a lot to move into it.

Originally I'd hoped to live with a family and had been disappointed to have a house to myself. Now I discovered that most Anaktuvuk homes had just one room and bed for the whole family to share. Occasionally a cot was set aside for an older son or daughter, but there was no privacy. Everyone seemed to crave togetherness.

"What's privacy?" asked Richard Ahgook, a tall, skinny perpetually grinning lad of about thirteen, who in the early evenings favored my place to his home at the post office.

"Privacy is being able to lock your door and have nobody bother you," explained Betty Kakinya, Marie Paneak's daughter.

"What if they look through the window?"

"Pull the curtains."

Richard looked distressed. "We don't have any curtains," he said.

"Well, take off your pants and hang them up," Betty advised.

Although I lived in continuing fear of being caught on my honeybucket by a visiting neighbor, I settled fairly easily into this pattern of semicommunal living. By the end of my first week, nearly every child in the village had tried on my hat, used my hairbrush, counted my pencils, and inspected my groceries—to pronounce them as meager as their own. Marilyn Sikvayugak even ate my toothpaste one day when I was doing

*Babysitting made easy.*

my best to ignore her, then brushed her teeth with my finger-nail brush.

One day I found Doris Hugo scraping a caribou hide for masks with a magnificent willow-handled tool made long ago by her uncle. I asked if I could photograph her but her husband would not allow it. Some oil company had taken an excellent picture of her the year before which hung on their wall but no one had paid them for its use in an oil industry handout and the experience had soured them. They did agree, however, to have their portrait taken as a family with whichever of their five children happened to be available and it was an endeavor of which we were proud. The Hugo boys were winsome and adopted sister, Marlene, was a real scene stealer even though, as her mother joked, sometimes her hair looked like a little porcupine's.

I also began to appear at various houses, notebook in hand, in an attempt to record some of the problems that plagued the village. Then Robert Ahgook and the village elders apparently gave some thought to what my reporting might do and invited me to attend a village council meeting.

For years I had covered stuffy, formal council meetings in large cities and Anaktuvuk offered a pleasant change. I arrived to find six men lying on their backs on Bob Ahgook's shiny kitchen linoleum, smoking pipes and cigarettes in front of the warm kitchen stove. Riley Sikvayugak, taking notes, was propped up against a big teddy bear in the corner, a toy no doubt abandoned by one of Bob's many youngsters, and Riley and Betty Morry were on the couch watching daughter Kathleen dismantle the place. Riley gave her his watch in an attempt to distract her. She threw it on the floor; but he didn't even look pained. She was an engaging youngster. Her mother put her on the honeybucket and half an hour later the child sat on it again on her own, wetting right through the pants she'd forgotten to drop. But she didn't disrupt the council meeting which was being conducted in unhurried Eskimo.

The problem of the evening was how to explain the federal settlement of the Alaskan native land claims suit to the villagers. The natives had just received $1 billion and 40 million acres of land as payment for relinquishing aboriginal title to Alaska. It was to be parceled out by regional corporations over a twenty-year period and the congressional bill explaining it ran forty-eight pages of complicated legalese. The luckless Sikvayugak got the job of translating the thing into Eskimo and he suggested I might be elected in his stead.

"Heck, I don't pretend to understand it even in English," I told him.

"I'll have to go through the dictionary and get all the long words," he warned fellow council members. "It will take a long time but I'll try like hell, all right!"

The meeting was called for the following Monday, three days later. David Mekiana, who had gotten over being mad at me, told me it would be the first time all the villagers had assembled since 1968 and I was very much looking forward to it. The appointed hour was 1:30 P.M. in the log community hall. I showed up at 1:45 P.M. but found the meeting place empty. Puzzled, I finally went to the post office where I found a crowd. The community hall hadn't warmed up enough to meet, Lela Ahgook explained.

"We're going to wait and hold it in the spring," Bob Ahgook told me with a dead-pan seriousness I grew to appreciate as humor.

Riley Morry was stomping around all sooty and mad. His stove had gone out the night before and he couldn't get it fixed. Said he was going to resign from the council. Everybody looked pretty surprised at that. The job was without pay, but Morry was a leader of growing stature and really concerned about the future of his people. Now he explained that Betty was threatening to vacation back in New Mexico with Kathy and never come back, and she meant it. He traveled so much as a village representative that Betty had to spend too much time alone, he added pointedly. And the people hadn't been good about helping her when her fuel ran out.

There was no rebuttal. Everyone was uncomfortable and the crowd wandered off. But at 7 P.M. the land claims meeting came to order. Adults sat along the walls and no children were allowed except for toddlers who stomped around the middle of the floor and yelped at one another. Raymond Paneak, juggling his young son on his hip, announced the coming election of two new councilmen. The stove, which had been on all day, never did warm the room so we could take off our coats. When anyone opened the door we were engulfed by a white cloud of cold air engulfing the youngsters who shucked their coats in the ice fog and seemed not to notice.

The meeting lasted two hours. Riley Sikvayugak explained in Eskimo, with Riley Morry as back-up. There would be no per capita dole with the settlement, they said. Each native would receive instead shares of stock in their regional corporation.

"You get one hundred shares each," they said.

"How much is a share worth?"

"We won't know until we see what our corporation [the Arctic Slope Native Association] is worth."

"Can we sell now?"

"Not for twenty years."

"What about half-breeds?"

Answer in Eskimo I couldn't fathom.

"The Arctic Slope will get 5 million acres, $32 million, and we have only 5 to 7 per cent of the native population," Morry noted in English.

"Can we claim a township down by the oil shale?"

"Yes, but we don't get subsurface rights."

"Pet Four?" (That was the federal Petroleum Reserve No. 4, currently being claimed in court by the Arctic Slope regional corporation.)

"That's federal government," Morry smiled. "Kind of hard to get at."

"But where were our fathers before the government came in?" demanded Jack Ahgook, a savvy hunter who spent a better-than-average amount of time in Fairbanks.

"Our fathers were there when the government came."

Then, in Eskimo, I heard "pipeline," "$150 a gallon," and

some general talk about oil spills. The trans-Alaska oil pipeline
was slated to go through near Anaktuvuk and a survey company had left barreled oil stored near one of the local lakes.
The oil had leaked and the spill killed the fish. The Eskimos
were apparently aware that companies might be made to pay
for such damage although they wouldn't discuss it in English
for the newspaper, because oil companies might also mean
jobs.

Roosevelt Paneak, one of Simon's bachelor sons, spoke
briefly on surface damage caused by a state-built winter haul
trail in the area. Then Robert Ahgook rounded out the evening
by talking about the tapeworm problem. On the surface it
didn't look like much political action, but I was encouraged.

For some time the Arctic Slope regional corporation had
slapped Anaktuvuk's name on a series of law suits and press re-
leases against oil companies and the like. Often the villagers
didn't know about this until they read *Tundra Times* and they
never saw their regional representatives. But recently the village council had sent word to headquarters that unless they received a visit from the regional leaders Anaktuvuk would pull
out of the organization. I'd been in Barrow at the time and
knew their ultimatum had surprised and shaken the regional
office. Without Anaktuvuk, the Arctic Slope was just three
coastal villages with little or no claim to the oil-rich interior.
Since that time, the regional men had paid more attention to
the isolated Anaktuvuk group, and questions asked during the
local meeting led me to hope that the villagers really had
enough awareness to become involved in the politics of the
settlement.

The wisdom of the Anaktuvuk council showed itself in
most facets of village life. There was a high premium on hon-
esty and cleanliness. By cheerful, mutual consent (abetted by
a stiff system of fines), there was no drinking and poker playing was outlawed. And the council scheduled a steady round
of activities like church, bingo, Audie Murphy movies, pool,
mothers' club, more Audie Murphy. . . .

*A game of musical chairs at the school.*

Privately the Eskimos exhibited a passion for social card playing. "It's fifty per cent of the culture," observed one of the schoolteachers as he battled his way through a "dirty eight" marathon with the Robert Ahgooks.

And visiting made up the other 50 per cent. Several families who moved from Anaktuvuk to large settlements had returned because they missed this companionship. Although there was a growing concept of private property, Anaktuvuk was still like one big family, sharing its fortunes, its game, and its children.

Because of this I found myself inadvertently running a social center and a preschool class. The first Eskimo word I learned was "nelek," which means "fart" and is used pretty often when you're entertaining fourteen very young children in an eleven-by-thirteen house. Delighted with my pronunciation (Eskimo with a New England accent is apparently the funniest thing going), the youngsters set about seriously improving my vocabulary and soon I could speak quite graphically on a number of subjects that rarely surface in polite society.

My young guests were never bored. They played endless Eskimo pantomime games like "Mack," designed to make a hostess laugh, and invented their own versions of games I suggested like "Hide and Sneak" or "Cracker Meeting" and "Twenty Answers."

The older prepuberty set often played "House" or "Husband" which proved much more specific than the Victorian variety I'd grown up with. In fact, it was pure, simulated sex, but quite healthy and in good spirits. When they wanted variation, they'd team up little Freddy Ahgook, five, and Louise Paneak, four, and the resulting wrestling match was a joy.

Another, more subtle contest was staged for my benefit when Joe and David Mekiana paid me a joint call. Watching them, sitting either side of my stove like bookends, it was hard to realize they were brothers. The two men had nothing to say to one another and talked to me on totally different subjects, each as if the other wasn't there. One night Joe began with a long discussion of the BIA and how much good it had done the village. Quietly, David waited to tell me of his "vacation" down in the timber at 30° below zero. He had broken his back longshoring in Barrow and had had to go into the hotel business in lieu of subsistence hunting; but he loved the out-of-doors.

"Dat was wonderful. It is good down there," he said happily. He had gone with a cousin to check his trap line. He had caught a little lynx and seen a porcupine.

"But we not hurt him, that poor fellow. So cold he could hardly walk."

They had seen a weasel which came up behind them to scout their tracks but kept safe distance. They dined handsomely, though, on frozen sheep they had cached from a previous hunting trip. And, he reported enthusiastically, he was trying a new wolf bait which he'd found advertised in a white man's catalogue. His cousin set his traps with the traditional bait (smaller wild game) and David was using the experimental type. Neither of them had caught anything as yet but we'd know in about a week.

Joe brightened as his brother went on to tell of buying a trail bike (a motor bike for rough trails) in Barrow. When it arrived he had had to learn to ride it and it "got him good. Nearly took off his leg."

"I sure thought I'd made a mistake," David said.

"He even admitted it," Joe added happily. But finally man conquered machine and David even taught Joe to ride it.

As usual, David waited for Joe to finish and then ended the evening himself, telling me a little of his early life. He had quit school after the second grade to follow his uncle, John Hugo, who let the youngster walk behind him while he hunted and trapped. He recalled that John would never wait for him, small though he was, but expected him to catch up, and when he finally could keep pace, Hugo made him go off on his own.

"That's why I never went to school," David said. But he added that if he had children, he would send them off to get an education, perhaps because his brothers (whom he had taught to hunt after their father's death) made fun of his lack of schooling.

In defense of his unlettered self, David hit upon the essence of the Anaktuvuk problem and I was anxious to explore it with others.

"In the old days whole families camped for days at a time," Rachel Sikvayugak told me. "But now, because of the school, it's impossible and the youngsters don't get much chance to learn to hunt and trap."

Times were harder now, too. Over 90 per cent of the village was on welfare. It was taken for granted, now, that welfare came with the winter season as surely as snow blew down the pass. But food stamps were useless when the supply plane couldn't land and the meat caches stood nearly empty.

"It's too bad we can't eat the ravens," Rachel joked. "We would have plenty of fresh meat if we ate ravens." For only unpalatable ravens remained. In the spring and fall the caribou migrated through the pass. In fact, "Anaktuvuk" translates to "place of the caribou droppings." But in winter the game had long since learned to detour the village and the men had traveled as much as sixty miles from home the month I was there, to come back empty-handed.

February was a hard month in the old days, too, Rachel recalled. She had been raised by nomadic parents and knew the life to be rough. But the old people called February "Sikinasugruk," month of longer sunshine, and they were free to follow the game with their families.

Heat was also a problem now. The willow supply that once provided ample fuel gave out in the mid-1960s. The BIA met the emergency by providing free oil stoves and free oil, but nothing was free any more and a fifty-five-gallon drum of oil that cost $74 wouldn't last a month.

Roosevelt Paneak, in his mid-twenties, summed it up well for his Inupiat generation.

"I am lucky to have lived before it began to change. We moved. Lived in dome-shaped tents—caribou fur on the inside, canvas outside. There were six of us. It was a good life.

"I read *People of the Deer* [Farley Mowat's account of the extinction of a Canadian Eskimo tribe] and I knew how every

scene would end before I finished it. They lived like our grand-
fathers did, following the caribou, living on them . . .

"At first there was no welfare," he recalled. "One of the
traders introduced it. I don't know what is going to happen
but I worry it will get worse. Some people have grown to depend on welfare. If it should stop, I don't know what they'd
do."

He worried, too, about the children who were not learning
to speak enough Eskimo or to hunt or trap as well as their fathers.

Louisa Morry, slightly younger, talked of alternatives. She
had been in the federally funded Upward Bound program
(similar to Head Start but for older children) and later gone
to high school in Fairbanks where she nearly qualified for the
Olympic ski team.

"Upward Bound was good because it made me realize there
was something beyond village life. A lot of people think they
can't make it anywhere but in the village, but there are a lot of
good things in the city."

Yet well as she knew them, she had elected to come home
and marry a local man. Now she taught "Children's Cache," a
modified Head Start program for preschoolers, and her future
seemed as vague as everybody else's.

Church is a must at Anaktuvuk. Not only is it an affair of the
spirit—for many Eskimos are true believers—but it is social—a
chance to see everybody and also to cut your fuel bill for the
evening.

Services were held in a pretty little log building on top of an
abrupt hill that was so slippery I often had to negotiate it on
my hands and knees. On my first night the building was
packed and Roosevelt Paneak, a church elder despite his scant
years, gave a good Presbyterian sermon in both English and
Eskimo, checking the hard Eskimo pronunciation with the
older people. There was lots of singing, too, including "Blood
of the Lamb," although they left out the verse that begins
"Would you be whiter, whiter than snow?" My favorite num-

ber was "Onward, Christian Soldiers" in Eskimo. I had difficulty with the verses, but the chorus ended "Ta-ta, rah, rah,
Jesus!" which I liked enormously because it sounded like a
spirited cheer.

After the service about seventeen kids came to visit with
Mrs. Jane Young and her son Rodney who was about eight.
Jane looked as if she'd had a rougher life than most of the
Anaktuvuk women and I noticed the kids watching closely to
see how I would treat her. They were always picking on Rodney and apparently I was expected to treat his mother accordingly. Instead I offered her a cup of coffee which she accepted and went her way happily. The boys, who never
showed any qualms about sharing eating utensils, refused to
drink from the cup she had used and I wondered what her
story could be.

I later learned from the villagers why Jane Young was in a
class by herself. It seemed she had not only married a white
man but it was also her first marriage and she had had four
children before she ever met him, thus defying the church as
well as tradition. Her father had told her "not to marry until
she had experienced everything," she later explained to me,
and that seemed reasonable enough. I liked the woman. She
spoke of her husband, Kenneth, with a combination of awe,
wonder, and love that made me root for her. He was a retired
Army man, she said, who'd grown tired of the outside world.
He'd tried settling in several places but none of them were
right. Then, two years earlier, he had settled here and through
a near-miracle they had gotten together. Like me, she noted,
he was shy about visiting people because he was afraid he
might bother them. A weird excuse, if the Eskimos ever heard
one. But she defended him, kept their sod house spotless, and
willingly drove her dog team many miles to fetch wood for his
stove. Rumor had it she neglected Rodney to do it, but I knew
Young was proud of the youngster and I decided to stay clear
of the issue.

There had been puzzlement, originally, when villagers
learned I was neither a teacher nor a missionary. Gradually

they'd come to accept the fact I wasn't bent on enlightening them with my wisdom or moral judgment, and I wanted things to stay that way. It very much surprised me, however, to learn that the local white schoolteachers felt the way I did.

In the beginning I had avoided Pat and Mike DeMarco; I wanted to wait to see what the villagers thought of the young teaching couple. If they weren't liked, I didn't want it to rub off on me.

As it happened, the Eskimos not only liked them but considered them an integral part of the community. The trust was well placed. The DeMarcos loved Anaktuvuk and they seemed to understand its people. When they'd first taken over the state-operated school that fall, Simon Paneak had asked Mike if the village could hold a dance in "Mike's" school. Mike said it was the village school and of course they could use it. The De-Marcos believed Anaktuvuk had native leadership with a good potential and that it was a "coming" village. It was a great temptation to take over and do things for the Eskimos, Mike observed. A lot of people had done that—built themselves a little empire, made the villagers dependent on them, then departed, leaving Anaktuvuk no better off than before. Mike and Pat were anxious to help with any technical problems, but they believed the major decisions of Anaktuvuk lay with the Eskimos and they didn't do much lobbying. Anyway, education was their number-one priority.

Though bilingual, the village youngsters couldn't really speak or think well in either English or Eskimo and didn't know the basics, the DeMarcos reported. Previous teachers had lectured the pupils as much as six hours a day and forced them to memorize the parts of the body, the names of the states, etc. Since none of that was relevant to life at Anaktuvuk, the children had forgotten it all and didn't have much to show for their work.

The children were generally well cared for and well fed, they added. Although their diet consisted mostly of pancakes and caribou meat with no vegetables, the meat was a rich diet in itself. Only when the hunting was poor and the villagers were forced to eat old meat did they suffer, for old meat has little nutrition.

The state-operated school with its adjoining apartment sat high on a hill outside the village and was complete with a generator. Often I'd envied the electric lights in that "ivory tower" but now I found that, for all their modern conveniences, the DeMarcos envied me. They didn't like living apart from the village. It was a long walk for friends to visit and they would have preferred to live within the community. They'd tried unsuccessfully to buy David's sod house and hoped by summer to be rid of their electric lights and the problems that went with them.

Cold weather set in and I watched sadly as the children—so healthy and bright complexioned when I first met them—became thin and sallow for want of food, which was now in short supply. And I saw the same thing in my own face—dark circles under the eyes and patchy skin. There was little fresh meat to barter for. Everyone had borrowed pilot bread (a bland cracker that is a staple in the Arctic) until no one had any left and my neighbors were down to eating the thin legs of old caribou.

A pilot from Bettles, the nearest big village, flew in grocery orders occasionally, but the prices were prohibitive—two small boxes of Kleenex, $1.25; four rolls of toilet paper, $.91; ten pounds of sugar, $2.64—and there wasn't much money.

Jobs in the village were always few. Some men successfully sought work in the big cities, but they missed the Arctic and usually returned. Those who stayed in the village could sometimes earn $1,500 to $3,000 a summer as fire fighters in a dry year. But these paychecks wouldn't last the winter, for the concept of saving was alien to these people. Most villagers could pick up extra money by selling caribou-skin masks for $15 each —the unique faces had been originated by two hunters for an Eskimo dance several years before and were now much sought after by tourists. David had paid for his hotel through such

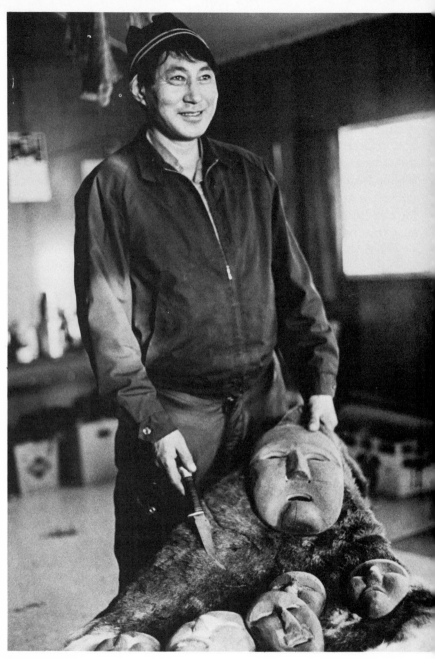

*John Hugo with carved wooden frames he uses to make caribou-skin masks.*

sales, but in the winter there were few tourists. I bought what I could, hoping to trade them later for board and room, but I didn't have much more money than the Eskimos.

Still, life in the pass was pleasant and I found myself becoming more and more engrossed. The villagers showed me how to sew furs and make masks, and Simon told me Anaktuvuk legends about a giant sled dog and people with webbed feet and hands. The others grumbled he'd made most of the stories up himself because anthropologists kept badgering him for the Inupiat's cultural heritage, although, being independents, they really didn't have any.

Mothers' club, which met every Thursday in Pat DeMarco's electrified living room, was another pleasure. It was about the only respite the Anaktuvuk women got from their large families and I loved to sit among them and listen to their soft, happy chatter. One night I watched Rachel Sikvayugak painstakingly put together a fine ruff. Doris Hugo worked on a caribou-fur parka, several others knitted mittens, Pat struggled with bead work, and I was making lace with a shuttle. Talk turned to the early days and Trader O'Connell who had helped establish the village. Rachel and Ethel Mekiana, a girlhood friend, remembered traveling all day by dog team to visit him and the marvelous meal he fed them, which they described in such detail that it made our mouths water.

"We'd run errands for him just for the littlest lick of a Sugar Daddy," Rachel told us. How times had changed. Today, candy and Dr. Pepper soda pop came out of the food stamps and youngsters had grown to think of them as their due. And there were tourists now, not just occasional wayfarers. They started coming to Anaktuvuk on a North Slope tour two summers ago, though no one was sure exactly what to do with them.

A favorite story was of two women tourists who had come to Rachel's and sat down uninvited, "perhaps to find out some things." Rachel was doing her best to be a good hostess when Riley Junior came along, taking his position on the honeybucket directly between the two visitors.

"Pretty soon comes the smell. I didn't know what to say," Rachel recalled. "And Riley Junior sat there and just smiled. They left on some little excuse and never did ask those questions."

In another fascinating session at Pat's house they told stories of the old Eskimo magic and of a medicine man who could throw his gloves across the river and have them fetch back a load of willows or dig his knife into the floor and produce water. It made me shiver, even in an electrified living room. But the stories were not being passed on to the children. No one would say why. Perhaps the Bible had replaced them.

On other evenings Joe Mekiana would tell stories and I came to appreciate him. When he was young he had been adopted by Trader O'Connell for a year. He had dropped out of school early but gone back at the age of twenty-five to finish the seventh and eighth grade. To support himself he'd gotten a job maintaining the school generator. The Anaktuvuk teacher, who was a pinochle nut, kept him up each night playing cards, but somehow he'd managed to earn his diploma and go to Chicago to take a job. Now, at thirty-two, he was back in the pass again. He'd written the BIA in hopes of obtaining a city job, but the mail planes came and went without an answer. And his mother, the widow Rebecca, who worried about him considerably, was doing her best to keep him home.

She was an industrious woman, out in the foulest weather to gather wood or water or tend the dogs. This morning early, she'd decided to build a new entryway onto Joe's sod house and went at it with hammer, timber, and sheet metal. He slept through the racket and when he woke up he walked bang into the addition and nearly knocked himself out.

With Joe I could speak English freely and indulge in an occasional nostalgic discussion of indoor plumbing or city lights. But I was also acquiring enough Eskimo and local pidgin English to talk with the old timers. Once I had found conversation with Doris Hugo, very difficult although she spoke a little English. Now, when I was stranded with Elizabeth Ahgook, who spoke no English, I used Doris as my interpreter. At last, I decided, I was fluent enough to visit Elijah Kakinya, oldest man in Anaktuvuk.

"He is the only man in the village who always has enough meat," Jane Young told me. "Younger men often laugh that he is too old but whenever they run out of meat they run to him. The old people told him if someone comes to you who needs help, you give it and do not make them pay for it and you will be lucky in catching animals. And Elijah believes that. He always gives and he never gets anything from anybody."

Last year some of Jane's relatives had been camping on the other side of the mountains and found seven fat caribou someone had shot and abandoned. They weren't equipped to take them home so they left them for the ravens but later happened to mention it to Elijah. He had gone up and taken the animals himself. When things got tight this winter and Jane's family ran out of meat, Elijah had come to them and said, "I have seven of your caribou. Come down and help yourself."

Kakinya's frame house was on the remote outskirts of the village surrounded by huge snow drifts. Mae, his weathered-looking wife, watched with amusement as I floundered through and she continued to stare out the window at the birds. Betty and Minnie Ahgook were curled up on a cot, squeezing the last gasp out of the dying batteries of their tape recorder. Elijah I caught napping on a big bed.

He was a strong, sturdy hulk of a man—the one man in all Anaktuvuk, I thought, with whom I would cast my lot against the Arctic. He looked a match for the country. And Jane had been right. He did believe in giving and, as the old people had predicted, he was lucky at catching animals. Although well over seventy, he braved the fiercest weather, brought home the richest pelts; his dogs were well fed and his meat cache was well filled.

Elijah awoke in an expansive mood to tell a surprising history. At the age of thirteen he had worked for Vilhjalmur Stefansson, the Canadian explorer, washing dishes and shooting game. He, his father, mother, brothers, and a sister had traveled widely with Stefansson's Canadian Arctic Expedition while it was in Alaska, until about 1917 when Stefansson moved back into Canada.

Digging under his mattress, Elijah produced an old hand-bag with a carved plastic clasp and brought out a pile of fad-ing photographs. They showed most of the adults in the village as children: David and Joe Mekiana hardly bigger than a cari-bou rack, with David looking just the same as he did today, though on the verge of tears. There were Rachel Sikvayugak and Lela Ahgook in thick, ugly wool stockings with no hint of the beauty they would later mature to. And there was Simon Paneak looking not unlike his son Roosevelt, with his first wife.

Elijah's father was pictured, too—a lithe old Eskimo with a trim mustache like the one Elijah now wore. And there was Elijah, himself, as a young dandy in Fort Yukon, with a Mo-hammed Ali stance and a glare in his eye. He was wearing knickers, a vest, watch and chain, sunglasses, and a brimmed cap—the "now generation" of the twenties. As the photo se-ries progressed, he began to appear more Eskimo. In one shot with Mae and two children, he is wearing the traditional atigi (caribou-fur parka); his wife and children are holding fox skins but Elijah carries the latest model of Kodak camera. To-day's tourists, who regard him as the personification of Eskimo tradition, would certainly have been surprised to see him then.

Walking back to the village I stopped at Ruth Rolland's to warm up and found her three-year-old son wearing only cow-boy boots, a shirt, and a cowboy hat and carrying a cap pistol on his naked hip.

"I want to keep him in so I take away his pants," she ex-plained sheepishly.

"Does it work for husbands too?" I wondered aloud. She giggled and said it did not. On her table was a new garden catalogue showing fruit trees, rose bushes, and strawberries. She had tried to grow a garden once but it had failed. Now she planned to try again, using a plastic shield. We pored wist-fully over the colored pages. How good the strawberries looked.

But Olive Morry had finally sewed my mukluks and I could

*Mrs. Elijah Kakinya in her kitchen.*

enjoy Anaktuvuk without strawberries. My snowmobile boots were oversized and heavy, but the mukluks of warm caribou fur were fantastically light. With them I dared travel several miles from the village in search of occasional privacy.

One afternoon I discovered a glacial lake about a mile and a half south. The day was gray but the ice was an astonishing mint green, set about with flat white mountains. In the middle of the lake was a patch of blue ice and I headed for it, losing all caution in the excitement of the find. Suddenly there was an enormous cracking sound and the vapor of open water ahead. Frightened, I crept back to shore, feeling too much alone.

A week later I returned, escorted by a large flock of ptarmigan in the track of a wolf, to find open water where I had walked so boldly. The day was magnificent. Wet streaks on the shore ice reflected bright blue sky. A gust of wind drifted lazily through the pass, carrying a cloud of delicate mist. The sun was so bright and the sky so clear that the snow was blue. I crumbled some of it in my hand and it stayed blue to the core until the sun dropped and flooded the pass with golden light in the late afternoon.

The silence was broken, then, by the roar of Robert Paneak's snowmobile. After nearly a month's tinkering he'd figured out what was wrong with it and now he was as happy as the winner of the Indianapolis 500. With a wave of his hand he disappeared, to return shortly with Marie sitting behind him. That night to celebrate I baked them a loaf of bread, since they didn't have an oven. When I delivered it at their house I interrupted the children searching Marie's scalp and I wondered if there were lice in the family; but they were only looking for white hairs which Eskimo women pull out. The house was immaculate and so were the Paneaks. Next morning when they ran out of soap they borrowed mine but I had borrowed their washbasin; we had a good laugh getting it all together.

The last days of my stay were the best, for people spoke more freely and I understood them better. Lela Ahgook, whose marriage was said to be the last arranged match in Anaktuvuk, told me of the beginnings of the village when the radio was all static and Andy Anderson, a valiant bush pilot, was their only real link with the outside world. Her mother had died in childbirth when she was eight. Then there had been a flu epidemic and five of the villagers had died.

"I kept the baby alive for two days with a spoon. But then it died. We didn't have bottles then . . ."

She had married when she was sixteen and Noah Ahgook was seventeen; it seemed a good match, with a wealth of children. She had been taking care of children ever since she was eight, and her house was never without guests.

In vain I had tried to find out how the Eskimos felt about their exposure to radioactive fallout, and that answer came, too, in the last week. The people were not worried about fallout but about the white men who were sent to protect them from it. The first to take radiation counts had visited them off and on for several years and they liked him enormously. But he had run off with the white schoolteacher's wife and they were scandalized. The man sent to replace him was thought to be in love with one of the Eskimo wives and she with him. Had she asked me to write him a letter, an elder inquired? She didn't know how to write but they were worried for fear she might be trying to communicate with him. Her husband wanted the villagers to stop her if she tried to run off.

"In this village no one has ever put a wife away," the elder said. "We like this man but we want to write Washington and ask them not to send him any more." He smiled. "Next time he comes, I'm going to tell him I'm going to get that radiation job, maybe get me an English woman."

Then there was the problem of the airport. Several years back the state had taken land in the heart of the Anaktuvuk township and leased it to Wien Airlines. Wien was supposed to maintain it, and they did for the small planes they flew. But they could hardly be expected to put it in shape for the big planes chartered to beat Wien's freight rate of twenty to fifty cents a pound. Several times the Eskimos had unsuccessfully queried the state land office to find out what the terms of the Wien lease were. Now they were wondering if they might lease the airstrip themselves . . . daring to dream of Eskimo power for the first time . . . and I promised I'd help research the venture.

On my last day I stopped to interview Raymond Paneak about the now extinct VISTA program and found myself the target of an interview.

"Well, at least you're spending a little money in the village," he noted, for the checks I'd signed to purchase masks had been turning up to pay fuel bills. Then, out of the blue, he made an eloquent speech thanking me for what I would do for his village and saying how people had enjoyed having me. It was a long speech and caught me quite by surprise, for there were days when I hadn't been sure anybody liked me or had the vaguest idea that I might be trying to help—and it was debatable whether or not anybody *could* help.

"Their fate doesn't seem to be in their own hands," one BIA official had told me. "They have to call for help so often. They're always in the news with airlifts of food, fuel, dog food . . . One day the government is going to have to decide whether it is going to continue to subsidize Anaktuvuk or let it go."

The Inupiat life was filled with confusing contradictions. I watched one morning as Roosevelt Paneak shaved with a battery-powered razor, followed up with a splash of English Leather, and then donned his caribou-fur parka and boots to go hunting.

At mothers' club my neighbors sewed traditional footwear with dental floss while they discussed the problems of melting enough snow to handwash diapers and the advantages of owning a wig. Joe Mekiana told me he had to take a crash course in writing Eskimo before taking the job in Chicago so he could write home to his mother who reads no English. And with my rent money David had ordered twelve frozen chicken TV dinners and some beef which he stored in his traditional outdoor cache.

The Inupiat had found a precarious balance between two worlds—a balance that depended, unfortunately, on the whims of the caribou herds and the welfare agencies. Like my stove, there was no telling when the balance would blow up.

There was no timber, little game, and the cost of living was out of sight.

"Why, why do you live here?" I asked Simon Paneak.

"My family raised me up in the Brooks Range. Traveling all over," the old patriarch said. "I have never been to a school in all my life. . . . When the school is set up we've got to stay where the school is. We like to have our kids learning a little something."

Of course he reserved some nostalgia for the old ways.

"We never had to worry about money then. We traded. Nobody worried about money. A lot better, too. But right now no one can go without some money for the picture show, bingo. We got to buy groceries and fuel oil is expensive."

But he had made the transition from a caribou-fur tent to a plywood house with seeming ease and considerable dignity. He had learned to write well enough to put down some of his favorite legends and sometimes, on winter evenings, he met with the younger men in the village to keep the old songs alive to the beat of the Inupiat skin drum.

I visited one night to listen to the music and was happy to watch his young son and daughter shyly practice the age-old dance motions in imitation of their elders. The next day they would go to Cyrus Mekiana's and listen to his tape of "Jesus Christ Superstar" with the same enthusiasm. Maybe it would even out.

On my last night in Anaktuvuk I was granted permission to photograph the church service. Charlie Ahgook got a dramatic nosebleed, though, and seemed to be wherever I pointed my camera, so finally I just settled back to listen to the service. Zack Hugo was in the pulpit preaching in Eskimo and I couldn't get much out of it. Gloomily, I contemplated the church stove which was balanced precariously on four wobbly tomato-soup cans. It seemed a kind of miracle—if we lost faith, it would probably topple and we'd all go up in a sheet of flame.

"Oh, please God, get me out of Anaktuvuk Pass alive," I found myself imploring silently to the Maker. And at just that point Zack favored me with the only English of the evening.

"You shall be saved," he said firmly.

It was a clear, beautiful night and I didn't want to go back to the hotel when church was over. Instead, I wandered the hills around the village, trying to get some perspective on the little settlement.

Why had the Inupiat stayed in this pass? This place at the end of the earth? Why did they stay to suffer the cold and watch their children grow thinner?

Then, suddenly, I became aware of the moon which was as bright and full as an Inupiat face and of the mountains which stood close around me in the awesome beauty of its light. Who would believe that man could survive to enjoy this place? And what a feeling of strength to know you can survive it, conquer it, live with it, feast off it . . . or even endure it.

# Point Hope

## A WORKABLE TRADITION

*The Arctic village of Point Hope is set on a game-rich finger of land in the Chukchi Sea, on one of the oldest, continuously inhabited sites in North America. Little is known of its first inhabitants except that their artifacts are quite unlike any others and that they managed to support an unusually large population (over 2,000) by hunting and fishing.*

*About A.D. 900 Siberian Eskimos introduced the seal-skin float, making it possible to keep the heaviest sea animal buoyant after the kill so the carcass could be retrieved. With this invention, the inhabitants, backed by the security of having an increasing herd of caribou, began to develop techniques for hunting the abundant whales that migrated annually past the point.*

*The people flourished from this whaling industry with virtually no intrusion until 1886 when the first Yankee whaling station was established there. Eskimo Chief Attungowruk imposed a demarcation line between Point Hope and Jabbertown, a colony of sailing men and adventurers that grew up around the American whaling camp. The line kept the whites from Eskimo whaling waters but it didn't stop a lively traffic in alcohol and women that grew up between the two settlements.*

*In 1889 the commander of a United States revenue cutter found Point Hopers "in a most degraded state, physically, mentally and spiritually" as the result of contact with the white man. "Each visit of a whaling* ship was followed by riot and drunkenness; the women were carried off to serve the lusts of the sailors and officers," he reported to the mission division of the Episcopal Church. "Although under the flag of the United States, there was nothing but chaos and paganism."

In response, the Episcopalians dispatched the Reverend Dr. John Driggs. The Point Hope people, still very much in control of their boundaries, refused to let the missionary land in the village, ruling that he must stay a mile from town. At the end of the winter, they said, they'd decide whether to kill him or let him live among them.

Driggs had his work cut out for him. His Eskimo dictionaries didn't include the Point Hope dialect. He had no place to live except an improvised shelter of barrels and canvas, and many of his supplies had been swept away by the sea when he came ashore. Eventually, though, according to his own account, he captured a native boy on the beach, took him home, taught him the alphabet, and baked him a cake. The boy's report of the adventure inspired other Eskimos to visit and they displayed an interest in Driggs's educational program as long as it included food.

In mid-winter the missionary was called to cure the chief's son of an illness that the local witch doctor had failed to diagnose. If Driggs failed, the Eskimos promised he would be killed, but being an excellent physician he cured the boy and was allowed to move into the village.

Driggs stayed with his ministry until the turn of the century when the Church retired him on the grounds that he'd "become a bit strange" and that "a man should not be alone too long in the Arctic." But Driggs hadn't been alone. He'd simply gone Eskimo. And though retired, he stayed on, living in a sod house like the rest of his people.

Driggs heartily endorsed the traditional Eskimo

*Point Hope.*

*ways, refusing to let the young men of the village at-
tend school in hunting season. But he had also placed
a high premium on formal education and through his
teaching the Eskimos had become literate and developed a workable balance between their own and the
white man's culture.*

*For three generations Point Hope prospered. A mod-
ern village was built and became a fourth-class incor-
porated city. In 1958, when the Atomic Energy Commission developed a plan to evacuate the settlement
and blast an atomic harbor off its coast, the Eskimos
were strong enough to fight it. Joining forces with
other endangered villages and with the Association of
American Indian Affairs, they eventually pressured
the AEC to abandon the project. One highly literate
Point Hope man was elected to start a newspaper and
watchdog for further encroachments on the valued native lifestyle, while the rest of the Eskimos went back to
whaling.*

*Point Hope's respite continued until 1971 when out-
side conservationists moved to stop the killing of sea
mammals. American efforts had failed to limit the annual taking of thousands of bowhead whales by the
Japanese and Russian factory ships, so conservationists
turned instead to the Eskimos. The natives took only a
few dozen bowheads each year, hunting from their
primitive skin boats, but the conservationists demanded they end their tradition.*

In the spring of 1972 I was signed on as assistant cook for the
whaling crew of Bernard Nash, a Point Hope Eskimo. Usually
Eskimos do not allow white men on their crews and white
women are even less welcome, but Nash's wife, Ruth, was the
sister of *Tundra Times* editor Howard Rock. It was Rock whom
the villagers had chosen a decade ago to monitor any infringe-
ments of their rights, and Rock realized that if conservationists

could gain congressional support, this might well be the last whaling season for his native village. The Eskimos did not understand his concern, nor did they welcome his reporter, but, apparently as a family obligation, the Nashes accepted me as a member of their household.

Ruth was at the Point Hope airstrip to greet me but left on the very plane I arrived on to consult an eye doctor in Kotzebue, the nearest large village. Her absence was to my advantage, for it gave me an immediate chance to show my worth. There was a family of five to be fed and cared for, as well as the whaling crew and neighbors who were working to ready the Nashes' gear.

Point Hope, a village of four hundred Eskimos, looked like a modest suburbia displaced to the bleak tundra some 140 miles north of the Arctic Circle. All the houses, with one exception, were of modern frame construction and wired with electricity. The Nashes' home, perched near the Chukchi Sea, was a delight. They had painted it indigo which brightened even the grayest days and it stood out smartly in the conservative community. It boasted three bedrooms, a sizable kitchen and living room, and a washroom with a chemical toilet; and it was well insulated and warm.

Nash had built it himself, he said, hiring the Assembly of God missionary to finish off the inside when he got a high-paying job in summer construction. The money spent on his house had been put to good use. Except for indoor plumbing, we did not want for material comforts. A big electric deep freeze and a new gas range dominated the kitchen. We still cooked on the old oil stove, since it served as a source of winter heat and the gas had yet to be hooked up. But Ruth stored her tablecloths in the new stove and it was a prestigious fixture.

Other signs of prosperity included an electric can opener, radio, and tape recorder. The freshly painted walls were decked with family photos, religious pictures, calendars from politicians, and a plush wall tapestry. The house was comfortably furnished throughout.

Preparations for the traditional whale hunt were in stark

contrast to these modern surroundings, however, for the ritual had changed little in a thousand years. A week before the whales were expected, the women sewed new covers of the skin of ugruk, the bearded seal, over boat frames of driftwood. Paddles were readied, since engines made too much noise to hunt the great whales. Now our men inflated the sealskin floats and cleaned their ancient harpoons. Their weapons had been patented by Yankee whalers in the late 1800s and I suspected some of them were originals. All the harpoons were fitted with crude black-powder bombs which the men loaded by hand in the living room.

This would be Nash's second year as a whaling captain and he had yet to get a whale. He was an excellent hunter and had been harpoon man on the crew that killed Point Hope's largest whale, a sixty-five-footer, but becoming a successful whaling captain takes considerable experience and cash outlay. Last year, for want of funds, he had left his crew part way through the season to take a construction job outside the village. This year's hunt was being outfitted with about $700 from his income tax refund, unemployment checks, and food stamps.

Most of our equipment came from Laurie Kingik, a successful captain who'd been forced to retire because of poor health. Kingik's wife, Sarah, was Nash's sister, which created a close bond between the two families, and Kingik spent hours in the Nash living room carefully overhauling his gear.

With Ruth gone, there was plenty for me to do, too. I relied on her capable daughter Judy, nineteen, to give direction and to care for the younger children, Elizabeth, aged eleven, and Jack, seven. Judy was inexperienced at baking, though, so I kept the family supplied with fresh bread and worried about most of the meals. And there were endless pots of coffee to be brewed for our visitors.

The ice finally began to move and the first navigable water opened April 12. Now the big bowheads could begin to pass through the leads (channels through the ice) on their northern migration and the whole village became tense with the excitement of getting out on the water. Children spent a lot of time on the rooftops gazing out at the sea ice, and young Jack practiced throwing his broomstick harpoon at the snowbanks when he thought nobody was looking. Our nearest neighbor got overanxious and set up ice camp prematurely. It was hard to contain ourselves as we watched him take down his umiak (skin boat) and strap it to his sled. But we waited—the nearest lead was still ten miles out and that was too far.

The next morning open water moved closer and the whole village came alive at 6:30. Our crew descended with wives and mothers and Esther, our head cook. She was twenty-seven, unusually tall for an Eskimo and lanky. Some of her front teeth were missing and her face defied all the standard criteria of beauty yet came off as simply marvelous. Despite the fact that she was born and raised in Point Hope, she spoke English with such a polished accent that her "no" came out "new" like a Boston lady. But she was easygoing and I liked her immediately.

We served breakfast in seemingly endless shifts until the last setting was finally determined by the arrival of a snowmobile bearing the "preacher" to bless our boat. I was laboring over some scrambled eggs at the time and arrived late, to find everybody kneeling in the snow around our umiak in the face of a stiff west wind. The preacher was a solidly square matron wearing a full-length fur-lined parka of wildly flowered cotton. She spoke briefly in guttural Eskimo and apparently to the point. Our crew hit the trail as soon as she departed. Our camp was to be four miles out on the ice.

Two dog teams went first, followed by snowmobiles hauling sleds of supplies, our grub box, and the boat. Esther and I hurried into our arctic gear, thinking we would surely go with the grub box, but the men said no. They'd come back to fetch us after camp was set up. Disappointed, we settled back to wait.

Although she was much sought after as a cook, Esther had not been on a whale hunt in four years. She was Laurie Kingik's daughter and had been born restless; she had received her education at the Bureau of Indian Affairs school in Mount Edgecumbe in the southeastern part of Alaska, near Sitka, gone north to work in a bakery in Nome for a year, then lived on Little Diomede Island near Siberia until her father asked her to come home. Somewhere along the way she had married a hard-drinking Eskimo from Barrow, but the marriage had ended in divorce. Now she had a second husband of whom she was very proud, a man from Michigan who had come to Alaska as a heavy-equipment operator. The match kept her in Fairbanks but she had grown homesick for the whaling season and her husband had let her come back.

She was almost as excited as I was when the men came to take us to camp an hour later. Secretly I had feared that we might be left behind and she seemed concerned, too. Now the false start was forgotten and we were ready for action.

It was my first long snowmobile ride. Esther assigned me to the back of a flat wooden sled tied on behind the machine, handed me a tin teakettle, cover ajar, and sat in front of me, feet out straight. Clutching my teakettle like a sacred trust, I grappled to snap up my hood to keep it from blowing off. To get a better grip I shed my fur mittens and my hands began to freeze. Finally I got the hood up but the wool-brimmed hat I was wearing underneath it kept slipping down and covering my eyes. All vision was obscured except for a tiny peephole and that shortly went blank because my breath steamed up the sunglasses I was wearing to prevent snow blindness.

Somehow I worked my hands back into my mittens, just managing to stave off frostbite, and hooked one arm through some webbing I'd tangled with on the back of the sled. For an instant I heard the snowmobile slow down and hoped for a reprieve, but I quickly learned to respect the sound. We had topped a drift on an ice ridge and didn't hit the trail again until we dropped some three feet. Fortunately my elbow was lodged in the webbing and I wasn't thrown. Then my glasses cleared and I found to my relief that I still had the teakettle and cover. "I'll probably freeze to death right here, clutching the damn thing," I thought wildly and had to giggle at the

*Two would-be "boys" catch a ride to camp.*

*Whaling camp on ice at Point Hope.*

idea of being interred wrapped around a tin pot in a crouching position.

We rode for what seemed like an hour but was probably only twenty-five minutes. I got only glimpses of the huge pressure ridges and large ice chunks. Most of the time I found myself looking at the inside of my hat brim.

Finally we stopped and I unsnarled myself from the webbing, carefully setting the teakettle on the ice. The wind snatched it out of reach. I hustled after it, reclaimed it, and was brought up short by a string I'd tied to my mittens to keep them handy. It had tangled in the sled runner and I worked a long time to get myself sorted out. Straightened out at last, I worked my way out of the hat and hood for my first look at the camp and was almost knocked out at the beauty of the site.

There was a new white tent, ten by twelve feet, with smoke perking from a metal chimney set in a shield at the top. The guy ropes of the shelter were tied to crystal ice blocks with holes chopped in the top. Our two dog teams were staked out neatly on either side of the snowmobiles. The skin boat was ready and waiting, poised in the direction of the open water and Bernard stood lookout high above it. Back of the tent was a sheltering pressure ridge glistening with virgin snow. To my right was a fierce black sea which gave off dark mists shot with flashes of brilliant sunshine and I stayed there for some time trying to reconcile the contrast of the heaving water and our serene encampment just beyond its reach. Finally I followed the crew to shelter.

The tent flap was tied down to a two-and-a-half-foot opening which I negotiated on my hands and knees. Suddenly my jacket caught and held me poised, face down, over a big pan of greasy seal blubber.

"Oh, my god, is this lunch?" I wondered. As if in answer, a boy fished out a piece with a fork and rammed it into a little homemade stove. It burned like napalm, the world's finest fuel in action. I'd read that ancient Eskimo winter homes were unbearably hot and had never understood why. Now I did. The tent was just thin canvas and a strong wind assailed it, but inside it was sweltering.

*Visitors in the cook tent.*

One of the men was eating raw frozen fish, cutting off chunks with his hunting knife, and everyone else was drinking tea. A flat sled had been brought in which seated four, and the folding cot, Bernard's one camp luxury, was set up at the far end to accommodate four more. There was also the big grub box where I perched myself. Everything was neatly arranged on three plywood planks that served as a floor and around them and between the cracks I could see the Windex-blue ice of the Chukchi Sea.

It proved to be the shortest long day I had ever put in, for there was much to be learned. Esther was a past master as a camp cook. Casually, without a recipe, she mixed a mammoth batch of yeast doughnuts in a dishpan and fashioned them without a cutter by rolling the dough in a ball, punching a hole dead center with her finger and fashioning the rim between her palms. Then she boiled up a batch of caribou stew while she was waiting for the dough to rise.

The men sat around the tent for a while.

"Who's watching for whales?" I asked.

"Too rough."

But finally the wind abated and by late afternoon they were on the lookout.

We would stay on the ice unless the wind shifted south, Esther told me. Then we'd have to move the tent.

"I don't want to move the tent," I said.

"Then you'll probably wind up in Siberia if the ice doesn't melt before you get there," she warned.

"I'm willing to move the tent."

After supper there was debate as to whether we women should sleep in the tent or go back to the village for the night. It was decided that the men would stay out until whale watching was more productive, and they moved to windbreaks by the ice floes. Esther and I were to commute from town, although after the morning ride I had such a horror of it that I almost volunteered to sleep by the floe. Mercifully, the night trip proved easier than my maiden voyage. There was no wind and I got my hat anchored before we set out.

The next few days were poor whaling. The winds were tricky and kept shifting the leads and it really was early in the season. The men were disappointed and so was I, but at least it gave me a chance to get better acquainted with them.

Bernard proved to have more depth than I had expected, with a gentle sense of humor and a steady temperament. The mark of an Eskimo is toughness and he had that, but he showed a concern for the comfort of his men that I found rare on the ice. There seemed to be a generally held Eskimo philosophy that a certain amount of calculated cruelty was necessary. Most Eskimos were particularly hard on weaklings, perhaps to strengthen them for the harsh environment—for the survival of the fittest. But Bernard had a kind heart.

His lineage was a quarter Portuguese, but he bore a startling physical resemblance to the pharaohs of Egypt. His face was fine boned and striking, but I never managed to get a decent black and white photo of him because his subtle dark coloring added much to his good looks.

His son, Sam, twenty-two, was strong and powerful but the glasses he wore made him look the stereotype intellectual. He had been named for his mother's grandfather Sam Rock, a legendary whaler and one of the first Point Hope Eskimos to be educated, and young Sam carried on in his spirit; he read every possible spare moment. While others enjoyed "Bugsy Bunny" comics, Sam methodically plowed through Zane Grey and Herman Wouk and James Michener. He kept so many books in his room there was scarcely room for a bed. Last year while outside the village for National Guard training, he had laid in forty pocket books for the winter and recently he'd joined a book club. It was quite a self-education program. Often he read with a dictionary in one hand. Yet he was agile on the ice and a good hunter. Too good, perhaps, to go on to school and complete his formal education.

Eark Kingik, twenty-three, was the most sophisticated of our crew, having served in the Army in Vietnam and vacationed in England with the anthropologist who sometimes hunted with his father. Had I met him in the city, it would never have oc-

*View of the Chukchi Sea from the cook tent.*

curred to me he was an Eskimo, but he was Laurie Kingik's son and had been trained early and well as a whaler.

Recently Earl had been hired as an enumerator, to enroll Point Hopers for the land claims settlement and he shuffled the bureaucratic paperwork with ease, carefully documenting every family's lineage and working out the difficult English spellings of their names. His assignment had a May deadline which meant he had an enormous amount of work to do in a short time, but he was determined to go whaling despite it.

Norman Omnik, in his mid-twenties, had lived five years near San Francisco where he worked as an auto mechanic. One season he had come home to Point Hope for whaling, only to be called into the Army. Now he was elated to be back and he was good on the ice despite his long stay in the south.

Gus Kowunna, Sr., in his forties, offered fine testimony that the older a man gets in the Arctic, the tougher he gets. Although little more than my height and weight, he was built like a rock and had a cast-iron constitution. A friend of Bernard's since childhood, Kowunna served as his "ice expert" although he might well have been a captain in his own right. We took his weather predictions as gospel, and his judgment on the movement of the ice and currents was uncanny. He also had the balance to walk on thin ice that lighter men fell through, which had earned him his title of "ice expert."

Rounding out our crew was Isaac Killigivuk, twenty-one, who had returned from an Indian high school in Oklahoma at the first possible chance and seemed thoroughly content to live by subsistence hunting. His eyesight—his ability as a spotter—was phenomenal and he was tough enough so that no one made fun of his long hair—something villagers generally condemned as being "hippish."

The least heralded member of our party was Gussy Kowunna, Jr., thirteen, our "boy," who had the rottenest assignment of all. It was his duty to cut the blubber for the stove, fetch snow to melt for drinking and wash water, tend the dogs, and stoke the fire all night while the men slept. He was also

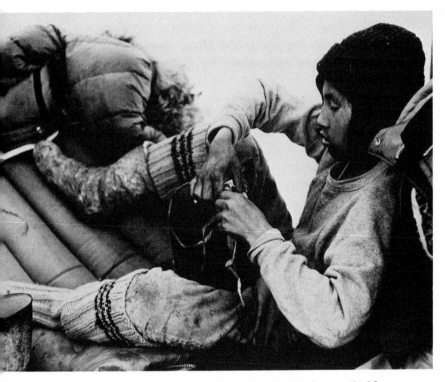

*Our "boy," Gussy Kowunna, Jr., trying to make his boots pliable.*

supposed to fetch and carry for the hunters and speak only when spoken to, but it was a coveted assignment and he carried it out well. If he hadn't, there were plenty of boys ready to take his place, for he was in reality an apprentice whaler and one day soon might become a full-fledged member of the crew.

As a baby—on the death of his mother—Gussy had been informally adopted by Laurie Kingik whom he regarded as his father. The crew reminded him with painful regularity that Gus Senior was his real father, but he didn't know Kowunna well and had little to say to him. Esther, who thought of herself as his sister, had considerable sympathy for the boy and managed to show it in ways the men would not notice. It was Esther who had gotten Gussy out of school for the hunt. She had simply written a note that said "Gustavo is excused from school to go whaling."

The crew was as curious about me as I was about them. They had heard that I had come from Anaktuvuk Pass and wanted to know what I'd been doing there. Some of the Anaktuvuk people had taped recorded greetings in Eskimo to their friends in Point Hope, which seemed to answer the question satisfactorily. As to my mission on the ice, I explained that Congress was considering legislation that would stop all taking of the bowhead for five years. There had been a rash of "poor whale" stories in the newspapers but nothing on the problems of the Eskimos, and I believed *Tundra Times* and other papers I wrote for might help.

The whalers understood but remained skeptical. One of the men recalled that once the government had forbidden them to shoot eider ducks, but they had hunted them anyway and finally the law was repealed. They would hunt the bowhead, too, he said, no matter what.

I argued that it was hard to hide a whale and that if the Department of Fish and Wildlife people confiscated their whaling equipment, they would be out of business, for it would take over $1,500 and many weeks of work to replace it. Yet as far

back as anyone could remember—indeed, for a thousand years
—the men of Point Hope had taken the bowhead. The whaler
was the most respected of men and it was hard for the Eskimos
to imagine him put out of business. Besides, they needed the
whale to live. I asked Bernard how much a whale would be
worth to him and his crew in equivalent groceries.

"Why, thirty to sixty tons of groceries," he said. Except for
small token gifts, the products of the whale was the only
recompense the crew would receive.

"And we use every bit of it except for the lungs and the
liver, which we give to the dogs," Bernard added.

For this reason, the hunters were conservationists too, but
they honestly believed the bowhead wasn't endangered. One
scientist had reported there were only one hundred bowheads
left in the world; another estimated fifty.

"If that was true, I've seen them all in a single day,"
Kowunna smiled. "There are plenty, as you will see."

Esther and I arrived on the ice late next morning to find our
camp in a new location. The men had awakened at 3 A.M. to
the grinding of bergs and emerged to find their tent threatened. Decamping in haste, they pitched again, only to have all
ice action stop.

"But we've seen four belugas, one bowhead, and two right
whale," Isaac reported.

"I never saw a wrong one," Kowunna added.

The men were famished for they'd pursued the animals for
hours without luck. Gussy made coffee for them, but it was five
hours old by the time they'd gotten in and they hadn't had
any solid food. We fed them the remains of the caribou stew.
Then Esther began preparing supper.

Hunters from a neighboring camp had just captured a beluga
and happily Esther fetched us a chunk of it that looked like
the fender of a Cadillac. Working carefully with her round
bladed ulu (the Eskimo woman's traditional wedge-shaped
knife), she cut all but half an inch of blubber off the tough
white skin. Then she chopped the muktuk (skin with blubber)

in inch-and-a-half squares. Over the chunks she poured boiling water, adding chopped onions and a thickening of flour.

The men were delighted. Some of them have been feeling queasy with the flu but the stew would settle their stomachs, they said. I was dubious and took only a small helping. To my surprise it rated as a gourmet delicacy, with a unique flavor somewhere between mushrooms and almonds. Although I realized it was a taste that would be hard to indulge later, beluga became my favorite food and it did help settle the stomach.

At the end of our first week of whaling, a south wind made the ice unstable and we hurried to decamp. The trail was crowded with other crews making a dash for the land. Ours was among the first to arrive in the sheltering lee of the point and I looked back to see a procession of snowmobiles, dog teams, and men steadying sled-borne skin boats. There had been nearly a dozen crews like ours strung out along the sea and they all came in safely.

The south wind prevailed, giving us a chance to rest and relax. It was a good time for storytelling and even the usually silent Sam Nash opened up after supper that night. When he was young, he recalled, he'd gone out with his mother and father and little brother to hunt seals. The ice had blown out to sea, as it had done today, only it was much later in the spring and there was more open water. They were traveling in a boat powered by an unreliable Evinrude engine and two miles from shore it threatened to quit.

"If it had, we wouldn't have made it. My mother was yelling and I was really scared," he confessed. And he had known fear again, even in manhood, going out last season with four men in the umiak in really rough water. They'd gotten a whale, but the wounded animal dragged them a long distance and it had taken them five hours to paddle home against the winds.

There was no shame attached to fearing the sea—it had sometimes taken the men of Point Hope, Sam's great-grandfather among them. He had been hunting with his son, Sam's grandfather, when a very large whale surfaced in a most extraordinary fashion and smashed their boat. The old man had yelled at his son to save himself—to swim—which the boy had done, buoyed up by the hollow hairs of his caribou-fur parka; but the old man had not had the strength.

Yet Sam loved whaling. It was his favorite season, he said, and his little brother, Jackie, nodded in agreement. He wanted to go whaling, too, but at seven they just wouldn't excuse him from school.

I talked to Tom Robinson, Point Hope's principal-teacher, and found him sympathetic to Jackie's problem. Although white, he was enthusiastic about the Eskimo traditions. In fact, he was trying to put together a dog team of his own and he got out on the ice when he could. Willingly he excused the older youngsters to serve a month's apprenticeship as "boys".

"It's as much of an education as they'd ever get in school," he maintained. The younger children couldn't afford to miss the formal education, but eventually he hoped to work out a plan by which they might start school a month early in the fall and then everybody could go whaling.

"The parents always give us the feeling they know school is important but the crews do need boys. What really is important is whaling and the kids take it as seriously as the adults. I don't know what villages do that don't have something as important as whaling."

Robinson invited me to stay and see a movie on the Netsilik Eskimo, a migratory Canadian tribe. The Netsiliks were presented as primitives who lived wholly by subsistence, making sled runners of frozen fish and hides and packing themselves about the Arctic with one or two dogs. The Point Hope youngsters thought them very quaint. Point Hope had a modern school with a modern audio-visual department and the youngsters were pretty much of the twentieth century themselves. Still, they were pleased to recognize some of the Netsilik Eskimo language as their own.

Ruth Nash came home on Saturday, wearing new glasses and proudly bearing a shopping bag stuffed with an enormous wolf skin she had purchased from an interior Eskimo for just $100. Bernard was very happy. His wife was a plump little woman with exquisite dimples and she looked as if she loved him very much. Immediately she set about baking bread and rolls to please him, and she pleased me, too—her bread was the best I had ever tasted.

In honor of Ruth's homecoming, some of last year's black muktuk (from the bowhead whale) was taken from the freezer. Boiled and served hot, it reminded me of tender sweet clams, incredibly disguised to look like pieces of automobile tire. It was eaten with a knife. I learned to cut all but half an inch of fat from the blubber side, peel off the thin outer layer of skin, and then cut it into bite-sized pieces. Some liked it with salt, others with mustard, and I ate it any way I could get it. Rations were short.

The wind was still south so we spent a congenial day at home. Gus Kowunna came over to admire the wolf hide, stayed to scrape it for drying, and soon the family was talking about old times. Out came the Bible with records back to 1890. Both sides of the Nash family had spoken and written some English for three generations, but they laughed to recall how Bernard's father had gotten confused by the new language and answered "absent" to the Rev. Dr. Driggs's first roll calls.

They told of the first vegetables the Eskimos had ever seen and how one old lady had bitten right into an unpeeled onion and how others didn't know what to do with flour and had sprinkled it on the ground. Then, about 1930, the first airplane had flown over, a biplane with no cockpit cover, they recalled.

"One old man looked up and fell right over backwards looking up," Bernard laughed. And Will Rogers and Wiley Post had actually landed in Point Hope for a brief visit.

"He is a good man, Will Rogers. If he had lived, he would have been President," Bernard maintained.

At Kowunna's suggestion, I went to the St. Thomas Episcopal Mission to see some more records. The mission included three large green buildings, straight out of turn-of-the century New England, and Donald and Lilly Oktollik were the first Eskimo preachers to run it.

I found Donald, a small, wiry ex-reindeer herder, laboring over a brand new Sears portable electric typewriter and putting out ten words a minute. His wife, the same woman who had blessed our boat, was working at a treadle sewing machine, surrounded by assorted children, none of which were her own. She told me that she had gone to school with my editor, Howard Rock, and that they had had to walk a mile down the beach to get there.

"It was so cold sometimes the small children cried," she recalled. "Howard was very smart, but his mother made him wear white man's shoes."

From a trunk she produced one of Dr. Driggs's record books dated 1895, in which he reported that school attendance averaged "20-16/25 scholars" and that in April "All boats from whaling stations gone out on the floe and many natives with them. Several of our scholars among them."

Later Driggs noted a "growing disinclination to hunt . . . Gave notice I would not receive at school *on any day when the weather was suitable for hunting,* any young man." (He offered night school for make-up.) Certainly he would have approved of Principal Robinson's plans for early spring dismissal, I decided, but I wondered what he would have thought of his epitaph, written on a plaque by a group of ladies from his home state of Delaware:

"To the Glory of God in the Memory of Dr. John Driggs, first missionary to Point Hope 1890–1908, who led the Pagan Eskimo from the darkness into the light and the Glory of the Gospel of Jesus Christ."

Happy to have a day off and not wanting to crowd the Nash family circle, I explored the village, ending up at the modern prefab co-operative store which offered everything from hair spray to artifacts and harpoons. Then, since I still felt like walking, I got directions to Nanny Ooyahtuonah's sod house.

It was on the very far side of the village behind some whale bone markers and was unlike any sod dwelling I'd ever seen. Twice I circumnavigated it without finding an entrance. A dog was staked beside it and an electric wire was connected from a pole to the snow-covered sod roof, but where in heck was the door? Finally, about a city block away, I noticed a second mound and a doorway. I had to crouch to enter. There were smooth flagstones leading down to another little doorway which opened into a spacious passage lit by a twenty-watt bulb and a little skylight and lined completely with ancient whale-bones covered with vagrant green mold. Stacked neatly along the sides was a fantastic collection of things—old stone seal-oil lamps, carefully chewed mukluk soles, frozen meat, ancient dishes, cans, boxes, a huge copper boiling pan with wooden handles and a graceful cover—more things than I could comprehend although I stood looking at them for some time.

Finally I walked the length of the passage and found a third door even smaller than the first two. I knocked, feeling that the Seven Dwarfs would certainly carry me off at any minute. There was a shuffle beyond and a faint "Hello." I let myself in to a tiny room furnished with two beds, a stove, and a chair. In the center was a small, childlike woman who could have been any age between thirty and fifty, and who looked as though she had been the victim of tuberculosis. She was kneeling on the floor, scraping its immaculately clean wide boards with an ulu.

"I spilled the stove oil," she apologized and went on scraping, and I couldn't get much more out of her except that she wasn't Nanny but Rosemary, Nanny's daughter. Nanny was visiting.

The experience seemed unreal in this modern village, and I arrived back at the Nashes' slightly dazed, only to encounter another surprise. A bush plane had just landed through the foulest weather to take eleven-year-old Elizabeth to the hospital in Kotzebue. She had been sick the day before and skipped school. A cold, I had thought. This morning she had been well enough, but in the afternoon, without a word to the family, she had visited the village clinic and the health aide decided she was having an appendicitis attack. There was no fever and the doctor in Kotzebue, contacted by radio, questioned the diagnosis, but the aide had been sure enough to demand a plane.

Now the little girl walked calmly to the sled behind Bernard's snowmobile and made the bumpy trip to the dirt airstrip without a whimper. She looked very small and lost in the back of the bush plane but her round young face betrayed no fear. The family was stunned but there were no big displays of emotion. After the plane disappeared into the swirling snows, we went home and deliberately talked whaling.

"How many crews on the ice?" I asked.

"Oh, my sister will have it all in her diary," Judy said. And so she had—the name of each captain, the description of each piece of whaling gear, and a camp supply list. There was all the research I had been meaning to do, compiled in Elizabeth's neat hand. To think I had written her off as just a chunky, sometimes beautiful little Eskimo girl who didn't understand English very well!

By Sunday the south wind was dead but church came before whaling. It was a High Episcopal service, with eight choir members in robes, two ministers, and three altar boys garbed in white and carrying gold candle snuffers. The church was large and old, with electrified Japanese-Danish type lights hung from the ceiling and real church pews. The service was in Eskimo, with singing in English, but I didn't care much for it. Compared to the simplicity of the little church at Anaktuvuk, Point Hope Episcopal seemed ostentatious.

After the service I went again to visit the sod house and found Nanny entertaining a troop of youngsters. She was a small, practical-looking woman of no definite age. Her hair was gray-white, her face lined but not withered, and her feet couldn't have been more than size three.

When she learned I worked for Howard Rock, she made me welcome, for she had liked him as a boy, she said. Being used to tourists, she spoke unhesitatingly, though in limited English,

*Nanny Ooyahtuonah working in her sod house, surrounded by children and grandchildren.*

entertaining the children as well as me. Her sod house had been built by the parents of her late husband, before she was born. She stayed there because she liked it, in the face of the general opinion that she should move to a modern house. Maybe she would try a new house next year, but here she met a lot of interesting visitors and occasionally sold them artifacts. She wasn't sure about her age, but she could remember when women thought it fashionable to wear a glass trading-bead strung through the base of the nose and she had known Dr. Driggs, too. A very reasonable man, she said.

Back at the Nashes' at noon, I gave some concerned thought to the problems of diet. Lunch was soup with rice, macaroni, and reindeer meat. Supper the night before had been frozen fish and seal oil. There were also fresh yeast doughnuts and I had to admit that when there was a choice between frozen fish and doughnuts, I leaned toward the doughnuts. It was too much starch and no vegetables, which the Eskimos generally don't eat. I had read that if I ate everything the Eskimos ate, I wouldn't need any vegetables. These people were quite healthy, although whites often got sick among them.

Well, there was no chance of sticking to my usual diet. My job as assistant cook included packing a share of the camp gear and I didn't have strength to carry my own provisions as well. Besides, from what I had seen of the Chukchi cold, I couldn't sustain myself on a white man's diet and do a full day's work, so I'd better get used to something new.

After lunch we were entertained by Principal Robinson who was trying to mobilize his dog team in front of our living-room window. The animals kept pointing in the wrong direction and tangling together, and the lead dog tried to sit on the sled. It was quite a show but no one laughed outright. You had to admire the man's persistence.

Then it was back on the ice for a second week of whaling. Open water was much further out to sea now—maybe six miles —but I made the long trip straddling the grub box and found my balance improving.

The men had improvised a little shelter at the edge of the

floe, digging in with the ends of two ice-testing sticks and hanging a wide strip of canvas between them as a windbreak. Later they built an ice-block wall in the direction of the prevailing wind and installed a sled cushioned with a caribou-fur blanket. Here they kept watch, taking turns cat-napping. It was the mark of a man to stay awake on the ice three days and nights, and our whalers—even little Gussy—were men indeed.

This day was wrapped in a cold white mist. Six boats slid soundlessly past us in pursuit of a whale we hadn't spotted. Nearby a fat seal showed his head. There was a shot. Its nose jerked up and I could see its blood spurting out. It hadn't occurred to me that I would have to watch animals die, but of course that was what this was all about. Our meals had been sparse because Bernard's unemployment checks hadn't come through, and we needed the meat and the blubber for the stove.

The cold was so fierce that ice formed instantly on the hulls of the umiaks when the men pulled them out of the water after each chase. The silence of the lead was broken by the dull thump, thump, thump of their paddles as they beat off the skim and then all was quiet again.

Then, far down the floe, the lookout from a neighboring crew made a wide swimming motion with his arm.

"Agvik . . ." The Eskimo word for whale came as a harsh whisper, and our six men, moving as one, launched the boat and paddled cross current, evading a sweep of jagged, fast moving ice blocks. Suddenly, square in their course a bowhead surfaced. Its black hulk was three times the length of the boat but our men moved without hesitation to attack with the thrust of an ancient harpoon. They struck, but the monster took only a glancing blow, sounded, and surfaced well beyond range.

They returned and hauled the boat out on the ice. The dull thump, thump of the scraping paddles followed me as I headed toward the cook tent.

Because the ice by the lead was untrustworthy, our main camp was made more than a mile away on a thick solid shelf. It was the cooks' assignment to fetch hot food from the tent to

*The hunt just before the ice closes in. Captain Bernard Nash in the*
*bow with harpoon.*

the hunters by the open water and it was a tough job. The pots of stew and coffee were hot and cumbersome burdens for such a long trek.

Foolishly I set out on the second run alone and lost the trail in the uncertain twilight. Soon fear and cold began to wear at me. I was packing a heavy shopping bag. My hands grew numb and my legs leaden; an overpowering desire to sleep came on me. It was the first stage of freezing to death. I knew it and I fought it, but never had I entertained a sweeter idea than the thought of just curling up on that ice and closing my eyes.

Finally Esther overtook me and I got control of myself. I couldn't let her know I was in trouble or the Eskimos would be too worried about me to let me back on the ice. So I forced myself to keep walking, thinking of only one foot at a time, and there at last was the tent.

The third trip to the lead that day I survived in good shape and stayed to watch a new moon appear like a shiny fingernail paring in the sky.

Ruth was there, too, and she and Esther and I made our way back in semidarkness. Nothing looked familiar and the light went out completely as we reached the tent. At midnight Ruth and I bumped back to the village, to find the stove out and the house gone cold. It would have been warmer to stay in the tent, but at least we had news of Elizabeth. Her appendix had ruptured. They had operated on her for three hours but she would be all right.

Next morning I heard Ruth coughing herself awake. Like most Eskimos she smoked too much, and I wondered why she had so much stamina. The cold air on the ice made me cough and I didn't smoke, yet she took it in stride, humming happily. Although several years my senior, she could outwalk me and manage a sled or a snowmobile almost as well as a man.

That day the wind was fierce but our crew was out on the hunt. Esther made reindeer stew, Ruth started doughnuts, Gussy took a nap, and I became Gussy, fetching and carrying whatever was needed.

The Eskimos of three generations back thought it was bad luck to eat on the ice or enjoy any comfort there, the women told me. They had just carried seal intestines full of water (under their armpits to keep the water from freezing) and a small poke of food in the boat and that was it. Women hadn't even been allowed on the ice. But eventually the Eskimos saw that the Yankee whalers ate better and had better luck and the present camp system developed.

The next long portage I made with food, I wished the Spartan way had prevailed, for I was miserable and too cold to eat. To keep occupied while I waited to collect the dirty dishes, I wandered off to take photographs and got back to find our crew in a rush to leave. The ice was shifting, pushed by a north wind, but they couldn't get their snowmobile started. We women left in haste, running into a twenty-knot wind. Esther fell, wrenching her leg, and my legs were stiff and sore.

Back in the tent, we began doing dishes. Bernard arrived and asked for tea. The wind was moving the floe but he didn't think the tent was endangered. The men arrived with the machine, drank the tea, and finished the stew. Then, fifteen minutes later, we struck the tent. The wind picked up to almost thirty knots and by the time we hit the trail it was hard to see. I was sitting on the sled atop a box of blubber. A washtub in front threatened to fall off so I inched forward and anchored it with my feet. Suddenly the coupling on our snowmobile let go and we had to pull off the trail to make repairs. The wind was wild and all the world went white. The other crews coming off the ice were just frenzied shadows. Finally our machine was repaired, but in helping dislodge the sled from a drift I fell heavily, cracking my knee. It was the roughest ride I'd ever taken and I was surprised to find I hadn't broken any bones.

The weather-bound vacation that ensued was a happy one, mainly thanks to Leroy, an Eskimo who didn't speak Eskimo, who was "in retreat" from the outside world. He had come home fresh from a cruise with a girl in the Bahamas (she paid) and was working on a neighbor's whaling crew in an attempt to forget her. Possession of liquor was outlawed in Point Hope, but Leroy still considered himself a resident of the Bahamas and had provided himself with a little cheer. Nobody got drunk—who could eat raw beluga for breakfast with a hangover?—but it was a good day off.

For some reason, there was a lot of talk about education. Most Point Hope adults had only had a chance at grammar school. The younger generation had better luck, and the Nashes were proud of Judy's diploma from Alaska Business College and of an older daughter who was working as an X-ray technician. Leroy lamented that his parents hadn't been enthusiastic about his schooling and finally changed the subject.

Amos Lane's crew was fishing through the ice this year, someone reported. Catching crab.

"How do they cook them?" I asked.

"Cook them? They just eat them raw," Ruth said.

"My mother used to say, 'You used to eat raw meat before you got civilized. Look at you now,'" Leroy put in.

The company started singing hymns in Eskimo. Ruth said they should pray that they caught the first whale. Leroy, being of another crew, said he'd pray they got a whale, but he couldn't quite ask that it be the first one. More hymns.

Leroy drifted into the living room to talk with some men who were visiting. Some children came by, peeked in the window, and saw his bottle.

"Little shits," he said. "Now they'll tell everyone."

They were followed by the police chief, but it turned out to be a social visit.

"How are you?" he asked Leroy.

"Horny," Leroy said placidly. "But that doesn't take too long to get over. Funny, once I went without eating eleven days and after the first two I wasn't hungry any more, but this doesn't work that way."

We asked the police chief about his new dog team, which he had purchased from an Anchorage musher. They were beautiful dogs, but city dogs in Point Hope amused the villagers and to date his animals had proved slow runners.

"They wouldn't eat seal meat when they came," the chief admitted. "But now they're getting on to it."

I relayed that one to Judy who had been watching the progress of the team closely. She giggled. "They're high-class dogs," she observed.

The next day we were hunting again. A longer vacation would have been welcome, for I was a mass of bruises—right thigh black, left knee blue and purple, right knee blue. Then Kowunna's snowmobile almost finished me off, bouncing into a crevasse on the trail and casting a two-foot U-shaped piece of iron sled runner within an inch of my head. The stove went overboard and I landed in a box of rancid whale blubber we were going to use for fuel and came up smelling like a real rose.

I walked the rest of the way with Ruth and Sarah Kingik, Esther's lanky mother, and her grandson who was known simply as "Junior." It was a clear day and I spotted the first whale as soon as I saw open water. It exploded on the horizon like black gunpowder and after that whales danced by all day.

The thick shelf of ice hadn't moved, so we reclaimed our original campsite and quickly set up shop to boil polar bear. It didn't appeal to me—it was rather like last Thursday's pot roast basted with cod-liver oil—but I swallowed three pieces and came to appreciate it. With a little polar bear meat under your belt, you can walk on the ice for five hours and never feel cold. Of course, you belch all day, no matter what you eat afterward, but that's a small price to pay to keep from freezing to death.

Mid-meal our crew took off to give chase and Ruth went back to camp to reheat the meat. I sat quietly by the lead watching the boats race to the horizon where the air seemed to separate the paddlers from their craft. Suddenly, almost within reach of my hand, six frisky belugas swam by. I was so pleased and excited I forgot about my camera but I recovered in time to photograph them as they obligingly swam back again.

Another bright part of that day was Sarah Kingik, who was an excellent storyteller. It seemed that although women are seldom allowed in the whale boats, she had a whale to her credit. As a teen-ager, she said, she had been out on the ice with two girlfriends when Jimmy Killigivuk spotted a whale. He didn't have a crew with him, so he took them along and they landed a big one.

At her request, I spent much of the afternoon knitting her a hat while she played solitaire and Ruth worked a pair of seal-skin boots.

Junior, Sarah's grandson, who wasn't quite four, had to answer a call of nature and nearly froze his bottom off. Then he couldn't get his pants up again—they had sort of frozen down. Gussy came to the rescue and dried his tears, but later, rather than face it all again, the child wet his pants and had to be sent home.

The cold was like acid, eating and eating at us. The wind went up to thirty knots, threatening the tent, and Sarah put up part of an old tent as a windbreak.

A rim of new ice began to form on the edge of our lead but the men were in good spirits, despite the cold and their lack of success with the hunt.

"Where did all the whales go?" I asked.

"The whales are up at Cape Thompson," Isaac said.

"What's going on up there we haven't got?"

"An Eskimo dance!"

Kowunna was talking to the sun.

"Thank you for shining, sun, and being happy. Even though it's winter, it's warm."

"Do you know why white people are always cold?" Norman asked. "Because they keep all their blubber in their heads."

"It's not our fault we're built upside down!"

At 7:30 P.M. we called it quits.

The first kill was made on the ninth day—a thirty-eight-foot bowhead, estimated to weigh a ton a foot. And it took an extraordinary amount of work to capture it.

We had been up at 5 A.M. and out early to find the lead still

*The whale hunt.*

icing. Earl had shot a seal and was waiting for the current to fetch it in. The men set up a casual competition to see who could skip a piece of ice the farthest, for there wasn't much to do but wait. About 5 P.M. we could see whales far out, and the crews began to attack the skim ice with their paddles, "making water" to float the umiaks. Then they worked from the boats, pulling them back and forth with ropes tied to the solid ice and gradually beating their way to open water. It was slow, painful work but a mile out, the whales began swimming en masse. At one glance I counted eight spouts and two black flukes (tails) plus some small belugas.

Finally seven boats gave chase. We women stood watching with cooks from neighboring camps, until our men disappeared over the horizon. For two hours we waited in the coming darkness, sometimes getting tantalizing glimpses of the chase. Finally from across the water we heard the echoing cheers of the crews. We cheered and yelled back and the Eskimos began laughing and hugging one another. Listening, I realized it was the first time I'd heard the women really laugh since we started on the ice. At last the tension was broken, and the boys began to dance.

The umiaks came home pulling the catch, hooked up to the whale like dogs to a sled. Billy Weber, the captain who made the first strike, was in the lead, but our crew was close behind because they had helped land the catch and would get a share.

Surprisingly, there was little talk of the hunt when the men got back to our tent. They said that when Weber got the whale hauled up on the ice he had thanked God. But that was all. It was 1:30 A.M. and I went outside. Our tent, lit by a Coleman lantern, glowed through the darkness and on either side were other radiant tents, dotting the line of the lead.

The next day Earl Kingik drove to Weber's camp to collect our share of whale. The animal had been completely butchered, its parts stacked in piles like the meat department of a supermarket. According to custom, the American flag flew over the site with the captain's whaling flag, and the place was crowded with people muscling huge chunks of meat onto sleds.

Back at camp there wasn't much to do except celebrate, for the ice on our lead had grown too thick to break, though not strong enough to walk on. A big batch of muktuk was boiled and a large number of guests arrived simultaneously for a feed.

Among them was John Bockstoce, an anthropologist who had hunted with Nash the year before. The Eskimos had spoken highly of him—he had once been on an Olympic boating team and was good with a paddle. He had also lived with the Greenland and Canadian Eskimos and our people liked his stories. Bockstoce was a jovial young man, six feet tall, over 200 pounds, and quite blond. A Yale graduate, he had just come by way of Nome from teaching at Oxford, and he was full of gossip from other Eskimo communities.

After the muktuk picnic I found myself in trouble with the Eskimos and I couldn't figure out why. I was all dressed for the ice next morning when Ruth told me I'd have to wait in the village until after they caught the next whale. Then she relented and said I could come along today, but she wondered just how much they were obligated to do for me.

There was no obligation, I told her—I didn't want to cause trouble and I realized that sometimes when I tried to help I caused work because I wasn't used to Eskimo ways.

She said that wasn't it—in fact, I worked too much. But they were mad because I'd taken pictures of them the day before when they were eating.

On the ice we used our hunting knives rather than silverware to eat because they were handier, but the Eskimos, who were sensitive about table manners, seemed embarrassed to be caught using a knife for a fork. And I had overdone the picture taking, I knew, but after my first bad fall from the snowmobile I'd feared I might soon break a leg or an arm and decided I'd better shoot while I could. Our crew had been patient, but when I'd pursued it before friends and visitors during a meal, it was just too much.

Throughout that day I took a lot of subtle digs from the men about it, but I held my tongue until everyone had assembled in the tent. Then Earl came near me, borrowing Esther's camera and pretending to take my picture as I speared a piece of muktuk with my Swiss Army knife.

"I'm sorry, Earl, that I offended you by taking a picture of you when you were eating," I said evenly, and all conversation died around us. "I never saw so many happy people on one beach. I won't use it if you don't like it but it was a good picture."

There was no reply, nor did I expect one, but the digs stopped and the air seemed lighter. Earl asked Bockstoce about congressional hearings to be held in Nome on the sea mammal protection bill. How were they going to be?

"Exciting," Bockstoce said.

"Will your pictures be ready by then?" Earl asked me.

"At least half of them," I promised.

Then Kowunna asked me to knit him a hat when I finished Sarah's and little Jackie stopped talking in whispers in my presence and, for the first time since I'd arrived, he actually sat down beside me. Further down the ice, another photographer was having problems, too. Later I learned that he had been banished from his camp and gratefully I went back to my cooking.

In three days the new ice on our lead became thick enough for experienced men to walk on. Carefully they carried our boat over it and set up a windbreak at the edge of a new lead a mile out. From the huge ice block by our tent I watched them play hide and seek with three big bowheads, but they didn't win.

"How fast can a whale swim?" I asked Kowunna.

"About fifty miles an hour if he puts his mind to it," was the answer. One of the Point Hope boats could go twelve miles an hour, a bit faster if the crew was good.

"When you see a whale, you gotta work, work, work. Work like hell to catch him . . . Work till you sweat!"

You must strike him from behind or directly in the front, because his eyes are on the sides, Kowunna explained. If he sees you, he'll move out. And with our old weapons, the crew needed the advantage of surprise.

But I would shortly see another technique, for Amos Lane, the captain of the crew nearest us, tackled a whale that afternoon just below our tent. It had shouldered its way through an incredibly small lead and Lane's men simply stood on the ice and harpooned it. Our crew converged on the scene to help and I made my way over the jumble of shore ice to get in on the action.

"Keep behind! It nearly did us in!" Earl warned me as he sprinted past. And it was good advice. Gus Kowunna was standing on the whale. He had just triggered a good charge with his harpoon and got covered with blood when suddenly the animal thrashed to life and took off, straight down, never to surface again. Luckily, Kowunna was nimble enough not to fall into the water but he was sorely disappointed.

For lunch that day we cooked up whale meat, muktuk, and intestine—what Bockstoce referred to as a "mixed bag"—and carried it out to the lead over the new ice. We had just gotten settled on the flat sled at the water's edge and begun the meal when one of the men saw the ice crack and gave the word to move. Being a slow walker I started shuffling directly for the hard ice. Esther yelled for someone to get the dishes. I shuffled back and got them, shuffled shoreward again. The men with the boat were at my heels and we had no sooner made it to safety than the spot on which we had been picnicking became open water. The men were calm but they said it had been a close call. Ruth said it was fun and everybody was happy because the ice hadn't moved for ages and we needed open water to encourage the whales.

The rest of the day was spent shifting the boat as the ice shifted. The sunset was red and I took a long walk by myself admiring the grandeur of the frozen sea. The snow was blue and the sky went mauve and I wasn't sure any of it was real.

For supper we took macaroni and cheese to the edge of the

*The ice is moving and the men are running for firm ground.*

new ice and some of the men carried it out to the others. Earl
and Bockstoce brought back the dirty dishes, Bockstoce falling
flat twice while Earl skated merrily around him.

"That makes ten times today," the big blond said cheerfully.

"Do you bruise easily?" I asked.

"No, I did this all last year," he answered.

The Eskimos called him "Sukpun" which means "seal oil."
The year before a doughnut he had been eating fell into the
seal blubber, but he picked it up and ate it anyway—which
was how he got the name. He was an easy-going fellow.

In the last light I climbed the ice block by our tent to survey
our coast. Four boats and four groups of men were out on the
ice waiting by the empty leads. Waiting and waiting. It was
10 below and getting colder, but they stayed.

Ruth and I went home to find that the stove had gone out.
While it warmed up, she talked about the whale that got away.
Because we had harpooned it, we would have gotten a big
share. Well, perhaps the carcass would float to the surface
later, she mused, but perhaps it wouldn't.

Watching her and hearing the anxiety in her voice, I recalled how she had looked out there on the ice, watching her
husband go out in their fragile boat. How she had watched
long after he and his crew had been lost to sight over the horizon . . . watching and worrying long after darkness had
fallen.

"Whales are hard to catch," she said mostly to herself. "It is
not easy to catch a whale."

When the mail came in for the tenth time with no unemployment check for Bernard, I finally got the Nashes to discuss
my rent. The cupboard was almost empty and I suggested $95,
which was the monthly rent I'd paid for an efficiency apartment in Fairbanks. They seemed surprised and pleased with
the offer, which they accepted, and we restocked the grub
box.

Earl and Bockstoce stayed in town that day which did not
please the captain. Earl's job as an enumerator was growing
more difficult because so many of the Eskimos he was supposed

to enroll were out hunting. He was doing his best by commuting between interviews and his place in the whale boat, but his absences made it hard for our crew.

Today, however, was a good day to interview because the cold was wicked and nothing stirred in the lead. Gussy was being visited by a friend his own age, a boy from another whaling camp. They played cards and downed "fizzies" mixed with melted snow. Then Kowunna Senior recruited his son to collect the remains of Weber's whale which had just been lying around on the ice. The neglected meat had been bothering Kowunna for three days.

"They're supposed to use all that meat, not waste it," he had complained the day before. "I think I'll go up there when it gets dark." Now he decided to brazen it out in the daylight. If anyone asked, he'd tell them it was for dog food.

Young Gussy had managed to ignore his father for some time, but the relationship was now changing. The previous night when Kowunna had instructed the boy to wake him at 3 A.M., Gussy found he couldn't stir the heavy sleeper and simply let the air out of Kowunna's mattress. This ingenuity made everybody laugh and merited praise from Kowunna Senior. Now they went off as friends and returned with an excellent selection of "dog food" which we cooked up for our supper.

Saddled with a cold, I took the next day off and went back to the village in time to welcome Elizabeth back from the hospital. She had lost four pounds but looked marvelous. All her friends were livid with envy for her adventure, and a copy of *Tundra Times*, which came on the same plane, added to her glory. It reprinted a letter she had written to Senator Ernest Hollings of South Carolina, protesting a proposed moratorium on whaling.

"I am an Eskimo girl who is eleven years old. My mother makes mukluks and my dad makes [whalebone] masks. They sell them at the store and we need that money for food and gas for the stove to keep the house warm. The sea mammal bill is terrible and we don't like it!"

Sam Nash came in at seven, chuckling. Norman had fallen through the ice, right into the freezing Chukchi.

"I was reading and I heard what I thought was a whale," he reported. "And there was Norman hanging on to the ice."

Since Norman didn't have a change of clothes at camp, Sam had brought him home to change, but they went straight back —the Lane's missing whale had been found. And it brought me back to the ice, too.

The animal, dead three days, had surfaced in open water about a mile from our tent and the Lanes had moved their tent to the site. A rope had been tied to the flipper of the carcass and butchering was just getting underway. About fifty men had started the dismembering, using ropes and a tug-of-war team to rotate the floating body. With sharp knives shaped like wide spatulas with six-foot-long handles, they cut the muktuk into four-foot-square sections, then piled it neatly. Grabbing my camera, I went in to get a shot where there wasn't a crowd. I soon found out why. Long-dead whales that finally surface are called "stinkers" and the open space was down wind. The muktuk of the animal would be good but the meat was fit only for the dogs.

Unthinking, I continued to photograph as the men cut off the big penis. There were several jokes made in Eskimo which I was just as happy not to translate, especially when I noticed I was the only woman around. The other women had discreetly disappeared.

Bockstoce was out with his camera, too, but his fate was even worse than mine. He had backed off to take a picture of a crewman and fallen into the sea beside the whale. Somehow he managed to hold his camera above the water, but he had to go home and change his clothes.

Butchering took about ten hours. When the men got hungry, they chanted, "Coffee! Coffee! Coffee! . . . Tea! Tea!" which would certainly have terrified an unprepared cook, but Mrs. Lane put out enough of both to float a whale along with a gross of cookies, pilot bread, cigarettes, cigars, pans and pans

*Butchering a small whale.*

of muktuk, endless doughnuts, and (God knows why) a gallon of blackberry ice cream.

If we got a whale, Esther told me, we would probably use about fifty pounds of flour just for making doughnuts to feed the butchering crew.

By now I was thoroughly sunburned and Ruth joked that I looked like an Indian. When I turned down ice cream at her table, she observed that I didn't like white man's food any more and I was surprised to find she was right. Whenever I tried something like fried chicken, I got sick, but I'd never felt better than on the ice.

Both Ruth and Esther called me "Lady" and Ruth occasionally referred to me as "my oldest daughter," but there was some doubt as to what Eskimo name I would have. Ruth suggested one that translated "White Lady." When I said maybe that wasn't much of a compliment, she was hurt—that had been the pet name of her grandmother who was an Eskimo.

On off days I began to make the rounds in the village, gathering information on how important the sea mammals were to the Eskimos. John Long, an ivory carver with five kids at home and three away at school, provided ample testimony. He tried to support his family by working half a day as janitor for the Head Start program, but that didn't begin to cover his costs. He also operated the only telephone in the village, housed in a booth in his living room, and in his spare time he hunted or carved walrus ivory.

"That's going to be pretty hard on all of us if we can't get the ivory and the meat and the skins," he said. "Most of us don't really have work all the time. I work at Head Start, but that doesn't go in the summer so I carve, sell sealskins, trade to get food for the kids. If we can't sell the sea animals any more, that's going to be pretty hard for all of us. Pretty hard time living."

"There's not much welfare in Point Hope," pointed out John Oktollik, Point Hope's mayor and a highly successful whaler. "Some food stamps, and right now a lot of unemployment

checks from summer jobs. But Point Hope people are proud
and independent. They live largely by their whaling and they
work for their whales, too."

David Frankson, who had been whaling for forty years,
said flatly there were at least five hundred bowheads left—as
many as there always had been. As he spoke, the village church
bell rang to herald another kill. Everyone in the village dashed
out of their houses to see who had got lucky and in came
Frankson's son and his wife with a whale fluke on their sled.

The best interview I had was with Jimmy Killigivuk, eighty-
one, who was still captain of a whaling boat although a stiff
leg kept him off the ice in bad weather. He wanted to write
a letter to Congress on the sea mammal bill but figured an
interview would do just as well, though he was worried because his English was poor. We took our time, with his son,
Eugene, and grandson, Jack, helping with translation. Finally
he directed them to fetch the whaling gear he had purchased
second hand in 1909; they had to go out to camp to get it because it was still in use!

The tension was now growing in our camp. Although our
crew had helped make several kills, they had yet to cast the
first harpoon and win the choicest cuts of the whale. The atmosphere was much like that of the household of a formerly
high-powered executive who suddenly found he couldn't get
a job. The first harpoon meant prestige and it also meant more
provisions.

Some of our crew began complaining about short rations. I
reported that the Nashes had a tight budget and some felt they
all should help supply the camp. There was some petty grum-
bling, but the overriding worry seemed to center on the belief
held by old-timers that whales won't come to people who are
mean and stingy.

Then came a blue, bright day when the sea looked like a
gentle lake. The sun was so warm that we took off our coats
and whales came by every hour and sometimes on the half

hour. The men were exuberant because they had helped take three whales and would get second and third shares.

Against doctor's orders, Laurie Kingik was among them, leaving his cane on the ice and manning a paddle for six straight hours. Perhaps he felt obligated to fill in for Earl, who was being forced by a deadline to spend more time on the land claims paperwork. Or perhaps it was simply that Kingik had been a great hunter and was still a great hunter and he couldn't resist going back to it. His family had taken his snowmobile, kidnapped his dog team; but there he was, back at the hunt, terribly tired but very happy, too. He was made of strong stuff and I understood why Gussy loved him.

Now the men stayed on the ice all day and all night. Bockstoce's nose was red and peeling and he said he was out of shape from sitting around Oxford too long, but he stuck to his paddle.

The weather grew colder but hunting was so good that it was decided the women would stay in the tent to keep the meals coming. None of us had brought a sleeping bag. Ruth took Sam's and Esther got Gussy's and I donned my parka and down trousers, which were too hot to walk in, and slept on top of the grub box. It was too short for me, but at least it was dry and warmer than anywhere else because of its elevation.

At 5 A.M. I awoke to see the sun rising in a feathery halo of pink clouds and John Bockstoce lumbering through the rosy glow. He looked quite frozen but he sought the warmth of our tent only briefly. Amos Lane had gotten a small whale at 3 A.M., he reported, and we would get a second share.

When hunting was good the women were expected to work nearly as hard as the men, making endless treks with food and coffee. We stayed on the ice during this period for two straight days, walking five to seven miles a day over the rough ice and getting little sleep. When a break finally came, I was thoroughly worn out, but all our sleds were full of whale meat and there was no room for a cook to ride to town. I set out on foot.

It was a long hike, four and a half miles, I figured, and I got confused about the trail. Finally I asked directions from a member of another crew, who took pity on me and gave me a ride to the edge of the village. That left only a quarter of a mile to go and I limped slowly along the beach, very much at peace with the world. A fine mist drifted through the settlement and the colors were unbelievably romantic.

I didn't fall asleep that night; simply passed out. But at 5 A.M. a persistent knocking brought me to. I tried to ignore it, thinking someone else in the family would answer. Nobody did. Perhaps they were still at camp. Finally I dragged myself to the door. I was wearing my only frivolous clothing—a short red nightgown designed like a football shirt with a big purple number seven on the front. My long blonde hair was in tangles and I must have been a startling sight, for the Eskimo visitor— a stranger—gasped audibly. He'd traveled all night by snow-mobile from the village of Noatak (about 125 miles south of Point Hope) and planned to stay with the Nashes. I was afraid that at sight of me he might turn around and go straight home, but instead he asked nervously for direction to Elijah Rock's, another relative of Ruth's.

Next morning I discovered Ruth had been home all along, heard the man knocking, figured he was drunk, and decided to let me deal with him. If he had stayed, I was planning to put him in her bed, I told her, and it would have served her right. The idea made us both laugh.

Before work that morning I bought a kikituk from Alex Frankson. It was a cunning creature carved from fossil whale-bone, with real animal teeth, a round head, trusting ivory eyes, and a body that was a cross between a dog and an alligator. The missionaries had banned the making of kikituks because the Eskimos believed if you gave one to an enemy it would steal his soul and make him a hollow man. Kikituks were not generally sold, but I'd asked Frankson to make me one. He'd been happy to, but he warned that his father had thought them to be powerful magic.

"He used to carry one under his armpit when he traveled to Siberia," he recalled. "It protected him from his enemies."

I put the little fellow in the pocket of my parka and told Esther about it as we set off on the long walk to camp.

"Why don't you wish for a south wind so we can have a vacation?" she suggested jokingly. Well, I was game.

"South wind, kikituk! South wind!"

We got so tired on that hike that we decided we didn't care whether our crew starved or not, but when we finally arrived at the tent at 1:30 P.M. we found the men hadn't eaten all day and our efforts were appreciated.

In mid-afternoon there were cheers from the water. Amos Lane had another whale and his brother, Jake, came roaring by our camp on his snowmobile with the flipper on his sled, en route to the village to sound the church bell.

Esther and I went to the Lane camp to find our men helping butcher, but they were watching for whales, too. Actually, we'd staked the site originally, but when Kowunna had gone back to town for our crew, the Lanes—innocently—moved in. The fact that they had gotten two whales there was hard for us to swallow. Our men were calm about it, but hunting, not butchering, was foremost on their minds.

The weather began closing in, casting a white film over the sun. The ghost of a south wind played over the ice, pushing vicious little icebergs before it to clog the lead. Often our men paddled among them and watching I felt a twinge of fear. I hadn't realized what a dangerous thing a south wind could be when I put in my casual request to the kikituk.

Down the lead, John Oktollik had just landed a fifty-seven-foot whale and was rushing to butcher it, working almost singlehanded. All the crews were busy butchering, taking as much meat as they could before the ice began to shift. Today, for sure, there was no extra room on the sleds, and Esther and I headed slowly back to the village. Both of us had stiff legs, so we walked haltingly through a world of new snow. It was so white and clean and quiet that it was hard to tell, except by gravity, which way was up. Occasionally we'd see the glint of green ice or a meat-filled sled ghosting by, but mostly we were just two comrades adrift on a frozen sea. We had walked fifteen miles that day.

The havoc wrought by my south wind was monumental. In less than an hour it had buried Oktollik's whale in ice and he never found it again. The crew had barely managed to escape and save the tent and, on hearing the news, I packed my kikituk away with considerable respect and swore never again to be casual about such magic.

During the bad weather that ensued, I caught up on village gossip. Principal Robinson had set off on a long, dangerous trip to Kotzebue with his dog team and run into trouble with unstable ice. A bush plane had rescued him and all his dogs.

Also from Kotzebue came rumors of a rift between Eskimo and white residents. The Eskimo regional organization was growing powerful and would become more so when it acquired funding from the land claims settlement. One of the Eskimo leaders was said to have boasted that the whites would soon be treated like the "niggers in Alabama," and the whites —whose record of tolerance was anything but distinguished— were said to be carrying guns in their cars.

The report turned out to be overblown, but it did foreshadow a wave of Eskimo independence, and some of the Point Hope teachers (all Caucasian) wondered aloud what would happen if all the whites pulled out of the Arctic.

To get away from the uneasy atmosphere I dropped in to watch Jake Jacobson, a red-haired dentist from Kotzebue, repairing teeth.

"The children's teeth are bad," he reported. "Their parents love them too much and give them too much candy. The further I go up river, the poorer the villages get and the better the teeth get."

Because he was working virtually around the clock, he'd developed a system of numbing one patient with Novocain while he worked on another. Some of the children mistook

Novocain for the cure and Jacobson never caught up with them to do the drilling.

Adjourning to a school typewriter, I met a talkative young teacher who was planning to leave Point Hope. It was like Grosse Pointe, Michigan, he complained. "Nob Hill . . . upper class Eskimos." He had done income tax returns for some people here and said there had been ten incomes over $18,000 and two over $23,000. Large families, of course, but even the poor could take care of themselves.

What was it Robinson had told me?

"If you feel like being a savior, this is not the place to come. This village takes care of its own problems."

The end of my month's stay coincided with a new run of good weather and my enthusiasm was still high for the hunt. My final day I would spend on the ice, but before going out I went to visit Nanny Ooyahtuonah to give her my leftover cache of candy bars. She was just polishing her false teeth for a visit to a relative, but she was gracious and took time to talk with me. Finally I got nerve to ask her about money— how she supported herself—and she showed me the waterproof boots she was sewing to sell Robinson. Her stitches were so fine it was hard to see them. Oh, her eyes weren't as good as they once were, she apologized. But Robinson seemed pleased to buy her work. And she was somewhat of an archaeologist, too. Villagers reported seeing her out many a morning wearing waders, digging for artifacts where the sea undercut the old village. Proudly she showed me some trading beads she'd unearthed. I admonished her not to sell cheaply, then felt silly. Like most Point Hopers, Nanny could take care of herself.

That last day on the ice was a beauty. Ruth and Esther both elected to stay home, but Judy went with me and, though quiet, she was good company. Kowunna took us out to camp, stopping along the trail as a wavering V of eider ducks flew over our heads.

There was little open water. The old, well-worn trail had

ended abruptly with a shelf of new ice and the men tested it cautiously with their ice sticks. No whales swam that day, so our men continued to down the migrating eiders. I watched five fall out of the sky. A female landed at my feet, swallowed hard, and died bravely. Nearby lay her mate, resplendent in bright green and gray feathers about the head and with a black V neck. Much as I liked eider soup, I mourned them both.

When it came time for parting, the crew lined up to shake hands and wish me well. If they got a whale, I promised to send champagne. Maybe, they suggested, I could come back and help drink it . . . and I wished I could.

I flew directly from Point Hope to the congressional hearings on the sea mammal protection bill in Nome, carrying a generous gift of beluga whale from the Nashes and smelling so ripe because of my blubber-stained parka that I had half a plane to myself.

Covering the proceedings turned out to be a painful, arduous task. Worried Eskimos had traveled for hundreds of miles —by dog sled, snowmobile, and plane—to plead their case. No interpreters had been provided and often there was confusion and misunderstanding. It went on, non-stop, all day and well into the night. Yet despite all difficulties the people spoke well for themselves.

Best, I thought, was the testimony from Point Hope. Perhaps I was biased, but David Stone, an experienced hunter, summed up the situation well.

"Our very lives revolve around the migration cycle of oceanic mammals," he began, reading carefully in labored English from a paper written by his village council. "There are virtually no jobs available in Point Hope. The 1970 manpower survey showed 64 per cent of our people have an average income under $3,000.

"The cost of living at Point Hope is double that of Seattle. Obviously it is virtually impossible to meet the cost of oil, rent, lights, and food without any monetary supply. Any money that can be gained from our limited use of sea mammal products is sorely needed."

Although Point Hope was the second largest whaling community in Alaska, Stone said the native store purchased only two thousand pounds of muktuk for resale last year. This averaged $23.53 gain per person, less than the cost of a barrel of stove oil. He added that they used the whole animal except for the skull which, by tradition, they sank.

"We have always hunted only for our need. We have been wise enough not to overkill. Is it fair to destroy our cultural heritage and our lifestyle by stopping all utilization of these mammals?" he asked.

He was followed by Art Davidson, a white man representing Friends of the Animals who surprised everyone by speaking on behalf of the Eskimos. He pleaded for co-operation between researchers and natives and for the development of more modern counting methods and more efficient hunting equipment. Then hesitantly, putting aside his text, he added, "You know, people are part of the environment, too."

And Congress finally came to agree, passing legislation that allowed for continued taking of the whale for subsistence use by the Eskimo so long as the bowheads continued to run strong. Which meant, I hoped, that I'd soon be sending champagne to the Nashes.

*Galena in the spring of 1972 after the flood.*

# Galena

*The Athabascan Indian village of Galena, on the Yukon River in the Alaskan interior, was established by white men in 1918 as a supply center for galena, a lead ore. Ivan Petroff, the census taker in 1880, found Indians making fish camp on the spot, but it did not become a permanent Athabascan settlement until the whites had moved out and a neighboring Indian village of Old Louden became overcrowded in the 1930s.*

*Construction of a major airfield near Galena in the early 1940s encouraged further settlement, and Indians moved in from all along the river to seek work. By 1970 the United States Census recorded 302 Galena residents, three fourths of them Indian. The village had become one of the most successful and fastest growing on the Yukon, yet one year later it almost came off the map.*

*In the spring of 1971 the thawing Yukon River ran wild. Below Galena it jammed, backed up, and rushed its banks, inundating the settlement with thirteen feet of water and smashing blocks of ice. The neighboring Air Force base sat behind a 136-foot dike that excluded the village, but its commander, unsure of the holding power of his World War II vintage earth rampart, evacuated 266 service men and offered to do the same for any Indians who wanted to go.*

*The majority of villagers declined. They had learned from past experience that evacuation can be a one-way trip—rescued natives without resources were often left to find their own way home. Besides, their people had lived on the river for more than a thousand years with no great loss of life from flooding.*

*The 1971 flood, however, was a sweeping, high-water record breaker, and in the early hours of May 22, Indians perched on the old airfield dike witnessed a spectacular event. Ice blocks bigger than buildings slammed into the village, tearing houses from their foundations, crushing everything that would not be pushed aside, and making a near-fatal assault on the dike itself.*

*Three days later the refugees were still waiting for the water to recede. They were short of food because they had cached their supplies below the new high-water mark and, although they had been visited by the governor, the Secretary of the Air Force, and numerous tourists, no one offered them so much as a cup of soup.*

*The skeleton crew left on the air base had been battling breaks in the dike but finally found time to bring the Indians a hot meal. The military was also considerate about providing water and fuel, but many villagers were hesitant to ask. The Indians remained short of food, tents, and blankets and made do with no sanitary facilities until the water subsided. Then things got worse.*

*The village was, in the words of its civic leaders, "a devastating mess," and so were the negotiations on rehabilitation that followed. Despite promises of aid from numerous government agencies, the red tape got deeper than the flood waters, and it was assumed—by everybody but the residents themselves—that Galena would not survive.*

On May 20, 1972, the frozen Yukon cracked open again and began a repeat performance of the previous year's flood. Ice

chunks moved out, meshed, and jammed and the water rose
within three feet of the top of the bank at Galena. Stoically the
Indians waited, seeking once again the dubious protection of
the airfield dike. Finally, after excruciating hours of suspense,
the ice jam broke and the river receded. But there was still a
lot of ice to be cleared and no one could call himself safe until
after "break-up" was over.

Grimly, the next day, I flew the course of the swollen river
from Fairbanks to Galena in a small bush plane. I had been
there in 1971 and seen the devastation in the wake of the
wild water, and I dreaded a repeat.

It seemed to be sort of a nothing village anyway. Although
the bulk of the population had moved in during the 1940s,
built homes and raised families there, if you asked a Galena-
born youngster where he was from, he'd tell you Nulato or
Huslia or Ruby or wherever his parents had originated. Nobody was from Galena, and I couldn't imagine the residents
would fight very hard to save it.

Still, something about Galena struck me favorably. Maybe it
was the spirit of the refugees I had found camped on the dike
the previous spring. They hadn't asked for any help and didn't
expect any. And it would be interesting, I decided, to return
and see how they had survived.

When I arrived the settlement was almost deserted. Families
were camping in trailers on the dike or in tents in the woods
along the evacuation route to high ground. Furniture and
prized possessions had been carefully wrapped in plastic or
tarp and stored on the dike; and snowmobiles, motorcycles,
and washing machines decked the rooftops.

After a lonesome tour of the village, I learned that the
Sidney Huntington family, with whom I was to stay, had
moved to military housing within the protection of the dike. I
knew very little about the Huntingtons. My living arrangements had been made by John Sackett, a young Athabascan
leader who was a personal friend. He had purchased a lodge
in Galena two years earlier and it was partly his concern for
the village that had caused me to cover the 1971 flood. Now

he was occupied in Fairbanks as president of the Athabascan native organization, Tanana Chiefs, but he assured me that the Huntingtons were the best people with whom to survive a flood and I sought them out with no misgivings.

They were camped in style in a furnished house designated for base personnel. I found Gilbert and Tommy, two teenaged sons, watching television with their younger brother, Charlie. It was hardly what I had anticipated as the life of a refugee family, but they offered me a Coke and I sat down to join them. Sidney arrived shortly and mistook me for the Avon Lady. Well, either way, I was welcome, for everyone, I soon learned, was welcome in that household.

My host was a bespectacled man, light complexioned, of medium height and middle age, without an ounce of fat to spare. He looked more like a Maine farmer than an Indian, but I didn't let that distract me for Huntington was reputed to be proud of his Athabascan heritage.

We were not living behind the dike because we were in dire peril, he assured me immediately. We were living behind the dike mainly to see if the military would allow it. Sidney was employed as head of the base carpentry shop. Most of the white employees enjoyed on-base housing and he wondered if an Indian would be accepted. Permission had been granted, all right, but no one in the family was particularly happy about it. They were used to living by the river. The dike made them feel claustrophobic and they wanted to get back to the bank of the Yukon, even if they did get their feet wet.

"Family," I discovered, was a term applied rather loosely to about twenty-five people who continually wandered in and out of the Huntington kitchen. Number one was Angela, Sidney's wife. She was a tall, amply endowed woman who looked exactly as you would want the mother of the world to look—capable, and with more understanding of humans than is generally allowed. She and Sidney had twelve children, all handsome and highly individualistic. Then there were half a dozen or so offspring from Sidney's earlier marriage and wandering strays who were attracted to the warmth and happiness of this large circle. And there was Grandma, Julia Nelson, Angela's diminutive stepmother. She was a neat, tidy woman, unquestionably of Athabascan descent; she was visiting from the small village of Koyukuk, the next stop downriver.

Supper for this mob was an outstanding production. Angela, with older daughters Agnes and Betty, served it with seeming lack of effort, in shifts determined by the size of the dining table. The menu was beef sirloin with vegetables and mashed potatoes. They would have preferred to serve us moose, but that was stored in a freezer in the village and there had to be some concession to our refugee status. Until the flood scare was out of the way, we would just have to make do with beef.

Never had I felt so at home so quickly. There was no ceremony to stand on here and no distrust. Angela promptly introduced me as "my newest daughter" and let me man a dishtowel. Sidney then settled in to tell me the history of the village and everything else I needed to know without my having to ask.

Currently a new village of Galena was being laid out at Alexander Lake, about a mile outside the old village, on slightly higher ground. It was to be a model community, with sewers, running water, and modern houses, but Huntington and a number of other villagers were determined to remain at the old site even though they could not receive federal loans for building in the flood plain. Sidney predicted that houses in the new location would soon sink into the boggy tundra and that, really, the houses would be no safer than those by the river because the elevation wasn't much higher.

"Besides, we like to watch the river," Angela said.

"You just can't see anything from up at Alexander Lake," explained Art Kennedy, a neighbor. "Of course we don't want to go."

After supper we got into Huntington's flower decal-decorated World War II army truck and drove around the dike to town where Sidney and the kids optimistically began spring house cleaning. I wandered through the village, finding little islands of activity. A few families like the Huntingtons were

*Sidney and Angela Huntington, with one shift of their family building crew and a new house in the making.*

using the evacuation break for clean-up and repair. And over the bank the Yukon began showing signs, at last, of performing an orderly run-off.

"My father told me back in 1928 that the Indians have it better than anybody else," Sidney recalled. "We only have to work hard a small part of the year. In November, a little in December—fishing, do a little trapping in the winter. You can live all year on that. You can live here on ten dollars a month for utilities and catch all you need to eat in moose and fish. This is the richest poor town in Alaska."

I was intrigued by the philosophy, but Huntington didn't elaborate further. He earned about $40,000 a year to support his brood. It was hard to figure where it all went, he said, but it didn't go far enough and so he always had something going on the side—a motorcycle dealership, coffee shop, house building.

And don't talk to him about government handouts, he said. He was dead set against them—this was a village of independent Indians.

I had seen this confirmed in a notice on a bulletin board in the middle of town:

To the People Of Galena—

It is your responsibility to move your own belongings away from areas which may be flooded. There is no money to move you. No money to put your things back after the flood. Goods you received from Galena Rehabilitation (after the last flood) must be moved. DONT WAIT UNTIL THE LAST MINUTE!

As additional proof, Huntington took me to visit Max Huhndorf, a successful, self-made Athabascan businessman who was building a handsome home, store, and lumberyard just outside the new village site. Huhndorf and his wife, Beverly, had been raised in traditional fashion along the river but had somehow obtained a good formal education and gone off to work for some years in Anchorage and Fairbanks. Now they were back with a stake. They had picked Galena to invest in because they believed it was the "goingest town" on the Yukon, and they also believed it was a better place than the city to raise their two children.

"The children, I feel, have much more freedom here," Beverly Huhndorf said. "I'm sorry we didn't move back years ago."

No flood worries there. They had faith in the new village site and also, Sidney was pleased to note, in the American free enterprise system.

The Huntingtons found a mattress for me in their borrowed house at the base, but I, too, found I didn't want to move back behind the dike. As the sun set, about 11 p.m., I climbed again to the top of the rampart for another look at the river. It was still running strong, casting off its winter coat of ice in massive chunks and sweeping before it trees, derelict boats, and rubbish. But by the next morning it had slowed and the ice chunks were smaller. Possibilities of a jam became more remote and, with noisy rejoicing, we piled the army truck high with household possessions and children and moved back to the village.

The Huntington house was really two houses ingeniously pieced together. The kitchen and a small room off it, to which I was assigned, had once been the top of a roadhouse, and the living room and two bedrooms had been another building. Sidney and Angela had a bedroom to themselves and the children claimed assorted bunks and couches in the other bedroom and the living room. Partitions were missing—the walls had gone out in the last flood—but Angela had sewn curtains in their stead which afforded some privacy.

There was plumbing, too—a real triumph in tundra country. Sidney had dug the cesspool himself through fourteen feet of frozen ground. Every few inches he had had to build a fire to thaw the dirt. And when a GI from Michigan, Howard Gillette, had asked to marry his daughter Alma, Sidney agreed on the stipulation that his future son-in-law would dig the last three feet.

Running water came from a shallow well nearby and hooked into a hot water tank for showers, but tannic acid made it unpalatable for drinking. Like the rest of the village, we relied on the military chlorination plant for drinking water which we fetched in big plastic garbage pails with the truck.

Galena itself was a motley collection of log and plywood houses and outhouses strung out along the river bank and huddled against the dike. Repairs and clean-up were still in progress from the flood of 1971 and it still looked like a disaster area.

The main street was the waterfront and a small, dusty dirt road the width of a car paralleled it. The country beyond was flat, although dumpling hills showed on the distant horizon across the river. Traces of snow still remained and there was no green yet, but swallows swooped and dived through the village. Inside the dike in a marshy field beside the jet airstrip I found a family of plovers enjoying a pool formed by a leak in the rampart, and beyond the military compound and the village, the woods of birch and willow were teeming with wildlife.

The first person on my list to interview was Bessie Wholecheese who impressed me with her calm during the last flood. Bessie had had twenty-two children, lost eight, and looked in better shape than the average society matron. She managed an unusual but well-accepted living arrangement with Edgar Noliner who had almost as many offspring as she did and I liked their style. This spring Noliner had built four rafts and a storehouse that would float on empty oil drums in the event of high water. The construction and loading of the evacuation fleet must have taken months, and all summer would be needed to clear it, but that was immaterial to Noliner and Wholecheese. Relaxing on their readied river boat they congratulated themselves on an orderly break-up.

Noliner, one of Galena's first settlers, had built his log cabin

*Bessie Wholecheese and Edgar Noliner relax with her grandchild after the flood scare.*

in the woods a considerable distance from the Yukon, and the fact that erosion now presented him with a river view did not alarm him.

"We like to watch the old Yukon," Mrs. Wholecheese explained.

"It scares a lot of people," Noliner admitted. "But we're used to it." Then he chuckled, remembering when the military had moved in to build the air base. The Indians had warned the builders about the river and told them it was a bad location, but they wouldn't listen. And in the flood of 1945 the troops had had to evacuate to the top of their gravel pile because the rest of the base went under water.

"We used to go out and paddle around the pile with our canoes," Noliner recalled. "After that flood, they built the dike."

I opined that it was niggardly of the military not to include Galena in the protection of its rampart but the Athabascans shook their heads. Behind a dike was no place to live. You had to keep an eye on the river. Besides, I learned shortly, some Indians believed there were better ways to rout the Yukon than with a dike. It was spoken of only in whispers, but Agnes Jimmie got credit for stopping this spring's flood with something called "powerful medicine."

Agnes was seventy-four, a squarish lady with a face like a sad Buddha and the skin of a young woman. Her grandparents had lived in a fish camp across the river from Galena, she told me. And when her mother was little, "not a woman yet," a Tanana native had come and kidnapped her for his wife. The match produced four children including Agnes. Then the Tanana Indian died and her mother had had a tough time, living by tanning moose skins and giving the children up for adoption until she finally found a white man to marry and support her.

Agnes knew well the old ways of the river. She had married a river man, but he had died sixteen years back and she had had to work like a man herself. Now she was too sick to fish, too crippled to sew, and found doing nothing unbearable. She had no immediate family to look out for her either, which was why the medicine thing had come up.

Mrs. Jimmie had been wiped out in the flood of 1971 and a new little house had been built for her with government funds. This spring as the waters rose, she had asked visiting government officials to move her house to higher ground and they refused. Publicly she had cursed them out. Then, seeing it was hopeless, she told them, "Never mind," that she would make medicine to make the Yukon drop.

I asked her stepdaughter about it and she was horrified.

"My mother doesn't do that any more," she informed me. "Where did you hear that? Don't you know you're not supposed to talk about it?"

"No, I didn't," I said defensively. "And what's so bad about making medicine if it keeps the village from a flood?"

"You're not supposed to talk about it," she warned. "Something bad will happen if you do."

But I liked Agnes Jimmie and found her to be a reasonable woman, so I did ask her.

"Before the first flood my husband and I had trapped all winter," she explained without fear. "We had done well. Bought a gas boat, stove, a big phonograph . . . and we lost everything. Nobody help us. Now my husband is dead. I have no one to take care of me. The second flood, last year . . . well, that was just too much!"

Between interviews and household chores I busied myself reading the best-selling *On the Edge of Nowhere,* a *Reader's Digest* condensed book selection with half a dozen American and European printings to its credit. It had been written by Sidney Huntington's brother, Jimmy, and proved an excellent history of his family and his people.

Their Athabascan grandfather had been a trader and their mother, Anna, had traveled with him, going once each year to a strip of neutral ground to meet an Eskimo trader. It was a dangerous assignment, for both Indians and Eskimos were traditionally committed by old wrongs to fight each other to the death. But the Indians needed salt from the Bering Sea and sealskins for waterproof boots and the Eskimos needed inland wolverine fur for parka ruffs and a soft red rock found only along the Koyukuk River for painting their snowshoes a brilliant red. To make the trade, a two-man truce was annually declared, and it proved to be fortunate for young Anna that she'd borne witness to it.

She had married happily but her first husband was shot by a white man and she was called to Nome to testify against the killer. Her testimony failed to convict him, however, because he was white and the court would not take an Indian's word against his. Heartbroken, Anna refused government transportation home and set out alone on foot, walking one thousand miles through the dreaded Eskimo territory in the dead of winter. All that had saved her was the fact that the Eskimos who captured her remembered her and her father from the trading days, and her survival marked a tenuous beginning of peace between the two groups.

Anna's second marriage was to James Huntington, a white trader who'd come to the country in the gold rush. Sidney and Jimmy were children of this union, which was a happy one, but the tragedy that befell them became a legend of the river country.

The Huntington children were raised at an isolated trading post on the Koyukuk River near Galena, and when Sidney was seven and Jimmy five and their little sister, Marion, was not quite two, Huntington left his family to do some trading. Shortly thereafter, Anna got food poisoning, falling dead on the threshold of their cabin. The children were not strong enough to move her body and were forced to abandon the house when it began to decay. Somehow the boys managed to keep themselves and their little sister alive for two weeks until a river boat came to the rescue, but it was an experience of nightmarish dimension.

Their grieving father sent them to boarding school down river for a while, only to summon them home again because he was lonesome. When Sidney was fourteen and Jimmy twelve, they spent a winter running a trap line with him and an old prospector, and they never did get back to school. Their education was completed in the woods. Sidney recalled that first winter when they read and reread a stack of *Saturday Evening Posts* about fifteen times.

The Huntington story, though dramatic, was not atypical of other river families. The difference was that the Huntingtons were more articulate and literate than some and, perhaps because of old Jim Huntington, a little more successful in weathering the cultural changes they had encountered over the years. Jimmy, at forty, had become a famous dog-sled mushing champion. He had gone through a series of unsuccessful marriages and a financial disaster when his house and trading post in Huslia burned, but he had pulled himself together, moved to Galena, and was now mayor of that town.

Sidney's career had been less spectacular but, some felt, even more successful. He had cured himself of a serious drinking problem to become a man of means and a powerful community mover behind the scenes.

Life along the Yukon settled into a curious blend of two life-styles—old Athabascan and contemporary American. With Angela's help, I learned to knit a fish net as Athabascans had of old, tailoring it specifically to the width and depth of the stream I wished to fish. To begin, I worked a small net for the children to play with. Angela started it for me, using unraveled army webbing, while two neighbors looked on, telling of nets they had made. One said she had unraveled sugar bags to work her first one. That was in the days before commercial twine, when you had to use what you could get.

Happily I hooked my net to a nail next to the Huntingtons' television set and worked away evenings like an Athabascan Penelope while I watched "Mod Squad" and "Ironside" on the military television station. Somehow the combination symbolized life in Galena.

Meals were cross-cultural, too. The traditional Athabascan foods—smoked fish, bear, and moose—were highly prized but there was also room on Angela's table for fried chicken, pork chops, and hamburgers.

Language in the household was also mixed.

"Do you kids speak any Athabascan?" I asked one night.

"I know more Eskimo," Gilbert allowed. He had picked it up when he went to boarding school with Eskimo youngsters.

Angela spoke Athabascan easily with her neighbors and the older people. Sidney was less fluent but it wasn't lost to him.

"But if one of the old-timers came back into this village, no one would understand him today," Sidney told us. He could remember as a boy hearing an old-timer giving a long speech and understanding just a few of the words. Athabascan was a tough, complicated language and most of the old, long words had been lost.

I reported that there was an Athabascan language course just starting in Fairbanks but Sidney was dubious.

"Grhr . . . ," he said in sort of a gargle. "How can anyone write down that? Athabascan is all 'grhr . . .'"

"Eskimo is easier," the kids assured me.

Then Sidney launched into a story about an old-timer named "Cheechako John," an Indian who, at the age of fourteen, was sent to a federal prison for seven years for rape.

"When he came back home he didn't know how to do anything—how to camp or hunt. He had to start right from the beginning. That's why they called him Cheechako." (In Alaska "Cheechako" means "newcomer.") Which was the same thing as today when the native kids got shipped away from home to attend high school, he added.

The coming of spring was heralded by enormous mosquitoes and a tantalizing lightness in the air. Now the ice was out of the river and I found a sheltered spot on the bank where I could watch both the river and the village without being noticed. But Galena was no town for solitude. It was a social town—"the drinkingest town on the river," they called it—and after analyzing it from the riverbank, I determined to roll up my sleeves and get involved.

The place to start was Hobo's Bar and I had been warned early to stay away from it. Hobo was a white Harvard graduate, gone bad, sober folk warned me. Once he had lost $20 when one of his customers was shot—not because it drove business away but because he had bet that the victim would take fifteen minutes to die and he had taken twenty. And only the week before, an innocent lad had been hit on the head and lain on Hobo's floor with a concussion for twenty-four hours before someone noticed he was worse off than the ordinary drunk.

In the winter Hobo sometimes let the old people sleep in his bar because their houses were cold. That could hardly be held against him, I thought, but he had bodies all over the place, it was argued, and he encouraged the Indians to drink. He also encouraged prostitutes on the premises and, in addition, his well had become mixed up with someone else's sewage system and it was dangerous to drink the water.

With such a build-up, it took considerable nerve for me to enter Hobo's, although it looked innocuous enough. I had once cased the place when Carl Huntington, one of Sidney's older boys, went there to fetch Grandma Nelson home. Three natives I had never met invited me in but I lost courage on the doorstep. Finally, after a ball game, a community raffle was held at the bar and I decided to go with the family. It was really delightful, with some good Jack London style murals done by one of Hobo's girl friends, a pool table, a long bar, booths, and a couple of benches.

Angela was playing pool. Although she didn't drink, she had learned to play at Hobo's and was a real shark. There she stood, sipping 7-Up, looking round and motherly and wearing—ye gods—a hair net, and the suckers could hardly wait to take her money away. However, she beat everyone in sight.

"It's embarrassing," an out-of-town visitor said sadly. "Embarrassing to be beaten at pool by that woman."

Grandma Nelson was in fine spirits. I found myself wedged between her and a towering black GI named Hollis.

"I'm going to buy Grandma a drink," Hollis declared.

"Agnes said she couldn't have any more," I warned him.

"You shut up," Grandma told me.

Then little Charlie came in to coax her home and the old lady became furious with Angela for allowing her young children in the bar. Finally she was lured home with the inducement of an unopened bottle of beer as a night cap and she left with dignity.

I, too, survived the evening none the worse for wear. The way to do it, I decided, was not to drink that bad water. Just stick to straight shots.

Sidney walked back with me that night and I found he was not unduly upset about Galena's drinking problem.

"If you live in any decent-sized city in the United States, there'll be bars and liquor stores," he maintained. "We might as well face reality. People are going to drink anyway. Always have."

Countering the evil influences of Hobo's Bar was an on-going organization called the Galena Sports Association which got a lot less publicity but was backed wholeheartedly by everybody in town including Hobo. It had been started two years ago when the village council undertook a sports promotion campaign to keep its youngsters occupied, but it had met with little success until last year when Sidney's son Carl got it rolling with the help of some enthusiastic friends.

Gordon Cruger, a civilian who ran the military water-purification plant, was one of the original movers. Unlike the majority of Galena-based whites, Cruger spent a great deal of time with the townspeople. He had even tended bar for a time at Hobo's and married one of Hobo's girls, and he was enormously well liked by the Indians.

They had come to him for advice on how to get people interested in the Sports Association and he'd told them to take politics and the council out of it and let the people run it.

*At Hobo's Bar in Galena.*

"These people are great people to work with," Cruger said. He was a big man, six feet three, and handsome despite a red birthmark on one side of his face, and there was a winning sincerity about him.

"Oh, you hear stories about the drinking here—and stealing. Well, I've never had one thing stolen and I keep a boat right in town. Never had so much as a busted glass. We have problems similar to those in a big city, but the Galena people are all right."

As for the Sports Association, the membership now numbered over two hundred, at $10 per adult member. They had rallied to support a basketball team and a dog-sled racing renaissance, and now they were working on a bush softball league. The next week, if enough money could be raised in a raffle at Hobo's, they were going to import an Eskimo softball team from Kotzebue for competition that really would be a first.

The impending visit of the Eskimos was awaited with considerable curiosity, especially by the old-timers. Charlie Evans, a one-time trader and riverboat captain, shook his head at the idea. He could remember the day when Eskimos were for shooting, but early in his lifetime, trade had begun with them in earnest. Sometimes the Eskimos had even come to visit the village for a couple of weeks.

"They were pretty slow to catch on to the trading," he chuckled. "We wanted their sealskins and seal oil and muktuk and they wanted our inland furs, particularly wolverine. At the store you couldn't get more than five dollars for a wolverine skin, but the Eskimos would trade for forty or fifty dollars' worth of goods. It went on for years until the Eskimos finally discovered the store for themselves. And that's about the last we saw of them."

The raffle at Hobo's was successful enough to buy one-way tickets to Galena for the Eskimos and they arrived to an enthusiastic welcome. It was so enthusiastic, in fact, that it became apparent during the first inning of the game that the

*Julia Nelson making fish net.*

visitors had lost the initial match before they even reached the field. They were the victims of Hobo's hospitality.

Our first-string team was surprisingly professional, with three good pitchers. The Eskimos, who had never played together as a team, took it all with good grace though.

"We don't care if we win or not, if someone will just give us a boat ride on the Yukon," their captain had insisted.

Everybody in town turned out to cheer our team on. I met Grandma Nelson en route and she was so dressed up I hardly recognized her. She had chosen a new flowered kusbuk (long cotton parka) for the occasion, with gold trim and a pastel scarf tucked over her white hair. I stood with her watching from the top of the dike, but soon she insisted we go down and get a closer look at the handsome Kotzebue pitcher. She seemed too frail, but I held her hand and she went spryly down the almost vertical embankment.

"Will you help me if *I* fall down?" I asked her.

"No," she said firmly. "I don't want to get my parka dirty."

Some drunks began to heckle her about being from Koyukuk and she informed them straight out that she was no longer from there but from Galena and she intended to stay. That would be good news for Angela who was worried for fear the old lady might become homesick for her traditional village. But Julia loved the excitement of Galena. After the game she headed for Hobo's with us for a celebration and another fund-raising raffle for return tickets for the Eskimos. It was a tiring day even for the youngsters, but when Angela finally got the old lady to bed, she was still anticipating.

"And tomorrow there'll be a lot more fun," she said as she drifted off to sleep. "Two more games and a dance!"

The next day was hardly softball weather. It stalked in, cold, gray, and rainy. But the Eskimos rallied, bravely drinking 7-Up, to win the game nine to eight. Then they dived into a bracing supply of beer with the cry of "Black Label is beautiful!"

The play-off game, set for 7 P.M., was diplomatically

avoided. Both teams suffered such severe drop-out problems
that they pooled players to make two teams of equal parts of
Eskimos and Indians. John Evans, a Galena Indian who had
lived in Kotzebue since 1964 and helped initiate the games,
wasn't sure at that point whether he should be counted as
Eskimo or Indian.

"What did they used to call those Indian-Eskimos?"
someone asked him.

"Every fucking thing in the book," Evans answered dourly.

"Indian devils," someone volunteered.

The night grew colder but the men played on, enjoying the
sport.

"We just came for the fun of it," the Eskimos said. And so
they had. But the match would have pleasant political re-
percussions, too, for many of the players were native leaders
who would, two months later, have to sit together and argue
out the boundaries of Indian and Eskimo lands for the federal
claims settlement. Surprisingly, the camaraderie of the Galena
visit would prevail and they would settle the matter amicably.
The real fight, the Kotzebue people were to discover, would
not be with their age-old Indian enemies, but with their Eskimo cousins to the north.


Bad weather stayed with us only through the softball tour-
nament, and Memorial Day, which followed, bloomed in the
full perfection of spring. The trees were finally showing leafy
points, grass was coming up in strange places, and the Yukon
looked unruffled despite an eight-knot current.

This was an important day for the Indian women. Early in
the morning Angela climbed to the cache in back of the house
and brought down several boxes of plastic wreaths.

"This one is for my baby," she said looking for a long time at
a delicate little spray of white flowers. "And this one is for my
sister."

Her close friend Hazel Strassberg had been planning to fly
to Anchorage, but when she realized it was Memorial Day,
she canceled the trip in favor of the dead. Together the two

*A Kotzebue Eskimo evens the score in a softball match against the Galena Indians.*

women took a boat and went up river to the cemeteries of Old Louden where their families were buried.

Sidney spent the day pouring cement foundations for the new house he was building directly across the street. It would be even closer to the river than the old one, but he planned a foundation solid enough to withstand even the giant ice blocks, along with buttressing steel I-beams. There would be offices for rent on the first floor and the family would live on the second floor so they'd have a good view of the river. A main feature would be a picture window in the living room. "Angela's dog-sled-racing window," he called it. From here she should have a really good view of next winter's races.

Most of the kids worked with him or helped ready the coffee shop for its summer opening. No Huntington child was ever allowed to stand idle for long.

"You kids got nothing to do?" was an oft-voiced question that should have put terror into their hearts, but they were forever good-natured and they worked hard. There was, I saw, a powerful lot of love in the family. It was a closely knit survival unit. Often after work the youngsters would talk among themselves into the night, making up for the time they'd missed together while they were off at boarding schools.

Most of the villagers were keeping an eye on the river at this point, for it was still running high enough to sweep the banks and runaway boats were worth chasing. I settled in beside Charlie Evans for a spell and he entertained me with river stories while we watched.

Charlie had always lived on the river. His father, Johnny Evans, had been white. He had come up for the gold rush— "just like everyone else. They all had their gunny sacks and shovels going to get the gold."

Evans, Sr., had sold thirty head of cattle in Idaho for a one-tenth share in a sailing ship. At the mouth of the Yukon his party had fired the captain and sold the ship for smaller boats. They had been frozen in on the Koyukuk that year and Evans stayed there and married a local girl. When Charlie was born,

*Charlie Evans and his camera.*

his father had been cutting trees to sell as fuel to the steam-ships, then later with two hundred pounds of flour and one hundred pounds of sugar, he started what was to become a successful store.

Charlie could barely remember the night when his mother died. She had awakened him and asked him to help her down the stairs. He was only five, too small to be much help, really, but he had held on to her hand and she stared out the window into the darkness. Then he helped her back to bed and she had told him to fetch his father who was playing cards at the neighbors.

"My father threw down his hand and rushed out," Charlie recalled. "Soon everybody came and started kneeling down and praying. I didn't know about dying but I got down on my knees, too, and started praying like hell."

"What did she die of?"

He shrugged. "Whatever you died of then; they just wrote down 'TB.'"

That year, 1905, he and his two brothers were sent to Holy Cross Mission, hundreds of miles down river, where they stayed for eight years. Speaking Athabascan was forbidden, but they did get a good basic education.

Later Charlie and his brother, Richard, had gone outside to high school in Oregon. Charlie had come home to marry a Galena girl, who was also a product of a white trader and native mother, and became a river-boat captain. He was thirty years on the river and did some trading, too, and also served nine years as schoolteacher for the BIA in Galena.

"I was a good teacher but I didn't know nothing about algebra," he said.

Joe Wholecheese, who had been river watching, too, snorted at that one.

"Charlie was my teacher and that's why I don't know anything," he volunteered. Charlie didn't deny it.

My river watch was eventually rewarded with the arrival of *Ramona II*, a small, homemade boat pushing a large barge. Crewman Claude Demientieff, Jr., a good-looking young Atha-

*Claude Demientieff, Sr., and his river boat.*

bascan in a Harvard sweatshirt, greeted me and gave me a ship's tour. His family had built the boat themselves, he said. They ran it with four men and his sister, thirteen, as cook. They had lived in Galena and owned a store but had sold it to go on the river. The family had had a small barge the year before but it was too small and they didn't make any money. This year Utana Barge, a large Yukon shipping company, had practically given them this large barge, and they figured the business might begin to pay. Freight charges were three and a half cents a pound coming down river from Fairbanks and two cents going up. The trip took seven days at best.

I asked about the Harvard shirt and Claude, Jr., said he had studied there a year but couldn't take Boston. He was finishing up at the University of Alaska.

His father, the captain, appeared carrying a case of beer. Claude, Sr. was an amiable man wearing a hearing aid. The locals hurried to help him launch his boat. Everybody enjoyed a beer which was apparently the traditional longshoreman fee, and the little boat chugged off again.

Sandrs Cleaver tied up a battered outboard in *Ramona's* docking space and unloaded fifteen wiggling whitefish. His wife and son helped lug the catch to the village and Mrs. Cleaver set about cleaning the fish with an ulu which was too large and too dull.

"You learn something if you stay in Alaska," she assured me as she hacked off a staring fishhead.

"I've been here since '59. Just couldn't get here any sooner!"

That tickled her. Her face was worn with hard living, but it was marvelous when she smiled.

"Why do you stay here?" I asked.

"Because it's my home. Because I *love* this country!"

Inadvertently she gave her thumb a big gash with the ulu and narrowly missed cutting off its tip along with a whitefish tail.

"Hope it doesn't get infected," she said casually, continuing to whack at the jumping fish. I wished she wouldn't scale them

*Sandrs Cleaver fishing up a slough on the Yukon.*

when they were still alive. It must have slipped her mind. She said she felt sorry for them.

Jimmy Huntington dropped by to divert my attention. I had interviewed him earlier and he had been a poor subject, but now he was in a talkative mood.

"The deep freeze is one white man's thing we Indians really do take to," he began, ignoring as usual the fact he was half white. "Before we couldn't store much. Now, with moose, fish, and ducks, you can live pretty good."

I mentioned that his father had said Indians had it better than anyone.

"Yes, but sometimes you get hungry," he reminded me. "I can remember when I was a kid I used to use a dog collar to keep my pants up. I needed a belt and there was this dog about as big as me. Stole his collar and it worked just fine. No worrying about diets in those days!"

Jimmy's philosophy on Galena and government in general differed markedly from Sidney's in that he believed strongly in the new village and planned to build there.

Despite the fact he was a relative newcomer in town, Jimmy had been picked to head its rehabilitation after the 1971 flood. He had combined forces with John Sackett, a former member of the State House of Representatives and of its powerful finance committee, and had taken a calm, no-nonsense approach to the red tape the village was snared in. Together the men raised $242,000 for flood rehabilitation through government agencies and the Red Cross and later returned $47,000 unused. The villagers had winterized their battered homes or replaced them and then voted by a 98 per cent majority to carve out a new building site.

Now Sackett was head of the Athabascan regional organization established to administer the federal land claims settlement and running for a seat in the State Senate (which he would win easily in the fall). This gave Galena and Jimmy Huntington a lot of political marbles to play with but, even when he was in a talkative mood, it was hard to pin Jimmy down on the subject.

It was obvious he had moved with dexterity to insure native control of the new site. Old Galena had been bought up pretty much by rich whites and Huntington wasn't about to see it happen again. There would be no sale of land on the new site, he said firmly.

"I'm suggesting land lease only. Not selling. That way we'll have an income for a good many years and be on a solid footing. If we sell, soon one or two people will become landlords over all the land." He hesitated and, for a revealing instant, the friendly face hardened.

"We've been dealt with by somebody telling us what is what for too long," he said quietly. "Now we've got a good strong council and nobody is going to tell us what is what! People running for the House and Senate are finding out where the vote is coming from. Anybody counting on the native vote is going to have to mind their Ps and Qs. We're getting more knowledgeable in this town. Throwing away our crutches."

There was no question but what Galena was learning to stand on its own feet. Although reputed to be a welfare village, its current annual income was estimated at over $1 million and only twenty-five residents were on welfare. Jimmy Huntington had been designated to handle the BIA welfare program, but anyone who came to him for a handout found himself offered a job instead and those reluctant to work were likely to be shanghaied to one of the Aleutian canneries.

"Anybody who wants to work here can work!" Sidney Huntington maintained. The area was strategic—the site of the U. S. Air Force base closest to Russia and two smaller Air Force sites. Military men stationed there numbered about five hundred and there appeared to be no danger of troop pullout. Because of the military installations, employment had always been higher in Galena than in the average Indian village, and now construction of the new village and a quickening of the economy through settlement of land claims would mean many additional jobs.

Also, through political maneuvering, Galena had been designated as the home office for a number of government agencies. The latest coup had been the establishment of a two-year high school. Most villages had to send their children outside to high school but last year Galena parents had flatly refused to do so. Sidney, who was president of the school board, explained with considerable relish that they had lobbied the legislature and in the last four minutes of the session had obtained $139,999 for freshmen and sophomore classes. And now they were planning to push for a four-year facility. The program had been so popular that the Huntingtons had taken an Eskimo from a northern village as a boarding student. He was a skinny kid who had never eaten vegetables, Sidney reported, but Angela had fattened him up and he'd grown six inches taller.

I wasn't anxious to interview the Galena teaching staff, which was all white. Rumor had it they were malcontents and —to the horror of the Indians—there was some wife swapping among them. The ones I came in contact with appeared to be happy with their lot, however, and they were enthusiastic about their charges. Galena's native children were far more sophisticated than most, perhaps—the educators speculated—because of the military radio and television station. And, they observed, the Galena youngsters were also more self-sufficient than the average white children.

Momentarily Galena was smarting from a story published in an Anchorage newspaper that claimed (among other indignities) that "the favorite game of Galena youngsters one afternoon last week was smashing muscatel bottles against Lucky Lager empties or kicking clumps of frozen garbage."

Now, two weeks after the flood scare, Jimmy Huntington in his capacity as head of the Rural Alaska Community Action Program (RurAL-CAP), had instituted a mammoth clean-up campaign, hiring twenty-four men to work thirty-six hours. Pyres of rubbish began to smolder from one end of town to the other and the scene reminded me of a movie version of London during the Great Plague. I sought out my river perch to read, but smoke got in my eyes and it was so cold my hands turned blue. A south wind was sloshing the Yukon against my section of bank, undercutting with an unnerving *glug glug glug,* and all the swallows had disappeared except for a shivering stray which had puffed up his feathers till he looked like a baseball.

Angela had left with sons Charlie and Henry for a weekend training course in Anchorage for families of the deaf and dumb. They were due back in a few days with Andrew, their youngest child, who could neither hear nor speak.

Roger Huntington, an older son who worked for RurAL-CAP in Anchorage, had come home on vacation but stopped only long enough to change clothes, collect his gear, and take his brother Gilbert beaver trapping. Agnes was plugging away at her typewriter in the welfare office where she was in charge of food stamps, and Betty, the next oldest daughter, had escaped work in the coffee shop and I hoped she was sneaking a rest.

Finally Sidney came back from work and livened things up by discussing witch doctors with his son-in-law, Howard Gillette, and Kathy Huntington, his niece.

Medicine men, he told us, were pretty much like all other churchmen—they took people's money. They had been people, usually, with a knack for prediction. They always had young wives. They'd say to a mother, "Give me your young daughter or I'll kill her anyway."

Talk turned to babies born crippled or maimed. In the old days they had been thrown away—put in a burlap bag and dumped over the riverbank.

"Pitka, Angela's adopted brother, got throwed away because his mother never married and she knew the father would never help care for him," Sidney recalled. "And your mother's mother went out and got that burlap bag and raised him . . .

"You know Little Eddie [a dwarfed but delightful young Athabascan vacationing in the village from a job in Fairbanks]? He never would have survived in that day."

Back a couple of generations, people were really tough, Sidney said. He could remember visiting an old-timer in the winter and seeing his young child wearing just a diaper and shivering with cold. When he mentioned it, the old-timer had told him he was just trying to toughen the kid up. And it worked. Sidney recalled an Athabascan woman who had given birth at midnight and won the women's snowshoe race next afternoon.

"As long as people stuck to the old ways and kept moving, they were all right," Huntington continued. "When they settled it was awful. Old Nulato in the twenties had no toilets. People went around their houses. Stools everywhere. And for toilet paper they just sliced a piece of lumber off the side of the house and used it . . .

"I can remember when Jimmy was tending store and a woman came in to buy groceries. She forgot something. Couldn't remember what it was. Jimmy named off all the things people usually bought including, finally, toilet paper.

"'Heck, no. There are plenty of sticks upriver,' she told him."

The next day I interviewed Colonel Gerald Evans, the base commander, who knew little about Galena except that it was bad news. His predecessor had reputedly come with grief because he spent too much time at Hobo's Bar, and Evans was determined to keep a safe distance from the village. I found him so honest, outspoken, and blunt that I finally asked him how he had gotten so far in the military.

"Mostly luck," he said cryptically. And he hadn't had much luck lately. Shortly after he arrived the previous March he had to withdraw base shopping privileges from locals living off base, as the result of a reprimand from the inspector general.

"Can't compete with local businesses by act of Congress, etc."

The ruling hit both whites and natives, but a visiting member of the Alaska Federation of Natives considered it discrimination and had written the commander a nasty letter calling him a racist.

"Good God, my wife is part Indian," he said. "Oklahoma Cherokee . . ."

He had no quarrel with Galena, he said. "But it's hard to run a base in the boonies. The natives have always been dependent on the base, which, of course, is just another headache to us. My first duty is to the military."

Actually, nobody seemed to bear Evans any ill will. The Indians were becoming realistic about "the system."

I now started working on a full-sized fish net. I had ordered twine from Anchorage, and Grandma Nelson promised to show me how to cast on the first stitches. The day my twine arrived, though, I couldn't find her. Angela joked that I would probably have to learn at Hobo's and it would cost me a lot of wine, but as I turned away from Julia's door, the old lady arrived looking sprightly in a long flowered dress and green sneakers.

First we had to find a board to make a net stick, she said. Not certain what was needed, I came back with an armload of lumber. My enthusiasm amused her but none of the wood was right.

"Need a gas box," she said, grabbing her cane, and off we went, Julia leading with a swift limp. After inspecting several rubbish piles, we finally found a wooden box that had housed a can of gas.

"Get hammer," she ordered. I complied and she whacked off the side of the box. Then, using a saw, butcher knife, and my jackknife, she fashioned a stick double the width of her second-finger joints, and we marched back to her house to start the net.

"Once I made one in one day. I had to. We really needed it," she recalled, as her gnarled old fingers flew. The net stick gauged the mesh size and she worked around it with a shuttle. "But I don't knit net since I go to the hospital."

She, too, had been down with tuberculosis some years ago, but it was not that that caused her limp. In childhood she had been forced to wear skin boots that shrank. But she'd grown up tough. A swift runner, they said, and a fast woman in a canoe.

Now, patiently, she showed me how to expand twenty-two meshes of ice net. The stitch was exactly right for dog salmon or whitefish, she assured me. She knit two perfect rows, then

dismissed me curtly saying she had work to do. She was bead-
ing a necklace for a paying customer at Hobo's.

Later in the day she slipped over to the Huntingtons' and I
found her drinking coffee in the kitchen.

"Did they throw out that bottle of wine?" she wondered. I
remembered having seen a bottle with about two drinks left in
it—not enough to do Grandma much damage. Angela appeared
and Grandma looked innocent as a babe. When she left, I was
ordered to keep watch while the old lady poured a thimbleful
of wine into her coffee; she drained it in one gulp, rinsed the
cup, and went happily back to work. Later I noticed Agnes
Jimmie sitting tearfully on a log by the river, with a friend lecturing her on the evils of drink. Expecting the worst, I stopped
by Grandma's. She and Agnes often toured Hobo's in tandem,
but Grandma was sober and her necklace almost finished.

After supper I went into Sidney's tool shed to make another
net stick and found Andrew playing alone. He was trying to in-
vent a game with the workshop hoist. Watching him, it occurred to me what a horribly lonely thing it was to be nine
years old and deaf and dumb. Even with a family as loving as
this one, Andrew was mostly on his own.

When he had perfected the game, other boys came to join in
and he was happy, but later, when they went off to climb
houses, he stayed on alone. The hoist worked like a swing and
I stopped to give him a push. It went too far, battering him
against the shed wall. I tried to warn him but he couldn't hear
my cry and I couldn't catch him to stop his fall. I felt utterly
helpless but he took it cheerfully.

He was a beautiful child, the handsomest of the lot, in fact,
and I asked Angela if he had been born with his disability.
No, she said sadly. When he was a year old he had gotten
meningitis, sleeping through two full days at home and three
more after they got him up river to Tanana Native Hospital.
When he had come back home the family noticed that he
didn't hear the other kids when they yelled and when someone
couldn't hear that, something had to be wrong.

"We banged our big metal frying pan behind his head and

he didn't even hear it," Angela recalled. "We called the Tanana hospital and they kept saying, 'Make sure he's deaf.' They wouldn't believe us. Finally I talked a social worker in Fairbanks into calling the hospital. She got him in the next November."

The next sunny day I pegged my net to an abandoned barge on the waterfront, and the sight of me working made Charlie Evans nostalgic.

"When I was single I started a net, but I was slow knitting so I hung it on my bedpost and whenever a woman came by to talk she'd sit and work on it," he recollected. "You know, I had that thing done in two weeks!"

"Say, Charlie, could you give me a recipe for white mule?" I asked. White mule was the traditional moonshine of the Yukon and I had heard that Charlie was a good brewer.

"Well, you take twenty pounds of corn meal, twenty–twenty-five pounds of sugar, one little yeast cake, and put it in a twenty-gallon barrel of water," he began. "Now, I'm giving you the *short* recipe . . .

"I was weaned on white mule . . . You had to keep the cover on it in Prohibition. You can smell it a long ways off . . . Let it stand six to eight days . . . I had a copper pot. Took a big fire extinguisher, cut off the top and soldered it to the copper pot for coils. Nobody was on the Koyukuk. Only me. It was during break-up and the Prohibition man couldn't get over the rotten ice.

"I wanted to make some good white mule. Them natives used matches but I got a hydrometer. The first batch came out 120 proof. Poured it back, mixed half with water and ran it through again. Next time it was 190 proof. I kept a couple of bottles of the 190 proof for shaving lotion. That's what the old-timers told me to do. But them bastards never shaved!"

Later in the day, as I wandered through the village taking pictures, a hand popped out of an open window offering me a bottle. To my disappointment it wasn't white mule but Black Label beer. The donor was Carlson Malemute whom I'd met at the Huntingtons' when Howard Gillette set up a barbershop.

Carlson, twenty-seven, was a Vietnam veteran. He had returned to find his girl married to an Aleut and then took off to diesel maintenance school in Chicago. The main thing he had gotten from that was a sterling silver Playboy Bunny ring which he wore proudly. He was a compact, graceful man, handsome as the devil, and charming. But he didn't seem to have any particular goals and I asked him why he had come home.

"It's so easy to live here. I can make it outside but it's so easy here. There's a lot about the life I like."

When the larder got empty, Carlson or his brothers or father shot a moose. In summer the family moved twenty miles up river to fish camp. His father, Jimmy, a former dog-racing champ, still raised dogs and in the winter they trained them. They also did some trapping "although it almost costs more to go out there these days than you make."

If the need for cash arose, there were construction or fire-fighting jobs or work in the canneries. Jimmy had legally staked out the family fish camp as his native land allotment, but Carlson, who had also been entitled to 160 acres before the federal claims settlement, filed no claim and did not regret it.

"I just don't want to be a landowner," he said. "Don't want anything to do with it."

As spring wore on, the river slowed and travel became easier. Now it was time for picnics and I was invited to go on a birthday celebration with the Edward Pitkas. There were two boatloads of us—eleven of us in Pitka's fourteen-footer and ten in a smaller power boat, with only one life jacket among us.

"Who here can swim?" I asked.

No one but me. No wonder the Yukon claimed some twelve people a year here. Today there were numerous drifting trees, but Arnold Evans, Pitka's son-in-law, ran the boat skillfully across the river and negotiated a lively tributary called Jack's Slough. He was a powerful young man and, despite the fact he had only one arm, he could handle a boat, drive, and hunt with agility.

*Carlson Malemute and a new sled dog.*

It was a great picnic and Edward Pitka enjoyed it most of all. He was father or grandfather or uncle to nearly everyone there and his pride was obvious and pleasing to see. Could this be the Pitka who had "got throwed away" down the bank, I wondered? How ironic that he should have survived to produce such a happy clan.

When we got home, Betty officially opened the Huntington coffee shop and took in $100 by 11 P.M. selling hamburgers, fried shrimp, soda, and french fries. The place had a pool table, too. That meant the kids didn't have to go to Hobo's to play.

Not that Hobo was all that bad. I interviewed him late that afternoon and discovered that he was a sincere Galena booster. He had, indeed, been a Harvard man, but quit to finish his scholastic career in Kalamazoo, Michigan. He had come to the military base twelve years before as a salesman for a bar fixture manufacturer and had become the silent partner in the village bar only to find himself running it. I knew him to be an easy touch and speculated he wasn't going to get rich here.

"I don't want to get rich," he said with certainty. "I'm rich now. Have lots of friends."

He was particularly proud of the fact that when there had been a hassle about renewal of his liquor license a couple of years back, the village council wrote a letter on his behalf. Those who disliked him pointed out that Hobo had been a member of the council at the time, but generally speaking, his stock was higher with the Indians than I had expected.

He didn't intend to move his bar to the new site, he said, although he had barely escaped with his life during the last flood.

"Of course, if the next flood moves the bar, that's all right," he mused. "Then it will be where it stops. We'll get in a boat and catch up with it and see if there's any beer left!"

That night he was first in line at a meeting of the Sports Association to plan events for the "Yukon 800" motorboat race. In past years the race had been from Fairbanks to Ruby, a village up river from Galena, and back. Now the Sports Association had raised $1,000 and induced race officials to make Galena the turn-around point. Naturally, the Sports Association hoped to make money off the venture, but mostly it was just going to be a good party.

Hobo suggested a pre-race, in which local people would jump in their boats, cross the river, gather fire wood, bring it back, and brew a pot of tea. They decided to call it the "Tea-Boat Race" and I threatened to write an article entitled "All you need is a boat and a little pot." The joke amused the younger generation, many of whom were quite fond of marijuana. Their elders, who maintained there were no drugs hard or soft in the village and actually believed it, got a smug chuckle out of the idea of a "pot" race too.

At the meeting I sat next to Jimmy Malemute, Carlson's father. He was delighted to learn that I had seen the world championship dog-sled race he had won a dozen years before and talked wistfully about going back to mushing. I liked the old champ. He had a shy gentleness I found uncommon in an Athabascan, but Athabascan he certainly was. No one could recall any whites ever marrying into that family.

Carlson invited me down to his house for a beer and after the meeting, I found him entertaining Ivan Supri, a young councilman from the village of Nulato. Supri looked stunned when he was introduced to me.

"I've been reading your articles in the *Tundra Times* for the last year and I thought you were an Indian," he said. And to make certain I wasn't, he pulled one hair from my head and checked the blonde root.

Another visitor was a young deaf-mute man with whom Carlson communicated in pantomime. I had never seen anyone joke in sign language before and it was amusing to watch them. The mute was one of a family of seven and had a brother who was also deaf and dumb. Their mother, formerly the village health aide, had just come home from the hospital to die of cancer. The father had been jailed for the rape of the oldest daughter, leaving the youngsters, aged five to nineteen, to fend for themselves.

Carlson's aunt, who was visiting from down river, wandered in, searching for food, companionship, and maybe a little beer.

She was Julia's age, a small woman with a skinny white braid down her back.

"No beer," Carlson told her. "Grandpa says no beer." But it wasn't easy to turn her down. She was fairly sober and quietly managed to take some when Carlson wasn't looking.

Some of Hobo's crowd dropped by, complaining bitterly about the last bastion of discrimination in Galena—Hobo's prostitutes charged the GIs $15 while the price for natives was $50.

We would fight it, I promised. Maybe we could take it before the Equal Opportunity Board or the Human Rights Commission.

After they left, some of Carlson's relatives arrived blind drunk and made a disagreeable scene, finally passing out on the living-room floor. Malemute's face hardened and rarely had I seen so much pain in anyone's eyes.

"I've got to get out of this place," he said quietly. "They say I don't do anything for them. Ever since I've been this high"—he gestured four feet off the floor—"I cut wood. Wood for the house. Wood for money. Seventy-five dollars a load. I'd go to the neighbors and ask if anyone needed wood. A lot of people used it then . . ." (And the Malemutes still did.)

"Quit school when I was sixteen. Stayed around like this. I couldn't get anywhere in grammar school. I'd go out every night on a party and I couldn't study. When I was about eighteen I decided to go away from here. Those papers your parents are supposed to sign . . . I signed them myself. The only thing that was open was Chemawa in Oregon. I liked it." (Chemawa was a BIA school.)

Then there was the Army. He had guarded a munitions depot, hit the rough spots, and was glad to be out, although he hadn't actually disliked Army life. He had met a Navajo who had insisted that it was an Indian's right to keep his hair long and gotten away with it, and so had Carlson.

"Then I came back here. Last winter I cut wood. Wood enough to last them. Then I just took off to hunt . . ."

He had been in jail. No big thing, but it soured him on the

cit y. He didn't give a damn for money, didn't want anything in particular except another beer right now. He was just drifting.

When the fishing season got active I talked Sandrs Cleaver into taking me with him while he tended his net. It ended up costing me $4.25 for gas and $2 for a jug for the captain but it was worth it.

Sandrs' little boat was so old that on sharp turns the top separated from the hull, but he had a reliable ten-horsepower engine and we took off fearlessly. The river was still full of drift but Sandrs expertly picked clear channels.

"You can't trust this river in the springtime," he said. And with reason. It had taken the life of one of his sons. The boy had been duck hunting. Sadly Sandrs showed me the spot where the boy's boat had foundered; but he brightened as we nosed up Jack's Slough. The banks were alive with ducks and geese and Sandrs watched them with the enthusiasm of a newcomer.

Two miles up the slough we turned into a creek where his net hung between two floating Clorox bottles. Another party of fishermen appeared in a boat further up, checked their net, and disappeared again.

"Do you think you can trust me?" Cleaver asked. The thought had occurred to me, too, for we were quite alone and it was a long swim home.

"Yes," I said firmly. "Angela said I could."

"She did?" he asked with pleased astonishment. "Angela said that?" I assured him she had and he was quite delighted.

The net was full of whitefish, each well over a foot long. Sandrs pulled ten out and left the rest for another day. Even out of water the catch clung stubbornly to life, flapping around in a large washtub. Idly I watched them as we drifted back down the slough. The sun was warm and the banks looked green and mysterious. Back where Cleaver's son had drowned, he spoke again of the accident. The fish struggled in their tub and suddenly I realized how closely the Indians lived with death. It was the biggest fact of their existence. They were seemingly carefree, quick to laugh, joke, and play. Yet death was always at their elbow, a constant visitor in every home.

I was reminded of a conversation I had had with Hazel. "TB," she said. "Tuberculosis. It took all my mother's sisters and a lot of our family. They died slowly. There were one or two in bed in almost every house. Then they started sending them to the hospital and they got better."

Back at the waterfront Agnes Jimmie greeted me and the dark thoughts vanished.

"You see net now. You find out?" she asked.

"Yes, Agnes. Now I know what the hell I'm knitting."

Jimmy Malemute had shot a bear near his fish camp and given Angela a hindquarter. It distressed her because she'd never eaten bear this late in the season and wasn't sure it was good. Twice she had planned to cook it and backed out. It reposed in the icebox and every time I opened the door a disjointed foot, pad and claws, gave me a jolt. Finally she decided to postpone the decision and I was elected to store the meat in the deep freeze.

Afterwards, Charlie Evans waylaid me and talked me into coming to hear some old stories. His brother Richard, Sandrs Cleaver, and Joe Wholecheese were visiting with one of Charlie's daughters and it was a long session. Some of the recollections were funny, like the story of Mrs. Happy and her lover who fell asleep by the fire and burned off their Eskimo boots and had to explain to Mrs. Happy's husband why they were barefoot. And how Charlie had challenged his daughter Hazel's suitor to a footrace and had to hold back so he wouldn't beat the young man. But some of the tales were gruesome, like the description of how one of Charlie's sons had been killed by the family dog.

Finally they told me of the Athabascan woodsmen, spirits even the most sophisticated Athabascans do not discount.

"It's an evil spirit . . . like the abdominal . . . I mean abnormal snowman," Charlie's daughter explained.

"I'd rather talk about an adorable snowwoman," Charlie grinned. "But then, I can joke because I never saw one."

There were recent stories about non-believers seeing woodsmen. One tale was about the "Dutchman" who had lived on the river in the 1950s and scoffed at the legends until one night he snowshoed twelve miles in the dead of winter to escape a woodsman and had nearly gone mad. There were reports of babies stolen by woodsmen and of the white supervisor of a fire-fighting crew who built an outhouse for his men, only to be frightened by a woodsman as he christened it. From the descriptions, I wondered if the woodsmen might be bears, but the Athabascans certainly knew bears when they saw them.

One busy morning Angela took time out to show me her family photos. I had been tempted to envy her her fine family and the ease with which she seemed to handle life, but sorting through the box of dusty prints I saw that it had taken pain and patience to be the mother of the world.

In the beginning, when she had married Sidney, living had been rough.

"Hard times those first eight years. Then we finally got a start. But our first two children we had to adopt out."

There were happy photos of bright-eyed children, of weddings and parties. But they were countered by pictures of the devastation of past floods, of her sister in a coffin, of friends now dead.

I asked about her adopted brother, Pitka.

"His mother had children and she wasn't married," she explained simply. "Each time her sister gave them away, but this time the father was a white man and the sister didn't like that. When it came time, they didn't want her in the house or in the village, so they made a place for her outside. Three women were with her at birth. Her sister said, 'Kill it!' It was a boy.

"My mother had never thought of taking a child, but her son had just died that spring and she thought, 'I wonder what my husband would think? Maybe he wouldn't mind since we lost a boy.' She took it home and put it in my father's shirt and wrapped it in his rabbitskin blanket . . ."

Sandrs Cleaver wandered in to interrupt her and she never

finished the story. I had just won a baby hat in the village raffle and I presented it to her.

"I wish I had a new baby to put in it," Angela said.

I'd decided to leave on Claude Demientieff, Sr.'s barge but
he was overdue.

"Claude's a good man and he's got a gold mine," a Galena
merchant told me. "I keep telling him I'll take all the loads
he'll haul this summer but you must know they'll get here.
Problem is he just can't pass a village bar without stopping for
a few beers."

Still waiting on a bright Sunday afternoon, I accepted Colonel Evans' invitation to drive to Campion, a neighboring military base. He asked a lot of questions about Indians, in much
the same manner that I would query a wildlife expert on bears,
but I knew he was well meaning. With the Huntingtons I gave
him a tour of the new house, which was shaping up handsomely, and Evans was impressed. Then we let him see the old
place. Noting that Sidney had twelve kids and there were no
walls, he wondered "how the adults in the family . . . er . . .
functioned . . . with so little privacy." I told him we played
the radio a lot.

This was Carlson Malemute's last day in town before going
for training on a fire-fighting crew in Fairbanks, and early in
the evening he borrowed his father's boat, packed two guns
aboard, and invited me up river to the fish camp. The water
was high and full of logs but he was sure and quick. In mid-
river the engine leaped off its frame, but he grabbed it in time.

"I had a metal boat one came off once and the son-of-a-bitch
sank on me," he recalled. "After that I always keep an eye on
them."

The sun was low as we passed the high cliffs of Campion
and turned down a quiet slough lined with emerald trees. Beyond it the river was rough and occasional waves chopped
over the bow. We passed the cemeteries of Old Louden, five of
them clinging to the hills of the ghost town. Carlson said he
had sisters buried there. His parents had been visiting a neigh-

bor when his brother Anthony had accidently started a fire. He had been little, but he'd tried to put out the flames, with no success. The memory made him quiet.

The sky turned soft rose and there was the smell of rich earth and sweet ferns. Geese flew in V formation overhead. With a grin Carlson offered me his shotgun but I shook my head, no.

The fish camp was a marvelous place, like a little town. There were about eight sheds, storehouses, and smokehouses and several cabins. The Malemutes' place was as well furnished as their home in town. His mother had built it one summer while Jimmy was working in the cannery, and Carlson and his brother, Anthony, had helped her. Then, by themselves, the boys had built a perfect little cabin next door.

We made coffee, ate dried fish, and climbed a big bluff behind the camp in the track of a large bear. From the top we could see a grand sweep of Yukon and the rich lake country beyond.

Carlson told me of berrying here with his brother. Of running down as fast as they could, grabbing branches to keep from falling. And how once, near the face of the cliff, a branch Anthony had grabbed broke off and he pitched almost a mile into a ravine.

"He wasn't hurt but he sure was mad as hell about spilling the berries!"

After the hike we did some target practice with a homemade .22. Carlson was right on target and I missed by a foot. And then, going with the current, we were home in forty-five minutes. Overhead two geese were making love on the wing. Inspired Carlson invited me to spend the rest of the night at his house and I considered it. I would be sharing a room with him and two of his brothers, which didn't upset me nearly as much as the prospect of facing Angela the next morning. Prudently I went home.

And still no river boat. Claude was reported to be at the Last Chance Bar with a broken gearbox, but I had my doubts. I feared he might feel duty bound to help drink the five hundred cases of beer he had to deliver there, and reluctantly I decided to take the plane to Fairbanks.

It wasn't easy to leave the Huntingtons or the village. If I stayed another few days I could watch Sidney crown his new house with a roof, and in another week I might go with Angela to the fish camp. But I didn't trust myself to stay longer for fear I might never leave.

And at least, I consoled myself, I could come back some day. The way Sidney was building his house—sturdy and strong— the way the village was rebuilding, it would take more than a flood to knock out Galena.

It was late that night when I got back to Fairbanks and I found my boss, Howard Rock, in Tommy's Elbow Room, our favorite watering hole.

"Howard, I finally escaped from the Indians," I greeted him happily. We had joked that I might never get out of Indian country, and although I'd planned to come home earlier, I'd postponed and postponed my return. Naturally, an Eskimo editor would worry about losing his reporter to the Indians, but the Indian woman he was sitting with wasn't in on our joke. A longtime militant, she accused me outright of bigotry against the Indians. I protested that, on the contrary, I had just spent the happiest month of my adult life among them, but she became nastier about it. Howard was put in the position of defending me and finally I got disgusted and left.

The Galena fire-fighting crew had invited me to look them up in Fairbanks. They had said they were sometimes in the Redwood Bar after working hours and since it was handy to Tommy's Elbow Room, I decided to find them. It was a dimly lit, cavernous place, packed with a fierce-looking assortment of Indians and a few servicemen. Once inside I had second thoughts. It was after midnight and I turned to retreat when someone tapped me on the shoulder. It was Carlson.

"This place is really scary," I told him. "It shakes me up so much I was just going to leave."

"Yes, I know," he said seriously. "You just can't trust those GIs."

# Atka

## THE FORGOTTEN ISLAND

*When the Russians discovered the Aleutians in the mid-1700s, every island on the chain was settled by fierce, proud natives. They were a people marvelously adapted to the world's worst weather, going without heat in their homes and often without shoes through gales and snow, but their primitive spears proved no match for the guns of the Russian fur traders—the* promyshleniki—*who cared only for the rich furs of the Aleutian sea otter.*

*In the early days, a single voyage to the Aleutians could make its Russian promoter rich, and so, carelessly, the* promyshleniki *slaughtered the fur-bearing creatures and plundered the Aleuts, killing those who resisted. Entire island populations were wiped out and sometimes the invaders killed simply to pass the time. One Russian commander wondered how many men a musket ball could pass through, lined up twelve Aleuts, and reported later, as an interesting footnote to history, that the shot stopped at the ninth man. In another village, by their own written account, hunters killed all the men and old women, sparing the young "to serve them." Then they kidnapped the women for their homeward voyage, dropping them overboard when they sighted the Russian mainland.*

*Atka in the Andreanof chain of the Aleutians, fared better than many settlements. The Atkans were forced to pay fur tax about 1762, but there was no mass slaughter. In 1825 the Russians established a permanent*

settlement on the island. A year later a number of Atkans were transported to colonize Bering and Copper
Islands near Siberia, but the village of Atka survived.

By the time Alaska was sold to the United States in
1867, the population of the Aleutian chain had dwin-
dled from an estimated 20,000 to 2,000. The sea animals on which the natives depended for food, clothing,
and skin boats were decimated on about the same scale,
and starvation and sickness became a way of life.

In addition, the Russians had almost obliterated the
Aleut culture, tribal traditions, and even tribal memories. To replace them they left the comforts of the Russian Orthodox Church and a written Aleut language,
but American administrators banned both from the education system.

About 1910 influenza halved the population of Atka.
Tuberculosis made further inroads, and then, on the
Japanese invasion of the Aleutians in 1942, the village
was evacuated and burned to the ground by the United
States Navy to deny facilities to the enemy. The Atkans
were moved to Killisnoo, an island in southeastern
Alaska, where their number was halved again by the
alien climate and problems of displacement.

After the war the survivors were joined by refugees
from the distant Aleutian settlement of Attu. The Attus
—some forty people in all—had been evacuated to Japanese prisons during the war and, like the Atkans, only
half of them survived. Now the United States Government refused to let them return to Attu, arguing that it
was the furthest western settlement in the Aleutian
chain and it would be hard for government agencies to
take care of them there. So the Attus were forced to
move in with the Atkans and together they began to rebuild the village.

*Atka volcano and geese in the fall.*

*Atka village.*

In the fall of 1972 Atka, with a permanent Aleut population of eighty-seven, was one of the most isolated communities in the United States. It had no ZIP code, no post office, no functioning dock, no airstrip, no scheduled transportation. Its only communication with the outside world was a temperamental fifty-watt radio and an old Navy ship dispatched once a month from Adak, 120 miles west, weather and military commitments permitting.

The ship was based at Adak Naval Base and military clearance was required for anyone who wanted to land there. I was told to make arrangements through the BIA office in Anchorage, but the office was vague about departure dates, not even sure there would be a departure during the month I wanted to go. Finally I called the Adak base and made my own arrangements. A ship was to be dispatched to bring the Atka teen-agers out in time for the high school term either in late August or early September. The authorities would be glad to take me over to Atka but they couldn't say when they could bring me back again—maybe in September, maybe not.

From all accounts, I was undertaking a hazardous venture. Every family on Atka had an active case of tuberculosis, one of the military medical staff cautioned me. If I drank the island water without boiling it, I was risking typhoid. I shouldn't even lick the postage stamps I bought from the general store, for there was no telling what I would catch if I did. Most of the Aleuts were said to be lazy drunks and few outsiders could fathom why I wanted to visit Atka.

The departure of the Navy boat from Adak was postponed two days, although the weather was fair. The Navy blamed the BIA and the BIA blamed the Navy. Finally someone got it all organized and we found ourselves chugging off at daybreak on August 27 on a World War II harbor tug. It had enclosed passenger seating for six and there were about twenty of us aboard, not counting the crew. There was no food. The Navy provided it when they made the run with the bigger ship, but that craft had been moved to another station and there was no room on the hundred-foot tug. We passengers

hadn't been warned of this, but you couldn't blame the Navy.
They had contracted with the BIA to provide Atka transportation only because nobody else would undertake the assignment.
It cost them $375 in fuel alone to make the run and BIA paid
them about $200 for the service.

It was a cramped, hungry twelve-hour trip but fortunately
the weather was fair so some of us could stay on deck. I spent
most of the run on a rubber life raft topside, studying the islands and lazy volcanoes as we traveled down the chain.

Michael Besecker, the new Atka schoolteacher, was aboard
with his wife, Roberta, and their two daughters—Terry, nine
and Tawny, twelve—and son, Douglas, who was a high school
freshman. They were fresh from Southern California and I had
my doubts about their survival ability. The wife was considerably overweight and had had trouble boarding and the trip
was a rough one on their big old dog, Bear, but their optimism
was astonishing and they were uncomplaining troopers.

So were the Aleuts. A couple of them had found no place to
eat during their two-day wait at the Adak base but there
were no gripes. In fact, they talked very little, even among
themselves.

I introduced myself to Larry Dirks, Jr., one of the younger
men whom I figured might speak fluent English. He did. It
had been a bad fishing season, he told me, and he was anxious
to get home to his wife of two years and their young son. But
chances of finding work on Atka was dismal. His father had
about the only paying job, as school janitor. Larry, Jr.'s training
was as an auto mechanic but there were only two trucks and
one car on the whole island.

I also talked to Dan Prokopeuff, a barrel-chested man in his
forties who was considerably taller than most Aleuts. He said
it was the worst salmon season he had seen in six years of going
off island to work, but that some had made good money in
halibut.

In mid-afternoon the sun came on strong and, to the astonishment of the captain, we sped along at 12½ knots before a
following sea. The usually conservative United States Geodetic

Survey sailing directions for the region claimed, "No other area in the world is recognized as having worse weather in general," but today the swell was moderate and the sea was the clear blue-green color of old telephone-pole insulators. Orange-billed sea parrots (puffins) paddled alongside, trying so hard to get airborne that when they made it, they were too tired to fly. Curious sea otters drifted by, one with a half-eaten crab in his paws which he proceeded to crack with a rock. And approaching Atka we sighted a whale.

The island was almost two hundred miles in circumference, upholstered apparently in soft green suede. Most of its volcanic peaks were modestly veiled in clouds but poked their heads out as we passed.

I felt disappointment as we came into Nazan Bay, for, not realizing how big it was, I thought the mountains seemed pretty small. Old Quonset huts from a World War II military base were strewn along the shore and I couldn't see any village. Then, suddenly, we rounded a point and there was Atka, cupped in sheltering green hills and backed by rugged mountains. The houses were mostly of weathered board, like an old New England fishing village, but overlooking them was a marvelous white Russian Orthodox church, capped with emerald-green onion domes and a red roof.

The Atkan passengers were smiling. Theirs was a quiet reception but a warm one. Aleuts talk about love with their eyes and there was a lot of love in their welcome.

Despite this, I delayed going ashore as long as possible. Perhaps it was all the health horror stories I had heard or the remoteness of the place. I felt uneasy so I hung back, watching the other passengers climb into the little boats that came out to meet us. Finally, a young Aleut with a square, chiseled profile came alongside and waited. His eyes missed nothing. He saw me in the shadow of the deckhouse and motioned me to his boat. I shook my head, but he waited. Finally I dragged my heels over the side. No conversation. Quickly he took me to shore. Should I pay him? He didn't give me time. Maybe I could do it later.

"What's your name?" I stammered. He was already headed back to the ship.

"Moses," he said. Well, maybe that was a good sign, to be fetched ashore by Moses.

I had written to Clara Snigaroff to check on housing but gotten no reply. Clara was supposed to be the village doer, friends told me. Most Aleuts were shy and retiring, but Clara was just the opposite, a real go-getter. Her parents had both died of tuberculosis, leaving Clara and her brothers and sisters to raise themselves. Her man had died at sea when the youngest of her six children was just a baby, and she had raised them alone. She had taken nurse's training, was the village health aide, and also managed the village co-operative store. Her house was the biggest in the village and looked pretty much like any Middle American home without paint. It was clean and roomy and so, for that matter, was Clara.

I found her entertaining Bill Vaudrin, a fellow passenger who represented the state-operated schools, and Sally Jamie, an Aleut League representative from Anchorage who had gotten quite seasick on the voyage. Now they were both wolfing down homemade bread, cheese, and Spam, and I joined them.

Clara, her son Ronald, and her daughter Sally were packing for the tug's return to Adak. Sally, a plump and rosy young beauty, was off to finish her final year at Adak High School. Ronald, a tall fifteen-year-old, had eye problems and flatly refused to go to school this year unless he had glasses, so he and Clara were making the twelve-hundred-mile trip to Anchorage to visit an optometrist. Her youngest, Danny Boy, nine, was to stay with the Dirks family, but Clara jokingly said she'd leave him to me. He looked like a Raphael angel and I said without hesitation that I'd take him.

It had been decided that I would rent the priest's house. He was in residence at best a month each year and his home was usually rented to visitors in his absence, to raise money for the church. I found it readily, for it was one of three painted houses in the village—white with a red roof, just like the church. It was wedged in between the church and the school, but the bathroom, entryway, and attic had splendid views of the harbor, and the kitchen, bedroom, and living-room windows surveyed the main village paths.

The interior of the house was painted light green throughout, with white trim and red floors. The place was modestly well furnished. Russian icons were in every room but they were cheery. The whole house was wired for electricity, too, but since it would take a constantly banging generator and an endless supply of fuel to produce it, I told the custodian, John Nevzoroff, that I didn't need it. It was luxury enough to have plumbing, not just a kitchen sink but a big, deep bathtub. It was the best house I had lived in for a year and a half, and all for $120 rent.

There was no time to settle in that night, however. The tug had originally planned to lay over in Atka two days. Now it was announced that departure time would be at 6:30 A.M. the next morning, which sent the visiting doctor, dentist, and bureaucrats into a frenzy. The dentist began inspecting teeth at once, under a weak light in the school kitchen. Having no dental chair, he used his hand as a head brace and, under the pressure, he lost a root from Danny Snigaroff's tooth during an extraction.

The doctor offered shots for TB tests. There was some confusion about this because villagers couldn't make him understand that they had been tested by another doctor a month earlier. Finally, so as not to disappoint him, everyone lined up and had it done again, the tests proving negative, as they had done before.

After a few false starts and several announcements, Mrs. Jamie and Bill Vaudrin got the villagers assembled for a meeting. The education specialist showed a movie on an Eskimo bilingual education program and asked the Atkans if they wanted to teach Aleut in their school. If so, would they decide by 6 A.M. who they wanted to teach it, whether or not he would travel to Norway to study with a leading Aleut expert, and whether he would teach the language in the traditional Russian (Cyrillic) alphabet or in the English one.

Then Mrs. Jamie explained that anyone from Atka could run for the board of directors of the Aleut League, a regional native organization which would administer the federal land claims settlement for the Aleuts. She also wanted to know if anyone wanted to train to teach an adult education course and if someone would serve on the Aleut League planning committee on early childhood education.

All the assignments involved traveling over a thousand miles to Anchorage where the Aleut League was headquartered, then hanging around the city for a month or so, waiting for the next tug home. Both speakers finally conceded that it would be impossible for the Atkans to make so many important decisions over night. Perhaps they could send their answers and representatives on the next tug.

Proceedings were interrupted when the schoolteacher's wife burst in to announce that their packing boxes, which had been left on the beach, were getting drenched in the rain and incoming tide. Everyone rushed to the rescue and returned muttering it wasn't nearly as bad as she had made out. The meeting continued. Clara Snigaroff said if she didn't have to teach, she would represent the village on early childhood education, since she was going to Anchorage anyway. The villagers assured her she wouldn't have to teach and added that they had already elected her while she was out. Mrs. Jamie explained that anyone from Atka who could collect twenty-five signatures could run for the board. Larry Dirks and a couple of others stayed on to talk with her, and a meeting of the Atka school board followed.

I went to watch the dentist until I was steered off by Lydia Dirks (Mrs. Larry Dirks, Sr.) and her daughter Barbara, who were worried for fear I might not have a ready kerosene lamp at the priest's house. John Nevzoroff was filling it as we arrived there and, with that taken care of, the Dirks invited me home for coffee and pirugâx, the island's traditional two-crusted pie of salmon and rice. It was delicious and I was ravenous for it was my first hot meal in twenty-four hours. Lydia topped the meal off with a piece of apple pie.

The Dirks's house was older than most, one of three that had escaped burning by the Navy when the Japanese threatened to invade the island. It was modestly furnished, with a few mail-order products, but neat and easy to live in.

At the end of the dining table was a handsome cake that had been decorated with "Welcome Home" for Larry, Jr. Next morning, though, Barbara and her younger brother would leave for high school in Adak, so there was sadness, too. The Dirks's lights, like other lights in the village, would burn long that night, for there would be a rush to pack and a month's mail to be read and answered before dawn.

It was still dark at six next morning when I lit my kerosene lamp and found my way to the bathroom. The washbowl had two faucets, one marked "Hot." Impossible, I thought—no electricity. Gingerly I turned it on anyway and to my astonishment hot water splattered forth. A miracle! The oil cook stove did double duty, heating a hot-water tank.

Groping my way through the village to the edge of the bay I saw a boy and a man loading suitcases into a dory. Then I checked in at Snigaroffs where breakfast was being served to everyone but seasick Sally. I got a cup of coffee and settled into a conversation on Atka's recommended reading.

*Birthplace of the Winds* by Ted Banks II was blacklisted. As a budding young anthropologist, Banks had visited the village during its troubled period of adjustment after World War II when refugees and survivors were struggling to get re-established. Also in residence at that time, Clara noted, were three hundred GIs who were helping to rebuild the village, and life was anything but normal.

"We took Ted Banks into our homes. Tried to help him. And the book lies," Mrs. Snigaroff said bitterly.

Banks had characterized the Atkans as little more than indulgent drunks and lost children. He had tried to take into account the changes they faced but had left leading questions unanswered.

Why had they given up the marvelous skin boats of their forebears in favor of wooden skiffs? Why did they eat canned fruit instead of picking berries? Why didn't they hunt more reindeer?

There were plausible answers—the shortage or inaccessibility of game, the tartness of the local berries which required so much investment in sugar that it was cheaper to buy jam—but Banks didn't pursue them.

"That's why people don't help writers with books," she said. "Some guy came from Adak last summer. His pictures were true but the rest was all wrong!"

This was, I realized, a roundabout way of explaining why she hadn't answered my inquiry about housing. But there was at least one book the Atkans liked, she added. *Aleutian Boy* by Ethel Oliver, their schoolteacher after World War II, told of a young Aleut boy who got shipwrecked on neighboring Amlia Island with a white visitor and how they survived by reverting to the ways of the old timers.

"It's mostly fiction, but it's so good it could be real," she concluded.

The departure for the tug was low key—a quick hug and the older children were gone and Clara with them. The tug made off quickly, finding itself in rough water. And with it went our last sure contact with the outside world.

I returned home to encounter my first visitor, Max Nevzoroff, brother of the church custodian. He sat down for a cup of coffee and an orange and offered polite conversation, during which he established himself as an eligible bachelor. Then, at 9:15, he left for church. It was, he said, some sort of religious holiday. Briefly I considered attending, but the villagers en route were very dressed up. The women were wearing dresses, something I had never encountered in a remote Alaskan community, and I had brought only blue jeans and slacks. So, instead of church, I elected to take a hike.

The steep, treeless hills made for rough walking, especially in a twenty-five knot breeze. I had read that there were mysterious, grass-covered holes on the island and that if you fell in, your body might be found days later on a beach miles away—or maybe never. In addition, the weather was fickle and so quick to change that sometimes even people who knew the country got lost in it. One Atkan, caught in a winter storm, had died from exhaustion within sight of the village. I plotted a cautious course along the south beach and bluffs but even that served to increase my respect for the country.

Tired and thirsty, I came home to study the water tap, glass in hand. Should I boil it or take my chances with typhoid? The natives weren't boiling their water and the island streams looked clean and fresh, so I decided to chance it.

John Nevzoroff appeared shortly to entertain me with some history, namely, his own. A widower for eleven years, he had just put his daughter on the tug for school and it made him gloomy. He was a wiry man, with a good face creased by long exposure to sea and wind. He had navigated the Aleutian waters with the late Squeaky Anderson, a legendary white who had helped the Navy chart this area at the outbreak of World War II.

"I am a full-blooded captain but I never got my papers," he assured me, without a trace of boast. "I know all the Aleutians. Every rock from here to Attu," but he couldn't read or write very well, he added shyly, so no papers.

Later, two bright, young faces appeared at my door—Danny Boy Snigaroff with his friend Michael Dirks, eleven. Michael belonged to Lydia and Larry, Sr. He was a strikingly handsome boy, tall for his age and as bright and sure of himself as Danny Boy. We compared jackknives and swapped judo tricks, and they tested my typewriter. Then they signed me up for a thirty-mile hike the next day. We would jig for fish with a string, they promised; eat them raw with salt. I was to bring the salt.

The wind blew so hard after dark that I slept fitfully, awaking at 4 A.M. after a bad nightmare. Dawn came with sheets of rain but it didn't stop the kids. They waited for a lull and then appeared with Danny Boy's big Labrador, Hippy. Resolutely, we set off along a deteriorating dirt road to the old military base, but the rains reappeared and chased us home. I knit fish net and the youngsters explored the priest's attic where they unearthed a set of snare drums.

Moses Dirks, my boatman, turned out to be Michael's older brother, and he dropped by with a friend, Mark Nevzoroff, to find out if the youngsters bothered me. In the course of conversation I showed them my Aleut dictionary and they quickly became engrossed in it. They took genuine delight in their language and were pleased when I offered to lend them the book. Earlier I had inquired for an Aleut teacher and now Moses volunteered for the job.

He was nineteen, had left Atka's grade school five years earlier with a sixth-grade reading level, to graduate with honors from Adak High School. Now he was home, living at subsistence level and enjoying the peace of the island, but he was still interested in education. He would tutor me every day when he wasn't hunting reindeer, he said.

With no electricity and no refrigeration, the Atkans were forced to forage constantly for fresh food. The island had a herd of four thousand reindeer, but they were wild and often inaccessible. Mark, who was thirteen and looked twenty, told of running out of meat the previous winter when his father was off island, fishing. He had cut school and floundered waist deep in snow to bag one animal after a hard day's hunt. The next day, part of the herd had made a rare appearance near the village but he hadn't taken any animals because, without a freezer his family had as much as it could use.

A break in my company did not coincide with a break in the weather, but something about Atka made me want to spend the bulk of my time outdoors and I decided not to be cowed by the elements. I had noticed some berries on an

*John Nevzoroff about to entertain.*

*Michael Dirks with Danny Boy carrying home the hunters' guns.*

*Moses Dirks takes his mother, Lydia, to fish camp.*

earlier walk, and, sticking a plastic bag in my raincoat pocket, I went after them. Covering the same ground that I had traveled before, I grew sure enough of my bearings to detour into the hills and discovered an idyllic lake above the village. The berries that grew on one bank were a sour cross between blueberries and cranberries and pickings were sparse, but Canterbury bells grew there too, with pink orchids, lupine of the brightest blue, lemon-sized sunflowers, and some exotic bell-shaped yellow blossoms.

Later I queried Nydesta (Nyda) Golley, the unofficial postmistress, about the plants I'd seen. Though a fragile-looking woman whose growth had been retarded somewhat by tuberculosis, she spent more of her time out of doors than most Atka women and I felt kinship with her. Now she assured me that I had picked my berries—*aangsus,* in Aleut—at the correct stage of ripeness. And, she added reassuringly, there was no plant on the island I could poison myself on.

Atka had movies, a surprisingly sophisticated run of oldies, shown on the average of every third night.

"Without television we need something to help educate our children about the outside world," John Nevzoroff explained.

The showings were held at the school and afterward my kitchen was a natural spot for the kids to congregate. Julian Golodoff, the oldest of the lot, often outlasted the crowd and I came to know him well. He was always impeccably dressed, usually in a white shirt, tie, and suit jacket carefully culled from the village Red Cross surplus box, which made him look like a model Aleut youth, circa 1912.

Julian was seventeen and the only boy of his age group not off island attending high school for he had gone only as far as seventh grade. He seldom volunteered information, but he gave intelligent answers to any questions I threw at him and I soon realized his grade standing was low because he spent most of his time learning to hunt and handle a boat. He was expert enough to take Douglas, the schoolteacher's son, in tow and was now patiently training him in the Aleut arts of

*Julian Golodoff after a successful hunt.*

survival. Often, too, he talked of reindeer, their habits, the preservation of the island herd, and hunting. He was destined for auto mechanic training in Anchorage but luckily the BIA had failed to make the arrangements. In October he would be old enough to work in the canneries with his stepfather and brothers, but he was considering going back to grammar school until gainful employment showed up. He liked Besecker and the eighth grade might be fun, he decided. Especially if they taught Aleut.

School was to open within the week and, under threat of it, Danny Boy and Michael determined to get in all the hiking they could. When a day dawned sunny, they appeared at my door early. The wind was up to thirty knots, but it served only to clear the sky and deck the bay with whitecaps.

"Adak people, they call this a storm," Danny Boy marveled. And we struck out, leaning into the gusts. In an hour Michael led us to a berrying spot he had found the year before with his mother. Picking was fair, and Danny Boy showed me dips in the bushes where he claimed crows had nestled to steal some of the fruit. I didn't believe him but later noticed bird drippings near the depressions. The idea of lazy crows lying around, scooping up berries, intrigued me, but I never was able to catch them at it. We did see them playing "chicken," though. Two of the big black birds would fly high over the bay, simultaneously fold their wings, and go into a stall. The winner, of course, was the one who waited longest before he started flying again, and sometimes they would come within inches of the water before recovering.

By noon we were a couple of miles south of the village searching for reindeer. All we found was last year's tracks but Hippy flushed an occasional ptarmigan as we poked our way down the coast.

The kids followed a "road" which was actually a footpath the width of a railroad tie. High in the hills it was easy, for grasses grew short, but in the lowlands the vegetation was taller than I, and I could follow my young guides only by ear

*Danny Boy Snigaroff hiking home after a morning of fishing salmon with a hunting knife tied to a stick.*

Hidden bogs and subterranean streams caused breaks in the trail and I found it perilous to put too much trust in my forward foot. Finally we headed back along the shore where it joined with a swift running river.

"Fish," Danny Boy cried, "qas, qas!" he yelled, lapsing into Aleut and grabbing a rock in each hand. The river was crowded with humpbacked and red salmon, and the kids went after them. Michael triumphantly speared a humpie with my jackknife. Then Danny Boy found an old hunk of gill net at the bottom of the pool and, using his bootlaces for hauling lines, the youngsters managed to catch six more fish. Judiciously they threw back the "girls" and neatly cleaned the remainder of the catch, throwing away the bodies of the humpies but saving the head and the hump. Michael strung part of the catch on a strong plant stem and Danny Boy carried the rest by their jawbones.

To get back to the village we had to ford the river. We had crossed it higher in the hills with little trouble, but here it ran wide and over our boots so we had to cross barefoot. I got the job of managing everybody's boots and the berries, along with my Nikon camera and an extra lens. The rocks were slippery and sharp, the current strong, and the winds gusty. Gingerly I picked my way across and it was a good half hour before feeling returned to my feet.

We came back starved and with a sunburn. Mrs. Dirks fed us homemade bread, butter, and jam. Then the boys followed me home. They had been pretty secretive about a little round box they hoarded. Now they confided that it was *tamaakax̂* (snuff). Their parents didn't allow them to chew it, but they kept a can hidden away. Generously, they gave me a good pinch. I knew it was supposed to be wadded in the side of the cheek, but the impulse to swallow was strong.

"*Don't* swallow!" they chorused, but it was too late. The stuff burned going down and laid a fire on my stomach.

The youngsters made me promise not to tell their mothers, but they needn't have worried. My own showing had been too poor to mention.

Lydia Dirks came to visit the following morning, just in time to sample the muffins I'd made of aangsus berries and sour dough and enthusiastically we talked cooking. She gave me her recipe for pirugax and told me how to cook octopus and she promised to lend me her cookbooks. She was quite fluent in English and pleased to explain that she, her husband, Nyda Golley, and three others in the village had worked last year to pass their high school equivalency tests. Her dark hair was touched with white and she thought in Aleut, she said, so it had been no mean accomplishment.

My Aleut lessons with her son Moses were going well, I was happy to inform her, and I loved her language. Aleut was a gentle tongue, so soft it was almost impossible to shout in it. And easier for me than Eskimo, though I did have trouble making the "tx" sound which is important in the Aleut word for "you"—"txin." Also, I stumbled on "itx̂aygis," the word for reindeer.

"It-x̂ay-gis!" Danny Boy and Michael would chant. "IT-X̂AY-GIS!" And their badgering helped, although often they'd get hysterical over my poor attempts to mimic them.

My lessons were interrupted at the end of the first week when Moses and his brother Larry, Jr., went hunting with Max Nevzoroff and Michael Besecker. I used the time to interview Nyda's father, Serguis Golley, seventy-four, who was the oldest man in the village.

Golley was tall, white-haired, strong of back, and firm of mind. Thirty years ago he had started selling supplies to trappers, and he still ran a busy general store in the front of his well-kept home. The exterior was smartly painted red with white trim. He couldn't afford to paint it all at once but managed to renew one side a year.

Golley had been born in Atka and could remember clearly back to 1910 when the first school was built and 1913 when a government boat dropped thirty reindeer off and forced them to swim ashore—the nucleus of the present herd.

Nyda, who lived with her parents and helped run the store, proved useful, too, in detailing village problems. There was surplus matting from Vietnam available for a new airstrip, she said. All that was needed was the labor of the men of Atka to lay it.

According to one estimate, islanders could have all the electricity they needed, free, if they tapped one of the spectacular waterfalls near the village for hydroelectric power. The Navy was willing to help with the planning. All they needed was from $13,000 to $20,000 worth of materials and the labor of the men of Atka.

There was material available to build a new co-operative store. All that was needed was the labor of the men of Atka to build it. And the same applied for the new village water system to replace the hook-up installed by the Navy in the 1940s. Again, the men of Atka would be called on for repairs. But how, Nyda wondered, could they find time to do all these things between commercial fishing off island for cash income and the time they had to spend subsistence hunting to support their families?

"Actually, we're hoping some rich millionaire will be interested in giving us an airstrip," she smiled. With that accomplished, the other problems might take care of themselves. If Atka could get regularly scheduled transportation, the government would allow them a post office, and with a post office, cannery boats would be interested in anchoring at Atka and providing work right at home. But no millionaire—or anyone else, for that matter—seemed interested in the remote community.

John Nevzoroff escorted me home to check my oil tank and we continued the discussion. The reason that it was so windy here, he suspected, was the moon shots. Those rockets must create a lot of wind when they took off and it had to go somewhere. Why not Atka?

Then he added a few terse words about the atomic testing they were doing only three hundred miles away on Amchitka. Everyone on Atka had signed a petition asking the AEC not to set off any more bombs there.

"They say they won't do it again but they probably will," he said glumly. "We wrote a petition to President Nixon but he never did answer. If it's so safe, why don't they hold those tests in Washington, D.C.?"

That night I borrowed Ted Banks's blacklisted book from Besecker (who thoughtfully enclosed it in a brown-paper wrapper), to see for myself how the anthropologist had viewed the Atkans. Noting the sharp decline in the Aleut population under Russian rule and later under the United States, Banks had written: "It is a picture that is all too familiar to anthropologists: a once-handy, populous group, admirably adapted physically and culturally to a rigorous environment—now impoverished, diseased, and spiritually weakened, their numbers alarmingly reduced and their former culture all but destroyed. The story of the Aleut might serve as a lesson to us, but it is a lesson that comes too late for our southernmost Eskimos. The Aleut seems likely to follow the Dorset Eskimos to extinction before our very eyes."

"He told us that, too," Nyda recalled wryly. "But we're still going."

The next day I interviewed Innokenty ("Popeye") Golodoff, who represented the Attu people of Atka and was married to an Atka native. Popeye, who was prouder of his nickname than of his Russian name, had spent three and a half years in a Japanese prison during World War II, and managed to keep from starving only because a Japanese nurse fell in love with him and smuggled him food. Today he hated rice. All the Attu people did, he said.

When the Attus were liberated by the Americans they were shipped to the Philippines, then to Okinawa, and finally to San Francisco where they were each given $150 for clothing and $200 for food.

"I spent most of it riding around," Popeye recalled. "And in the bars celebrating."

Surprisingly, he felt no animosity toward the government which forbade him to return to his native island.

Banks had reported that the Atkans regarded the Attus as primitives because they lived more off the land than most natives, and that the two groups did not get along. But the Attus had made a good adjustment, and their differences, except for the subtleties of their individual Aleut dialects, had apparently been forgotten. It was ironic, though, that had the Attus been allowed to return to their native island, they would have been enjoying twice-weekly plane service, for Attu had a Coast Guard station and its airstrip had been maintained by the government while Atka's had been allowed to rust away.

Popeye had not only adjusted to Atka, but also become well enough respected by the Atkans to be elected their treasurer. Every man who worked off the island put $2.00 into the village fund, he explained, and if they couldn't find work later, they borrowed money back. Although many Atka families qualified for government welfare, only two were enrolled. One was a woman with four fatherless children and another was an older man whose health had failed.

"Usually this village takes care of its own," Popeye said. "Right now we've got $200 left in the fund, but if all the loans came in, it would be up to $500."

By the second week of my stay I had settled happily into village life. Atka hunters and fishermen kept me supplied with meat without my asking, and I bought a fifty-pound bag of flour (the only size sold) so I could enter an informal bake-off contest with industrious Atka housewives. Danny Boy's cat, Zizzi, moved in as my house guest. Julian predicted she was "going to have pets," but pregnant or not she was good company. And Hippy became my watchdog, barking loudly at any luckless Aleut man who approached my door after 9 P.M. John told me a lot of people wanted to kill the dog when Clara was out of town. They said it chased reindeer and its defense of my honor hadn't helped matters. I warned him that anyone who laid a hand on the animal would have to deal with me first, and Danny Boy and I became strong allies.

Also joining my household on an occasional basis were Ruth Kudren, thirteen, and her sister, Molly, fourteen, who were my nearest neighbors. When I asked to meet their mother, Ruth said evenly that I would have to go to the cemetery. She had been dead three years.

They were comely, self-sufficient girls who lived in the care of their grandmother Mary, when their father, Dan Prokopeuff, was off island trying to support them. Mary was the island's oldest citizen and it was a toss-up as to who took care of whom.

I came to know Nyda better, too, which pleased me for she was close to my own age and temperament. Perhaps it was because I spoke to her personally of my own problems that I gained some insight into hers.

We were walking to her summer camp to check some basket grass when I confessed that I had been battling horrible nightmares since I had come to the village. It might be that I was too unholy to sleep in the priest's bed, I joked. But more likely it was because just before sailing for Atka I had broken with the man I had been planning to marry.

She had once fallen in love with an Attu man, she told me. His detention in a Japanese prison had weakened his health and he died of a collapsed lung while working in a cannery, leaving her with his son.

"My father didn't want me to marry him," she admitted. "Perhaps it's because I'm so small they never thought I was grown up."

Yet she had raised her son capably. Proudly she showed me the little cabins he had built around their camp. This was his first year away at high school and she missed him terribly, but the courage with which she faced the loneliness I could only admire.

She told me, also, of the Atkans' struggles as refugees during World War II.

"My mother, Jenny, couldn't get over how rough that first winter was. We lived in an old herring cannery and those buildings were never meant for winter. We had to boil our water. We were left to gather our own food. There were no boats to fish. We were just dumped off with the clothes on our backs. Later they dumped off a pile of winter clothing . . ."

On the walk home she showed me some of the plants her people used for food. One was a fresh, spicy seasoning I liked very much, quite different from anything I had ever encountered. She also showed me a feathery carrotlike leaf the old people used to stop bleeding. Over the hill a crow was talking and chuckling quietly to himself. It was a sign of rain, she said, and she was right. But you should never trust the prediction of a woman, she added.

Unlike the people in other villages where I had lived, the Atkans were early risers.

"My father always made me get up early," John told me when I answered his light knock just after dawn. "And I don't like to bother other people if they can sleep."

He had come at my request to teach me a new fish-net knot and stayed to entertain me with stories of the old-timers as I worked.

When he was a boy, before fuel oil was in use for heating, they had had to search endlessly for driftwood to heat their houses and cook their meals. Usually he had gotten up at 3 or 4 A.M. and rowed along the beaches for three or four hours each day to supply his mother.

One of John's happiest memories was listening to his father and his friends reminisce over tea. One would begin by saying he had paddled his bidarka (skin boat) to such and such a place, and another would top the story with a larger adventure. Sometimes the Atka men had paddled to Kodiak, nine hundred miles distant. At night they tied up together—eight or nine men in little boats—with lines of kelp seaweed, to sleep. And at sunrise they would start paddling again.

Originally, Atkans had built one-man bidarkas which re-

*Nydesta Golley sorting the monthly mail and finding a five-week-old telegram.*

*Hauling home the reindeer. From the left, teacher Mike Besecker, Julian Golodoff, and Dan Prokopeuff.*

quired constant balancing, like bicycles. There was a place to brace one's feet on the bottom and you put a knee on each side. Perhaps that's why Aleuts are bowlegged, John mused— unhappy was the bidarka paddler who wasn't.

In his youth, men had trapped the islands using inboard dories. They left Atka in November, going with the wind and tide and camping in barabaras (little earth houses) on each island all the way to Adak. It usually took them until January to get there.

As soon as the weather was decent, Dan invited me on a sea-lion hunt with Mike Besecker and Moses Dirks. I was delighted, for there had been speculation that I might become frightened and be a liability to a boatman. Now there were mutterings that the weather would be too rough for me, but we got off to a beautiful start, with an escort of puffins and cormorants. Out around the Army dock we turned stern to the sea and surfed along until the engine started missing. The generator head leaked, fouling the plugs, and Dan reluctantly decided to forget about making it to the rookery. Instead, we put into a rocky harbor where we sighted three seal. Dan headed the boat toward the rocks and ordered Besecker and Moses off. We left them and bobbed around, tinkering with the engine. I saw Moses shoot and miss, and Besecker's gun jammed.

"We won't pick you up until you get one," Dan warned, but he relented. When they were back in the boat I noticed Moses' gun had a metal peace symbol tacked to the stock.

"Did you do that?" I asked him.

"Yes, that's why I miss so much."

Heading back we drove squarely into bad weather. The sea had been gray, but now it was black with whitecaps and it slammed into us. The old boat was just fourteen feet long and it leaked. There were no life jackets. I wondered about the stress factor of fiberglass as one of the seats broke loose from the hull. But I admired the skill with which Dan handled the tiller. Finally we rounded a sheltering point and, bypassing

Atka village, landed on a small nearby island. Then we coasted among dozens of sea otters. Their fur was thick and beautiful. They were said to be good eating, too, but they were protected by law.

"There won't be any seal here," Dan said with disappointment. "They just don't get along with the otters."

Further east we beached in a neat bay to look for reindeer. Moses was away in an instant, bounding up the mountain with swift grace. Besecker said he had seen him outrun a reindeer, but today there were no deer to outrun. I climbed at a slower pace, reaching the top of the mountain alone to enjoy a spectacular view. At last I could see the south side of Atka Island studded with endless mountains, each with a little nipple at the top, and to the east lay the thrashing ocean pass between Atka and Amlia Island where a twelve-knot tide dashed over jagged rocks. Descending I followed a trail of fluffy ptarmigan feathers. Moses had shot the bird after Besecker had missed. His shot had neatly severed its neck but he apologized when he presented it to me, saying he had meant to hit it in the head.

Apart from hunting, church played the biggest part in Atkan life, and I inquired about attending. Since I was the tallest woman in the village, it was impossible for me to borrow a dress. Nyda's mother suggested I try the Red Cross box, but even if I found a suitable skirt, there was the problem of shoes and stockings to go with it. Finally I asked Poda Snigaroff, the church reader, if I might attend in my slacks. He decided it would be all right, "provided you are clean," but some of his congregation never did adjust to seeing a woman garbed in britches at their solemn Russian Orthodox service.

The event was marked by the tolling of a church bell which, I discovered, was really a young church member whacking a broken fire extinguisher with a crowbar. All Atka's bells had been destroyed when the Navy burned their church in 1942, and, although a church in Unalaska had extra bells, the Atkans couldn't afford to buy one.

The Russian Orthodox service was a stand-up one, women on one side, men on the other. I came in last and stood at the rear near an old-fashioned desk where Phillip Nevzoroff, an elder, sold candles and John recorded attendance.

The church was almost an exact replica of the one that had been burned except that the Atkans could never afford to replace the gold fittings and icons. They had an impressive number of candelabra of a lesser quality, however, and many printed pictures of saints and a photograph of the current bishop, all in handmade frames.

The church interior was painted in white, green, blue, red, and pink, with a dark red floor. Altar cloths were hand sewn and appliquéd with the Russian cross.

Deep within the church on the right, a choir sang the entire service in Old Russian. We couldn't see any of the singers except their feet and calves as they were concealed behind a curtain with Poda.

Next morning we attended church again to commemorate the beheading of John the Baptist, and proceedings were more elaborate. Willie Golodoff let down the candelabra and lit twenty candles during the service and Poda read in English from the Bible in a singsong chant. Everyone marched down the beige center carpet (which was covered with a plastic runner tacked down by cardboard stars), kissed a cross and a plastic-coated picture of Jesus, and put money in the collection plate.

At first, nothing about the services made me feel close to God, for they were far removed from any I had ever attended. Gradually, though, I felt more at ease and found the music— worn smooth by two thousand years of chanting—was a good background to think on the universe.

After the religious holidays the hunters went out again for we were low on meat. This hunt was on the north, Korovin, side of the island. Julian kept a boat in Korovin Lake three miles inland, and the party hauled it a mile downstream, then ran it along the north coast in search of game. The day they were due back at the inlet I decided to try and photograph them coming in, and, with Hippy in the lead, I made the five-mile hike just in time to meet Nick Nevzoroff and two friends packing four deer back upstream. They offered me a ride across the lake, which cut a mile off my return trip, but soon I regretted taking it because Hippy paddled along behind until I was afraid he would drown.

After crossing the lake, I left the men and picked my way back along to the village beach where I was startled by a playful whale and interrupted a young seal robbing Moses' net. It was a good trip and one that would alter the villagers' opinion of me, although I gave no thought to this at the time.

Shortly thereafter, Moses invited me to climb the highest mountain behind the village with him. I thought it strange, for his time was usually well occupied, but I was delighted to have a guide. The first steep grade was the roughest, but after I got my wind I didn't have much trouble keeping pace. He told me to rest any time I got tired and I did stop to take a couple of photos. The view was grand. Hundreds of islets hugged the mountainous coast, and from the top we could see the Korovin side and the curling spits of Old Harbor, the site of Atka's original Russian settlement. But we stopped only briefly. Moses had looked at his watch so often on the way up that I wondered if he had an appointment at the summit. Now I realized that my hiking speed was being clocked. After my solo trip to Korovin, the hunters had reported that I was a remarkable walker, and John, who had previously invited me to climb a mountain with him, backed out on the grounds that I was too fast. Moses was reputed to be the fastest walker in the village and he must have gotten curious.

"Well, we're making good time," he announced with satisfaction as we neared the village.

"How long does it usually take to make the trip?" I asked.

"Old ladies take three and a half to four and a half hours."

"How long have we been?"

"Two and a half hours."

"How long for you alone?"

"Oh, about one and a half to two."

If I had known that I was entered in the Atka Olympics, I

wouldn't have wasted all that time taking pictures, I thought.
Finally, in sight of the village, we slowed enough for casual
conversation.

"If there is reincarnation, I'd like to come back as a reindeer,"
I speculated.

"No," Moses said seriously. "It would be too hard."

"Why? All you do is run over the tundra and climb these
beautiful hills and eat grass and moss."

"Not in winter. In the winter it's hard. You have to dig
through deep snow for your food. It's cold. Hard to walk.
You're always hungry."

I hadn't thought of that and I was astonished at the man's
compassion for the animal he hunted so constantly. He cared
for the reindeer more than any Friends-of-Animals people
could ever understand.

The women of Atka were once reputed to be fine basket-
makers, but I had heard that the art was lost. Now I was happy
to find the old teaching the young. It was true that the war
generation had lost the skill, since they had had no grass to
work with, but now they were learning with their daughters.
The best teacher, they said, was Oleana Prokopeuff. She had
been born on Atka but had married an Attu and been taken
prisoner by the Japanese, with one child and another on the
way. She did not talk easily about it. Instead, she showed me
the difference between Attu weaving, a standard weave, and
the tight, wrap-around weave of Atka. The grass could only be
gathered in certain summer months, she said, and took many
weeks to cure. Baskets could only be made in good light under certain conditions of humidity and it might take months
to complete one. The old-timers had worked the tall, strong
grasses with a woody core, weaving capes and other articles of
clothing.

"They had strong thumbs," Oleana said. Today the art was
lost. They used the lighter grasses and removed the core.

Atka women could command $100 to $500 per basket. The
problem was that without a post office, there was no way to

safeguard shipping and their work often disappeared en route to potential buyers, leaving the weavers with no financial gain for months of work.

Also on my list of interviews was Poda Snigaroff, the soft-spoken church reader. He carried on in the absence of the priest for the princely sum of five dollars a month and he had studied hard for the assignment. Only he and old man Golley were qualified as readers, and, with Nyda, they were the only Atkans who could read the Old Russian required in their church service. That was why Poda stubbornly held out for the teaching of the Cyrillic over the English alphabet if the village voted to teach Aleut in the school. But it was strange for him to consider Aleut in the school, he said. As a child he would have been beaten for speaking it and even the teachers before Besecker disapproved when the children spoke it.

Poda had been reader since 1963. Just after he qualified he had been stricken mute and I marveled at the man's faith. A description of his affliction sounded like cancer of the throat, but he had regained his voice after a long fight and used it well.

In mid-month, during a visit with Mrs. Besecker, I brought up the village drinking problem. I hadn't seen any signs of it and wondered if I was blind or if it was as overblown as the rumors of tuberculosis. She said both. That weekend there had been a big party. She had been down to visit one of our favorite families and found everybody worse for wear and embarrassed about it.

"I don't mind if they drink, but it does bother me that they get embarrassed about it," she said.

That explained why certain people had been avoiding me. It had been an out-of-kilter weekend and I had spent it mostly with Hippy wondering what I'd done wrong. Finally Dan Prokopeuff dropped by, very sober and all spruced up. He was followed by John Nevzoroff who was not so sober but in a fine mood. Someone had twisted his arm and gotten him to take a drink, he lamented, but it gave him courage. When Dan left

*Mrs. Serguis Golley making a grass basket.*

*Poda Snigaroff in his church.*

he demanded to know what race I was and finally asked if my blonde hair was real. He inspected the roots just to be sure and finally allowed, "You are a good-looking girl, even if you are white."

Danny Boy and Michael followed him in, waiting for the entertainment they knew he would provide. Finally John brought out his harmonica and gave a lively rendition of "You Are My Sunshine," "Red River Valley," and "On Top of Old Smokey." "Smokey" was for his wife, he said, because that was where she had gone.

Ruth Kudren and Tawny Besecker arrived as he was taking leave and, to their amusement, he suggested I marry him so he could get his driver's license. Apparently he was a good heavy-equipment operator but couldn't get his license because of the written exam. If I married him, he speculated, I could pass the written part and he'd take care of the rest.

"Well, we'll be seeing you, Mrs. Nevzoroff," he concluded, and Ruth and Tawny teased me with "Mrs. Nevzoroff" ever after. But that was as much of Atka's "serious drinking" as I ever encountered. The villagers themselves worried about alcoholism. Their word for anything alcoholic was "piiuax̂," and piiuax̂ was a problem, they insisted. But there were other problems that seemed to me far more serious.

One morning Larry Dirks, Jr., came to monitor my Aleut lesson and spoke with concern about how many Aleut youngsters in St. Paul in the Pribilof Islands and on Unalaska no longer spoke their language. If people kept moving away, he observed, the villages would soon be empty. And if they stayed, there was a housing problem. Most of Atka's homes had been built on a crash basis thirty years before and were fast deteriorating. Atka had applied for a federal housing program, but because there were no Atkans to lobby for their regional organization, other villages gained priority although their needs were not so great.

Atka residents had never seen their legislative representatives and they'd never been visited by the president of the Aleut League.

"The problem is we are living like forty years ago," he maintained. It was hard to support a family. There were practically no jobs on the island. It was hard to hunt in winter. There was no electricity to make a young wife's life easier and no communication with your family when you went off island to work.

I said he was well educated enough so that he could find work anywhere in the United States. Why had he come back to Atka?

"Because it's so peaceful," he said. "Maybe it's O.K. in the city if you get used to it, but you've got to live by the regulations."

Larry's father, Larry Dirks, Sr., was also articulate, although shyer because of his lack of education.

"It's sort of like . . . Well, we've been forgotten," he began hesitantly when I came to interview him. And it turned out he had substantial reason to believe it. The year before, like some of his neighbors, he had filed for a native land allotment under a government ruling passed in 1906 which made it possible for natives to own legally the land they used and occupied. He could have claimed 160 acres, with additional tracts the same size for his wife and four of his seven children. Instead he filed for only forty acres around the summer campsite that had been used by his family for generations.

"I could have claimed more but there was a time limit," he explained. Passage of the land claims legislation ended the allotment program. "And I didn't need that whole mountain up there, anyway. We do want the campsite. It's been in the family for as long as anyone can remember."

But a letter from the federal land office had informed him this August that he could not have the land.

"On March 3, 1913, Executive Order 1733 reserved the whole Aleutian Chain . . . and set it apart as a preserve and breeding ground for native birds, for the propagation of reindeer and fur bearing animals and for the encouragement and development of fisheries," wrote the land office manager. "Accordingly, the application is hereby rejected."

The letter informed Dirks that he had thirty days to appeal the ruling, but that was no easy assignment. Villagers were not allowed to send personal telegrams via the radio they used to communicate with the state-operated schools office and mail service was spotty. Luckily, Dirks read his letter the night it arrived and asked Sally Jamie of the Aleut League to undertake his appeal. Other villagers were not so fortunate. Nick Nevzoroff had not received his notice until after the thirty-day appeal period had lapsed and Serguis Golley, one of the earliest filers, had been discouraged early. He had gone to the trouble of surveying and posting his family campsite in the late 1950s and his correspondence on the subject covered four years of bureaucratic confusion. In 1962 his claim was officially rejected and he was advised to apply for a five-acre homesite. Nyda located a copy of his reply which proved a classic example of the patience with which the Aleut people had handled discrimination over the years.

Dear Mr. Nelson:

I am a bit disappointed in receiving this copy attached [the letter of rejection]. After all the work I put in measuring and posting the land, I rather hoped I could, in the near future, raise sheep on the allotted land but I guess even that would be forbidden.

I do not wish to settle for five acres and I do not wish to pay five or ten dollars [the price suggested for a land use permit] to use my own native land.

Is there anything you can do for me in the way of helping get 160 acres and help me to understand this more clearly?

Hopefully waiting to hear from you I remain,

Very truely,
Serguis Golley

"I think we arrived here about the same time as the birds," Nyda said quietly. "There aren't very many birds on our campsite anyway and we don't do them any harm."

"They weren't so worried about the birds but what they set off an atomic bomb down here," fumed Michael Besecker. "What harm is it going to do for the natives to own the lands the birds fly over?"

On September 20 Mrs. Besecker dropped in with a radio report that the tug would arrive September 27 and the news depressed me.

"I don't want to leave this place," I decided as I drifted off to sleep that night. "I'll just carry on as if the tug's not coming."

Danny Boy and Michael had taken me fishing, using a hunting knife tied to a stick as a spear, and we had been quite successful. Now I decided to knit a net to their specifications. None of us knew anything about hanging it, though, and after John showed us how to fit it with floats and weights, it came out half size.

"Well, it will give the village something to laugh at," I suggested.

"It sure will," John agreed, looking dourly at the tiny piece of gear.

Undaunted, we trudged off to hang it, with Terry Besecker behind us all the way yelling, "Hey, fellers, wait for me!" The river was high and wider than usual. Michael, who had waders, carried Terry across and Danny Boy gallantly offered to do the same for me, but I made it barefoot. It took some time to pick a likely fishing spot and longer to anchor the net, and we got chilled to the bone. Terry whined until the boys got disgusted and abandoned her. I lectured the poor child all the way home on the fact that would-be Aleuts didn't complain. It was really a tough trip for the nine-year-old, but she straightened her back and marched the last mile like a good soldier. She had told me earlier that she had fallen in love with Michael and the color of anybody's skin didn't matter, so I had definite hopes for her.

In fact, I liked the whole Besecker family, for they had settled fairly well into village life despite rotten odds. About half their belongings had been lost in moving and, even though they had electricity and better furnishings than some, they had a lot of making-do to do. Also, they had been told when they took the assignment that a boat came once every two weeks. Now it appeared we would be lucky if one came by Christmas. But the Beseckers appeared unperturbed. Their kids lent their roller skates to the village kids who, in turn, lent them sheets of metal or cardboard for sliding down the grassy hills. Roberta started walking and picking berries, losing weight and making friends, and Mike proved a fair shot with bad luck, which put the hunters at ease with him.

Late one afternoon Moses Dirks came to visit in a very happy mood. The villagers had just voted that he would be hired to teach Aleut along with Nyda. When I had first taken him as a teacher, I had told Nyda that I thought he wanted the school job, not knowing she wanted it too. The village had voted between them and he had lost by two votes. John said Moses was too young for the job and I remarked, cruelly, that if the village didn't start giving some responsibility to their youngsters, they would leave the island and the older people would die off and where the hell would they be then?

But there was more to it than that. The older people were watching my progress as an Aleut student, and because of my funny accent and beginner's vocabulary, I guessed that they assumed that Moses was a poor teacher. To counter this, I told several elders what a generally poor language student I was and how, with Moses' help, I was making better progress than usual. That morning I had managed one of my more successful Aleut conversations with Jenny Golley. She had been merciless when I made a mistake, but that day I had done well and three hours later Moses was elected too.

And actually, Moses was a good and patient teacher. He had me thinking in Aleut. The only problem, in fact, was that he wouldn't teach me to say "no." He claimed it didn't exist in his dialect. And when I complained to the older people, they just smiled knowingly.

Word came that the tug's arrival would be delayed and Danny Boy began to show signs of worrying. He didn't like the thought of his mother riding the tug because, he said, his brother had been on one that had exploded and barely escaped. And he talked wistfully about hunting with his older brother Frankie, who was now working in a cannery. Despite his easygoing ways, Danny Boy was, after all, a nine-year-old and lonesome for his family. Nonetheless, he sensed my relief that the tug was late.

"If you want to, I'll hide you in the stove when it comes so you won't have to leave," he offered.

"I'll think about it," I said.

Taking advantage of the reprieve, I went camping on Korovin side with Molly and her father, Dan Prokopeuff. Amused by the idea of my sleeping alone with Dan, the girl threatened to back out at the last minute and giggled when I said I'd brain her if she didn't serve as chaperone. Their cabin was snug, with many homey touches left by Molly's mother. It was the first time since she died that Dan and Molly had stayed there overnight and I was glad I had come along to cheer them up.

Julian Golodoff's camp was next door, and we went to visit when he and Douglas Besecker came in from an all-day hike. Douglas was exhausted but Julian was still fresh, resplendent in a white shirt, blue satin tie with a pearl stickpin, suit jacket, and mildewed trench coat.

Dan tried to interest us in rising at 6 A.M. to dig clams, but we weren't receptive. Instead, we set off in Julian's boat about nine for Old Harbor. Running along the protective spit at the harbor entrance was awesome, for the hills had spires, like a Gothic cathedral, overgrown with moss. Inside we interrupted about seventy-five sea otters playing in the quiet waters. There was an Aleut legend that sea otters had once been people and I could understand it.

"When I was trapping I used to watch them make love and they made me so mad I'd want to shoot them," Dan recalled. "They are so human about it, caressing and hugging one another, it makes you mad when you're out there all those months alone."

Old Harbor was a classic Aleut village site on a narrow spit of land. Nothing stood now except two rusty iron crosses left on the old church grounds by the Russians in the 1800s, when they moved the village to its present location.

Going back to Korovin we beachcombed. Under a wrecked crab boat Molly and I were greeted by the hollow bark of a young blue fox. Lying on our stomachs, we could see him quite well but he didn't like our looks and refused the food we offered him.

A few days later a tremendous storm came in. I was elated—for the Aleutians were famous for rotten weather and all I had gotten was sunburn. But the storm raised havoc with the Atka houses. Julian's, which was highest on the hill, shook so badly his mother moved out and went to stay with a daughter. It was Julian's job to guard the place and he dreaded it.

"When will your father be back to help?" I asked.

"No man can come back to the island until he makes enough money," he answered.

The priest's house was newer than the rest, but it too pulled at its foundations. Larry, Jr., predicted that I would get seasick, and when Moses came by I jokingly asked him, "Do you want to fly to Adak with me and my house?"

"We couldn't land. We don't have military clearance," he replied with a straight face.

After three days the storm left us blanketed with snow. Danny Boy and Michael woke me with the happy news. The temperature was 40 degrees and dropping, but Atka topped with snow was a lovely place to live. Dan was planning a reindeer hunt from Korovin. Besecker clearly wanted to go, so I gave him the seat I had been offered and went off with Danny Boy and Michael in the other direction, following the river into the mountains and locating several superb waterfalls. I focused my camera on one in full sunlight only to encounter a small blizzard in my viewfinder. I looked up and over the ridge came the hazy silhouettes of Moses and Mark, packing two deer. They had walked nearly twenty miles on the hunt. Aleut fashion, they shrugged off fatigue. Proudly, Danny Boy and Michael carried home their guns.

Next morning I decided to surprise the Korovin hunters, and getting up at 5:45 I groped my way over the trail in darkness. When I came to the beach the sun lit the mountains of Amlia Island, but somehow I missed the trail in the half light and got lost in a marshy bog. Hail pelted down. I considered turning back, but after more blundering I found the path. Two hours later I arrived at Dan's camp, wet and cold but quite pleased with myself. The men were still in bed but mustered quickly when I told them of Moses and Mark's successful hunt. The weather grew fouler and the sea was rough. Our boat would not safely hold more than two men, and Julian and Dan were elected to man it. Besecker would stay and try his luck at shooting geese and Douglas, Molly, and I would tend camp.

By three in the afternoon the hunters were back with six whole deer and the hams of three more. It was rough pulling the load upstream to the lake and risky to make the lake crossing with six people, a dog, and a couple of tons of meat. We had three inches of freeboard to spare, but we made it—a mass of meat and men—for a truly triumphal return to the village.

The tug finally arrived on October 5 with a new load of doctors and dentists and three house guests for me. They had brought a fresh supply of groceries but left them aboard ship when they came ashore, and for two days the weather was so bad they couldn't get back to retrieve them. I fed my guests on reindeer and sourdough bread and berries that Danny Boy and I had picked in the snow.

The third day was fair, and the Navy people talked Dan

and Louis Nevzoroff, John's son, into taking their boats to the south side to hunt. Molly and I were invited.

At Amlia Pass our boats hesitated. It might be too windy to try it. Spray was blowing back off the breakers which looked like the teeth of hell. Dan studied the water carefully. Louis pulled alongside and there was terse discussion in Aleut. Finally Dan said we'd go.

Carefully he maneuvered our fourteen-foot boat, dashing before the giant rollers to take advantage of their power. They swept cross channel, towering over us on the port side, but at precisely the right instant Dan shot out of their reach. Nobody breathed. The Marine seated in the bow looked a little green but kept cool. Earlier he had offered Dan a beer but the Aleut hadn't touched it. Now Dan took a little swallow and looked pleased with himself. We were safe, and Louis, who followed close behind, also made it without swamping.

The south side was the magic side of Atka. While Old Harbor seemed truly ancient, the south side looked like a product of recent creation—as if rivers of hot lava had just poured into the cold sea and frozen. It was rich in wildlife, too. Sea lions surfaced like circus ponies and seal scooted in and out of sea caves, but we came home empty handed. We could see the reindeer but they were too high on the hills for us to capture before dark and the sea animals outmaneuvered us.

Departure time for the tug had been set for 6 A.M. the next morning, and many of the villagers would be leaving with me. The Atkans had never attended a meeting of the Aleut League, but now, to defend their interests, they had raised a delegation of seven for the annual convention. It would be a severe hardship for the village. Their families would have to fend for themselves for at least a month, or longer if the return tug was delayed. But it was a necessary trip if Atka was to remain a viable village.

Just before departure I took my leftover groceries to Lydia Dirks and stayed with her until Besecker warned me that the tug was about to leave without me. Lydia held out her hand and I missed it because my eyes were blurry with tears. "Kriisax," I muttered . . . the Aleut word for "rats." Then, wiping my nose on my sleeve, I turned without saying good-by. Michael was there and I nodded. Hippy I saw skulking in the shadow of the boathouse with his old adversary, John Nevzoroff. Danny Boy was long faced, trying not to cry. His mother had come home only long enough to pack again, for she was with the Anchorage delegation and he was to keep house with his brother Ronald, home at last with new glasses. The boys would have to hunt after school for their fresh meat. And Molly and Ruth would be alone to care for their grandmother, for Dan was with us.

Nyda Golley was aboard with us, too, as village secretary. Moses Dirks was also aboard, bound for Norway for Aleut language training, and Larry, Jr., who was to represent Atka for the Aleut League. That would leave Michael to be the hunter of the Dirks family, and he would probably bag his first reindeer before he was twelve. But it seemed too much responsibility to foist on the youngsters . . . and how painful it was to leave!

Yet the future of Atka hung in the balance.

"When I came back to Atka after World War II my buddy said, 'Why are you going to the Aleutians? They say even the seagulls are leaving there,'" Dan recalled. "I told him I was going because it's peaceful and quiet here. But if we can't get things straightened out pretty soon, I'm going to have to move."

His thoughts were echoed by Mike Snigaroff, village president, who had come home just long enough to check on his convalescent son Simeon and his family of five. Often Snigaroff had to travel hundreds of miles to find work to support them and he was considering moving to Kodiak where he often fished commercially.

"But I want to do all I can for the village first . . . To see if I can make it go," he said as we stood by the rail watching

Atka disappear behind the big volcano on the western end of
the island and the whole rock becoming a distant haze of
gray.

"I want to do my best by it," he said quietly. "But I just
don't know how it will come out."

*Waterfront on the Kuskokwim.*

# Bethel

## A BATTLE WITH THE BOTTLE

*From the time their legends began, the western, Yupik, Eskimos were rovers, launching their kayaks for seal and whale hunts off the Bering Sea shelf, navigating the broad reaches of the Kuskokwim River, following its tributaries through a patchwork of lakes and tundra.*

*In their travels the Eskimos made many fish camps, and Mutrekhlagamiut, on the north bank of the Kuskokwim, was typical. Although eighty-six miles from the sea, the site was rich in fish and a pleasant place to live in the summer. In winter Mutrekhlagamiut families traveled into the timber regions to escape the harsh river cold, but they always returned in salmon season. So when the first census taker came through in 1880, he recorded Mutrekhlagamiut as a village, noting a population of forty-one.*

*Neighboring fish camps—Kwethluk, Akiak, Tuluksak and Napaiskak—were recorded as villages, too, with populations double or triple that of Mutrekhlagamiut. But Mutrekhlagamiut was centrally located among them and when the traders and missionaries arrived on the heels of the census taker, it was Mutrekhlagamiut they chose as headquarters.*

*The Yupik translation of "Mutrekhlagamiut" is "smokehouse people" which referred to a peculiar type of house used by Eskimo villagers for smoking fish. However, the Moravian missionaries who came there in 1884 chose to rechristen the village "Bethel" from a biblical reference in Genesis 35:1, "And God said unto Jacob, Arise, go up to Bethel, and dwell there; and make there an altar unto God." The Hebrew translation of "Bethel" is "house of God."*

*The missionaries offered the Eskimos education in exchange for their souls, the traders offered white man's goods in exchange for the rich Kuskokwim furs, and both encouraged settlement. Because of its isolation and a lack of natural resources to attract pioneering whites, the area was slower to develop than other regions of Alaska, but Bethel's expansion was phenomenal for a western Eskimo village. Quickly it grew to be a transportation hub and service center for the entire Yukon-Kuskokwim delta, and natives from fifty-seven villages along the river network moved in. In 1910 the population of Bethel was 110. It doubled by 1920 and almost every decade thereafter, until by 1970 it was 2,500.*

*From the beginning, over ninety per cent of Bethel's residents were Eskimos who had formerly lived off the land, but such a concentration of people could not support themselves by subsistence hunting and fishing and there was little chance for natives to obtain gainful employment in the town. As a result, by 1967, Bethel reported one of the highest poverty levels in the United States and had similarly high rates of alcoholism and crime. The "house of God" was a shambles and its future looked grimmer yet.*

It was 1967 when I first saw Bethel. They called it the "armpit of Alaska" then, and worse things too, for it was the poorest part of a poverty-worn state. There had just been a nation-wide exposé of Bethel's living conditions . . . photos of the packing-crate and tar-paper shacks of the scruffy, tattered inhabitants of Lousetown, a Bethel suburb. Statistics showed that most western Eskimos never saw $1,000 a year or even $600.

I came to photograph the Lousetown houses, too, but I was shy about it. Was I to knock on one of those canted, battered doors and say to the lady of the house, "Let me photograph you in your wretched hovel?" I didn't have the heart, and so I sat dejected on a grassy hummock on the outskirts of Lousetown to consider. I sat so long, in fact, that the children of Lousetown found me, took me over, gave me a tour of their little homes, and topped off the day by offering *me* candy!

The houses were terrible, even by Alaska's permissive bush standards, but the children were happy children. They didn't appear underfed. And the parents I met, except for a couple involved in an all-out altercation on the waterfront, seemed reasonably happy, too.

In the spring of 1971 the Kuskokwim flooded and I was chagrined to report that Bethel suffered more damage from the wakes of the rescue boats than from the perversities of the river itself. The smaller settlements down river were harder hit, but that was mainly because they had been lulled into false security by inaccurate predictions from the Army Corps of Engineers and had failed to take to high ground as they usually did in the spring.

Then, in the fall of 1972, the Alaska Federation of Natives (AFN) held a convention in Bethel and I returned to find the city in a new mood.

A two-hundred-unit federal low-income housing project had just been built there by someone who knew (or cared) nothing about Alaska's shifting permafrost-shot tundra or the harshness of the Bethel winter. The buildings staggered, cracked, and came apart around the ears of the hopeful residents who had been "rescued" from Lousetown and made them long for the predictable misery of their tar-paper shacks. One Eskimo housewife testified at the inevitable government hearings which followed that when it rained, the water poured in one side of her house but that it was all right because the floor slanted and carried the stream out the other side where winter warp had provided an outlet between the floor and the wall.

The housing project was so much of a disaster that it actually became a joke and seemed to pull the city together. And Bethel had other things going for it, too. Its legislative representative in Juneau, George Holman, was a go-getting white who really championed the native's cause, and, backed by a coalition of native legislators, he had become chairman of the State House Finance Committee and was bringing home a lot of bacon. Not only had he promoted Bethel as the building site for a multimillion-dollar regional high school, but he had also secured federal funds to establish educational radio and television stations. The radio station was already in operation and broadcasting both in English and Eskimo. Now Bethel residents and people in neighboring villages could find out what was going on without traveling door to door. In addition, the city helped fund a newspaper, and for the first time the Eskimos were exposed to local, state, and national news.

Because of improved communications, the AFN convention had attracted from far up river Eskimos who were hearing for the first time about the Alaska natives' five-year battle for the settlement of their land claims against the federal government. The meeting was bilingual and mustered considerable "Eskimo power" from the bush. Still, the city remained rough and unattractive, and I carried some unpleasant memories.

In the fall of 1972, however, I was assigned to report on the problems confronting rural natives who moved into urban communities, and Bethel was an ideal observation post. The bulk of Bethel's troubles were caused by natives from remote villages who came to town in search of jobs or excitement and couldn't adjust to the faster pace of city living. Mainly, they drank too much, and when they fell drunk on Bethel sidewalks at 40° below zero they didn't last very long. To cope, Bethel citizens had opened a "sleep-off" and counseling center for alcoholics and I got a job as a counselor there.

When I arrived in late October, Bethel looked its worst, wallowing in between-seasons mud, obscured from the sun by a

*The sleep-off center from the front.*

*Tom Anderson, sleep-off center director.*

layer of gray scud and rain. I had wanted to come in the winter when the drunks were truly imperiled by cold and Bethel was beautified by a layer of snow, but the center was due to lose its federal funding within a week because of an across-the-board budget cut, and it was now or never, I thought. The Kuskokwim Inn rented me a dark, cramped room with a shower and honeybucket for $20.40 a day, and grimly I settled in for my new assignment, armed only with a quotation from Ben Franklin on the fate of the red man:

"If it be the design of Providence to extirpate these savages in order to make room for the cultivators of the earth, it seems not improbable that rum may be the appointed means."

As to my qualifications as an anti-alcohol counselor, they were not impressive. I enjoyed drinking and didn't believe it sinful unless it seriously incapacitated you or caused you to beat your family, and it was with considerable relief that I discovered this philosophy was shared by those who ran the sleep-off center.

Tom Anderson, the center's director, was a thin, weathered white of middle age with the look of a man who had once drunk too much or eaten and slept too little. That had, indeed, been his case and he seemed a better man for it. He had a neat, direct way of saying things and a rueful sense of humor. Originally he had come from Beverly, Massachusetts, but he had married a Bethel Eskimo. The Andersons had seven children and he definitely knew all about Bethel.

I was to work for him as a regular volunteer for two weeks or as long as I could take it, whichever was shorter. Mine would be the graveyard shift, from midnight to 8 A.M., starting the night I arrived.

"How long do your volunteers usually last?" I asked him.

"Sometimes they don't last a shift," he said cheerfully. "The last one survived just three hours."

After my talk with Anderson, Fred Pete, counselor supervisor, appeared at my hotel door. He was tall for an Eskimo, and his dark-rimmed glasses gave him the look of a college student, although he must have been in his late thirties or early forties. He had six children, he said, and one of them was attending college in Chicago. He spoke excellent English, but slowly, as one does when in the habit of dealing with people who speak it as a second language. He had been raised in traditional Yupik fashion, hunting and fishing, and his education had ended with his sophomore year at Mount Edgecumbe, the Bureau of Indian Affairs high school.

"He always tells people he hasn't had much education, which is true," Anderson had told me. "And he's eager to learn. But he knows more about counseling than any man I know."

"I think I've gone the route, if you want to put it that way," Pete admitted. "I've been through some of the hospitals. Been through some of the jails. I know what it's all about."

He had made his living mostly as a fisherman and was a reasonably reformed drunk when he spotted an ad for the counseling job posted in the Bethel post office. Like most Bethel people he had watched outside "experts" try and fail at dealing with Eskimo problems and, since alcoholism was something he knew about personally, he decided to try for the job.

Now he was working on his scholastic credentials. Just on the edge of 7 P.M. he excused himself to attend night classes at the newly opened Bethel Community College.

The sleep-off center was a tacky, four-room trailer complex with a narrow green lean-to, featuring a hand-lettered sign that said "Ekayurvik." Translated that meant "place of help" or "haven," Anderson said.

The first of the trailer rooms served as an office, with a desk, two overstuffed chairs, and a table with a large electric coffeepot. A girl was sleeping in one of the chairs, with her parka jacket over her face to keep out the light. By her side sat a young white man, anxiously waiting for her to wake up.

At the desk was Simeon Arnakin, a clean-cut Eskimo who carried himself with portly dignity. With him was Tom Michael, a quiet, trusting volunteer, reading a study on alcoholism.

The walls of the lean-to were painted bilious yellow and it was furnished with two couches of black fake leather. They had been new in 1971—I had seen them being uncrated—but now they were battered. One had a leg missing but it was carefully propped up. There was also a scarred desk, folding chairs, and, at the far end of the long, barnlike room, a washstand and shower. The sleep-off dorms were in the trailer—two for men and one for women. Each had a chemical toilet and bunks. The blankets were rather dirty but the rooms were neat and well-scrubbed. The odor of Lysol pervaded, although occasionally the underlying smell of urine assailed us.

It was a quiet night.

"Off season," Arnakin explained. The river, our only highway, was due to freeze any day now. Natives who traveled it were in danger of having their boats frozen out for their return trip and the winter was not advanced enough for snowmobiles.

There were times in the summer, he recalled almost nostalgically, when they had had so many drunks that there was no place left to put them. But that wouldn't be happening anymore, either, because the state had just passed a law that said you couldn't arrest a man for being drunk in public and if he came to the center he had to *want* to come.

The white man waiting in the office finally woke the sleeping girl. She was a pretty Eskimo in her twenties. Her name was Bubbles and she would have passed as a highly acceptable chick in any society. The white, who worked at a neighboring communications post, was apparently trying to save her from herself, for himself.

A few weeks ago the girl had broken up with her boyfriend and gone on a monumental drinking bout. The local Catholic priest suggested the center and she had moved in bag and baggage. Usually that wasn't allowed, but she had no other place to go and she had done so well under counseling that she now served as a volunteer counselor herself. She didn't like to sleep in the dorm because the company sometimes got rowdy there,

Tom Anderson said. Generally she slept in one of the office chairs, fully dressed, ignoring the lights and the action.

"Does she speak English today, Tom?" the communications man asked loudly. He had been needling her for about an hour with no results.

"I speak fluent English," she said indignantly, coming out at last from under her parka. But she was in a good humor and finally he talked her into going off to supper with him.

I read an English mystery novel I found in the office locker and came to about 6 A.M. The rain had stopped and I went outdoors to find the air as sweet as spring. One of our two customers had awakened and wandered out of the men's dorm, naked to the waist. He was young and well built, and so steady on his feet that I wouldn't have known he had been drinking if I hadn't gotten a whiff of his breath. He washed at the stand, checked the weather outside, told me to keep up the good work, and, giving my knee a gentle pat, went back to bed. I stayed until the morning shift came at 8:00 A.M., then walked the four blocks to the Kuskokwim Inn as dawn streaked the sky with light.

The town was deep in mud and accumulated rubbish but everyone seemed happy. No one passed on the street without a nod or a friendly hello. Who was I to tell them they should be miserable here?

The Rural Alaska Community Action Program office was cached away in a new building in a hopelessly mired part of town. The heat was off and Eskimo staffers were working with their coats on. The furnace had recently blown up and the landlord hadn't figured out how to put it back together. The employees' salvation was a gutless electric coffee pot which was good, at least, for instant coffee and a little warmth. Clara Kelly, articulate director of the Head Start program, offered me a cup and a good story about Ekayurvik.

The last winter one of Bethel's two hotels had closed and an outsider came to town to find the Kuskokwim Inn full and no place to stay. He was so desperate he went to the sleep-off center and begged them to put him up. The staff conscientiously explained that they were funded by state and federal grants that allowed them to deal only with drunks. So the young man dutifully went out, got totally drunk (for less than the price of a hotel room), and checked himself back in and everybody was happy.

A survey made of two thousand Alaskan natives by RurAL-CAP showed that 41 per cent believed alcohol to be their number-one problem and Harold Napoleon, director of the Bethel region, was in full accord.

"The bars are making a killing in more ways than one," he said. "Every year deaths connected with alcoholism are increasing. More people are freezing . . . Alcoholism is tearing our villages apart."

Part of the problem was the isolation of the region, he maintained.

"I just came from my village of Hooper Bay, for example, and they didn't know about the land claims until yesterday. That bill was passed without any input from my people. We're far from taking over our settlement. Unlike our Eskimo brothers in the north, at this time I don't think we're capable of control. We've got a big problem in terms of leadership.

"We have one hospital [the federal Alaska Native Service hospital] for fifteen thousand people [the Kuskokwim delta area]. In order for anyone from a remote village to get treatment, they have to pay their way in. People out there are lucky to see a doctor once a year."

As for the treatment of alcoholism . . .

"The type of program Bethel has now takes care only of immediate needs. In the villages I don't think you can start from that angle. A good education program has to be started."

Back at Ekayurvik I found Bubbles in a buoyant mood. Her old boyfriend had invited her out for steak. She had just had a shower and put together a change of clothes. And the jail had called and asked her to work the early morning shift as matron.

That would mean money in her pocket to tide her over until she started work as a secretary for the BIA the following week.

I was two hours early, but I stayed to talk poetry with her. She loved it and loved to write it. Seating herself at the center's electric typewriter, she dashed off a sample for me:

> Gliding through the soft, dazzling snow,
> The "Eskimo" travels with a-lot of go,
> In his sled he's in a "rush!"
> And to his dogs he tells them, "Mush!"
> "Gee" and "Ha" is his only change of gear,
> But, let me tell you those dogs can really steer!
> They need no gas to keep on the run—
> Just a little fish and a big shot-gun!

She had been raised in a tiny village on the Kuskokwim which currently had a population of three—her family. She was bright, fairly well educated and well traveled. She had worked in California and Chicago. The problem . . . well, maybe the problem was Bethel. . . .

At 11:30 P.M. she called a cab to go to jail, and I asked why, since it was only a short distance, she didn't walk.

"I don't want to get raped," she said matter-of-factly.

Counseling on my shift that night was Nick Frances, a sharp, local boy who had attended the University of Alaska with many of the bright young men who had become Alaska's native leaders.

"They're way ahead," he said thoughtfully. "I spent a lot of time trying to get out . . . with alcohol . . . with everything else. Then one day I woke up and realized *I'm important!* But now I've got a lot of catching up to do."

He talked of finding a fast way to the top, of making the big money his former classmates were now making, but as he talked it became obvious that money was not all-important to him . . . nor was power or status. He was still trying to make peace with himself, to find a useful place in the turbulent, changing world of the Alaskan native; and he had a strong compulsion to help others who were struggling along the bewildering route he had already conquered.

"Why do they drink?" I asked him.

"Living in a village can be pretty dull," he said. "If I lived there all the time, I guess I'd program a drinking bout in Bethel every so often, too."

Our discussion was interrupted by an exuberant trio, high and from all appearances quite happy. The woman, in her late twenties, was pretty except for missing upper teeth. Her clothes were ready-made, of good quality, and she carried herself with pride. Her young companion was also well dressed, but somewhat hangdog. And there was an older Eskimo who might or might not have been a member of the party. He arrived with them but quickly went off and sat by himself. His clothes were clean but shabby. There were neat green bicycle patches on his insulated rubber boots and the frames of his glasses had been rewired by hand.

The twosome—cousins named Brown—carried on a boisterous conversation in Yupik punctuated at every third paragraph with "Right on!" There was much laughter but after an hour they started to argue.

He had come from up river—a poor relative who, two months earlier, had left his family and come to Bethel where he found work at the hospital. She was well off, by Bethel standards, a respectable member of the community. So the poor cousin had moved in with her and her husband until he could earn enough to rent a house and send for his family. Tonight he had paid her $20 toward his keep, but she announced scornfully that that was all he'd paid her. He hadn't cost her much, he said defensively. He hadn't eaten anything. But she kept needling him, pulled his hair again, and made him really angry. He suddenly became menacing and swore he wouldn't let her touch him again. And then, unexpectedly, he began to cry.

"I came into your house with respect. Always respect," he told her. "I think of you as a millionaire."

"Hah!" she snorted. "Am I a millionaire? A millionaire?"

She taunted him, laughed at him, and called him names, but he was already broken.

"You know I am homesick," he pleaded. "So homesick there's times when I almost quit and go back. Three times I almost quit. I'm homesick for my hometown. You know that."

She continued to tease him, but more gently now. They were like children. Finally she turned her back on him. All her relatives regarded her as a millionaire, she said, and she was tired of it.

"Are you rich?"

"No," she said honestly.

"No fancy car?" I pressed.

"Just a truck," she admitted, which meant by Bethel standards she was well off indeed. She called a cab then. Her cousin, meantime, had gotten himself together and sobered remarkably. Nick lectured him sternly and the young man seemed grateful for it. He was wasting the taxpayers' money, Nick said. And, agreeing, the young man went his way.

That left us with the older man whom Nick counseled in earnest. The man did have a drinking problem and wanted to do something about it. They talked for an hour and then Nick let him go to sleep. He curled up on the couch, using his jacket as a blanket, and I asked Nick if we should move him.

"No, he feels safer here," the counselor said.

Next afternoon I managed to catch Tom Anderson for a formal interview. The center had been started in June of 1971 by a group of concerned Bethel citizens, he said. They found a trailer to house the operation and used volunteer labor to build on the lean-to. Local government agencies had kicked in some money and eventually it had been matched with $55,000 from the state and Title IV funding.

Currently the budget was $130,000 which would barely keep them. To date they had handled over six thousand cases, but they were only scratching the surface, Anderson maintained.

They needed additional funding for educational programs and for research.

"Why do you think the people drink?" I asked him.

"Drinking is a custom. It's kind of antisocial to turn down a drink. You get a couple of bottles and polish them off," he speculated. "A lot of people drink because it's a status symbol, I think. But there doesn't seem to be any real pattern. I don't think they drink any differently here than anywhere else. It's just that the Alaskan native is a little more honest about his drinking than a Caucasian. More apt to take a jug on the street.

"We have a great number of transients but they don't act much different than small town delegates to an American Legion convention in Atlantic City. There's the same kind of alcoholics here as there are in France or Sweden or New York. I think, because life's harsher here, alcohol is more likely to take a toll. You don't find many eighty-year-old winos in this country because they're likely to have frozen to death at an early age."

Anderson did believe that some of his Eskimo clients had problems in making the transition from subsistence living in their rustic villages to the fast pace of the twentieth century.

"These people have a foot in each world, and they can't decide which one to stay in. We try to help them decide which one they belong in and get both feet firmly planted. Sometimes we tell 'em 'Go back to your old ideas.' There's a lot of peace of mind in being able to walk on the tundra. To go fishing. To go hunting and berrypicking. I think there's nothing wrong with the way people have lived here for centuries. Nothing to be ashamed of."

Although originally inexperienced in counseling, Anderson's Eskimo staff had been surprisingly successful. His main prerequisite in hiring was that his staffers be rehabilitated alcoholics or at least have the potential for rehabilitation, but his own credentials were broader—Washington University in St. Louis and Lutheran General Hospital in Chicago.

"What we do is all the old things and a few of the new ones. First of all, we don't feed them anything. We feel alcoholics have a certain amount of dependency and that will add to it. We give them coffee and a place to stay. Figure they found somewhere to eat before they got here.

"We try to get the individual to realize that he is responsible for what happens to him. We're not. When people show they want to help themselves, we give them moral support."

Throughout Anderson's dissertation, Bubbles had been working at the desk and taking in every word. Now she volunteered her own analysis of what Ekayurvik did right. She had seen government social workers about her drinking problem but they didn't help.

"Social workers are kind of pressed for time," Anderson said. "They have hours, nine to five."

"No, it's not that. They don't share their experiences," she said. "*They* couldn't admit to any personal mistakes even if they did make any. I trusted Freddy because I knew he'd had his own experiences. I trusted him."

They went on to discuss the public health service hospital and how it didn't treat alcoholism as a medical problem.

"I don't know why it is. The people of Barrow love their hospital and here the people hate it," Anderson observed.

I told him of coming here in 1967 to check rumors that the head of the Bethel hospital had ordered the planting of birth-control coils in Eskimo women who came for postnatal check-ups, without their knowledge or consent. The story was apparently true, for there were whole villages where there had been no new babies that year. But by the time I got on the story, the administrator had been hastily transferred and there was "No comment" all around.

"They treat us like guinea pigs," Bubbles charged. "They've picked us because we're in a poverty area."

"Some of their young interns are trained in all the newest diseases and the most modern equipment, but we don't have either," Anderson said. "We've got things that are Dark Ages diseases and old equipment. We've had people die of pneumonia because they couldn't diagnose it."

Dave Elias, a white social worker, joined us. He was earn-

ing $900 a semester teaching at the community college and
had turned the money back for scholarships so Ekayurvik counselors could attend his classes.

"He tends to talk in terms of numbers, not individuals, but
that's a sociologist for you," one of the Eskimos observed.
"Otherwise, he's O.K. We wouldn't miss his class. It's a good
one."

Elias was president of the Bethel Council on Alcoholism, and
I sought his assessment of Bethel's battle with the bottle.

"Bethel is the Las Vegas of the Kuskokwim," Elias maintained. "It may not look like much to an outsider but coming in
from the bush is different. Many of the villages are dry. And if
you've got a little money, you can really swing in Bethel. A
man once told me his village had no booze. If you bring it in,
they take it away from you. But I've met people in Bethel from
his village so drunk they can't stand up. The implication may
be that it's O.K. to drink in Bethel."

Bethel was the headquarters for some eighty government
agencies dedicated to fighting poverty and improving public
health—as well as two bars, a pool hall, two department stores,
a new movie house, and an astonishing fleet of thirty taxicabs.
Although this was a poverty area, Elias said, with a population
of about 2,500, if you took the gross of all three cab companies
in a month, you'd probably have something in the neighbor-
hood of $50,000.

And it was nothing to have the liquor store do $2,000 worth
of business on a good day. Last Christmas Eve it stayed open
from 6 P.M. until midnight and grossed $5,000.

Back at the Kuskokwim Inn for supper, I found Terry
Gershon, a friend from New York City who had arrived in
Bethel the same day I had, to work as program director for the
new television station. She was living with two native girls. The
only thing they had been able to rent was a filthy house with
cockroaches and no plumbing, and they wanted to leave. Still,
Terry was enthusiastic about the country.

She was a young, good-looking redhead, extremely tall and

built on the proportions of Venus. I brought her back with me to the center and her looks caused quite a stir. She took a chair in the office, tried to be inconspicuous, and was soon in conversation with the sobering drunks.

The place was humming. On the first couch sat a parka-clad mother with her two-year-old daughter and a two-month-old daughter wrapped in a clean blanket and propped up by an ample supply of clean diapers.

Bubbles had been roped into volunteering—there wasn't much she could do about that because she was living there. But she wanted to go out, so I took over for her. She had black circles under her eyes from her stint as jail matron, but she fixed herself up, teasing her hair and spraying it to the current chic.

Tom Michael was working doggedly at the desk, logging everything but the sneezes on a desk pad as required by the center. Each visitor, each incoming and outgoing phone call, each pot of coffee brewed was noted. I never could discover what instigated this paperwork and wondered if the Eskimos were born bureaucrats or just trying to protect themselves from lawsuits and investigations. One thing was sure, not one drop of coffee would go unrecorded.

Nicholi Nicholi descended on us from Tuluksak, about twenty miles up river. He was young and quite drunk, but most of his faculties and a fine sense of humor remained intact. His English was good and he started a conversation on physical education with Terry.

I sat next to the Eskimo mother to hear what Fred Pete was saying to her. She farted, excused herself politely in English, then spoke at length in Yupik.

"Her husband wanted her to drink with him," Fred translated. "Then he got mad at her and threw her out."

She tried to tell me in English. She didn't want to drink because of the children, she said. But her husband made her drink five beers. Then he'd gotten mad at her and pushed her. Pushed the little girl . . .

"My Martha," she said fondly, looking at her beautiful two-

*Fred Pete counsels an Eskimo mother while her daughter rattles the candy machine.*

year-old. She had eight children, three at home with him right now. She had gone to the police. They brought her here.

She was probably in her mid-thirties and thin as a work horse. Her parka was new, well sewn with a band of ribbon around a bottom ruffle embroidered with "Love."

Fred offered to take her to a relative but she seemed to prefer to stay and talk. He took off his coat, listened carefully, gave advice in Eskimo, joked with her gently. She smiled, relaxed a little, then grew serious. More Yupik and she began to cry quietly. The little girl, Martha, took her hand, touched her face and her hair with baby fingers and tried to make the mother smile.

Fred spoke of alternatives—welfare programs, help from social workers. She listened earnestly. The baby had been sleeping, even when Martha smothered it with kisses. Now it woke and started to cry. Automatically the woman pulled her parka over her head, flipped a large, brown-tipped breast from her ragged pink cotton dress, and began nursing. Fred made a hasty trip to see about some business in the office.

The woman showed me the ripped sleeve of her skimpy, salmon-colored sweater. Her husband had done that, she said. But he wasn't usually bad. Only when he was drinking.

Fred returned and they talked at length.

"She doesn't know what she wants to do," he said. More Yupik. He listened with a patience born of a real interest in human beings. I guess that's why people trusted him. If Fred had told me to jump off the television tower, I'd have considered it seriously. If he thought it was for my own good, it must be.

"She wants to go home to her husband," he reported at last. "I don't know . . ."

He telephoned her house. The kids said their father had fallen asleep. Fred pulled on his jacket again and shrugged.

"Maybe you'd better take your six-shooter," I suggested.

"I don't like violence," he said seriously. The mother, quite sober now, was thanking everyone.

"Maybe you'll return this empty and bring us back a full one," I joked. Even Tom Michael laughed at that.

Suddenly a desperate, bespectacled white burst in. He had a drunk in his truck, he reported breathlessly and begged one of us to go out and bring him in.

"I can't do it," he added.

"With the new law I don't think I can do it either," Fred told him. "Maybe you'd better."

"But I don't speak any Eskimo," the white wailed. "Oh, oh, he's running away." And he dashed out, slamming the door.

"Well, at least he tried," Fred said. He was rounding up the mother's belonging, searching for something to wrap a wet diaper in. There was more commotion outside and I opened the door to see the white sprinting off into the darkness toward town yelling, "Harold! Come back, Harold!"

Then, in front of his truck, tottered a gnomelike figure, weaving like a dancer off balance, yet never quite falling down. Fred peered over my shoulder and the figure wavered in our direction, smiled directly at us, and gave us the finger.

"Harold . . . H-A-R-O-L-D!" came the distant cry.

"I wonder if this is the drunk he's looking for?" I asked Fred.

"Probably." Fred shut the door. Finally the man opened it on his own and stood glowering at us. He looked like a Chinese warlord, powerfully built despite his short stature, very menacing, and incredibly drunk. After trying to outstare us, he broke into a beaming smile, gave Fred a fatherly pat, and headed full tilt for the beauteous Terry, superwoman. She backed away. He followed like a thirsty man in search of water, grinning up at her in sheer admiration.

"You got 'usband?"

"No," she admitted uncertainly, still in retreat. He backed her almost the length of the lean-to before Fred and Tom Michael came to her rescue and steered him into the office. Fred left with the Eskimo mother and Terry was not far behind him.

"S-L-E-E-P it off!" Nicholi Nicholi advised the newcomer merrily. But when Nick Frances came in for the night shift, he shuddered at the sight of the drunk. It was Harold. He had

had him before, he warned. "Strong as an ox and psycho. When he gets started, you can't stop him."

Tom began getting Nicholi Nicholi down on paper, establishing that he had no job, no social security, no unemployment, and no welfare.

"I'm a *straight* man," Nicholi assured him proudly. He had come down river to pick up a new National Guard uniform. Was in line for a promotion and was going to Anchorage for training the next month. The Guard paid him about $80 a month, he said.

Bubbles came in terribly upset. She had had a drink with a girl friend and gone all to pieces. She went to the hospital and asked the doctor to give her some Valium, a tranquilizer she had been using. He said the pharmacy was locked up and he couldn't get any. Finally she had talked him into finding some, but now she was in bad shape, quite unsure of herself. Mercifully, she drifted off to sleep in her chair. Fred returned alone —the husband had been sleeping. Tom finished the paperwork on Nicholi, and now Fred Pete took over.

"I came here voluntarily," Nicholi began. At the sight of Fred he sobered rapidly. He might have "volunteered" but the police had brought him in, Fred reminded him; he had volunteered to keep from getting arrested.

Nicholi nodded sheepishly. His clothes were very dirty, Fred pointed out. If he wanted to keep out of reach of the law, he had to stay clean and to space his drinks. There followed a good, reasonable talk on how to avoid the police while drinking. Nicholi had expected a temperance lecture but this one interested him. He wanted to ask Fred some questions but the center was getting hectic. Harold kept butting into everything.

"I'll come back again and talk before I go to Anchorage," Nicholi decided. "I guess right now you're busy."

Harold was wafting around the office. Fred studied him.

"Do you think he'll remember when he sobers up?" the counselor wondered. "Sometimes even when people look sober, they don't remember what you tell them."

Harold didn't even look sober, but Fred decided to give it a try. The man had been talking about Vietnam. I suggested he might have someone over there. Fred tried that angle, but no—Harold thought *he* was over there.

He had come from Chevak in the delta to help build a traditional Eskimo heat bath (kuzigik)—like a sauna. The project was being sponsored by the Bethel Recreation Department and the worried white who had delivered him was his employer.

"I am millionaire!" he beamed at Bubbles, who came out of her sleep under his badgering. "You got 'usband?"

"He scares me," she said, shrinking into her chair.

"I'd hate to tangle with him if he goes off," Nick murmured.

"Well, I wouldn't," I said firmly. I was tired of being hassled, tired of the smell of Lysol and urine and booze, tired of being afraid of that Eskimo.

"You scared?" Harold asked, sidling up to me and standing almost on my toes.

"No, little man. I'm not afraid of you," I growled. "But you'd better be afraid of me. I can get pretty mean." He considered, then backed off to get some coffee.

"Were you ever in the Marines?" Nick wondered.

"No."

Finally Fred corralled Harold and spoke to him at length in Yupik. At one point Harold asked him a long, serious question and Fred had all he could do to keep from breaking up.

"He wants to know which one of you girls he should marry," he told Bubbles and me. Harold got up and pulled himself up full height.

"I millionaire. I millionaire. I strong!" he declared. Then he peeled off his shirt and his belt and started to haul down his pants. Fred talked him back into his clothes. They swapped positions at Fred's desk. Fred chuckled. Harold was lecturing him.

"He's got something there," the counselor said. "I've been asking what he'd tell me if I came in drunk. He says 'You've got to do what the people tell you to do!'"

Finally they got Harold to the men's dorm and Bubbles went to bunk in the women's, leaving a friend, Anna, the pretty Bethel librarian, to volunteer for night shift. She got into conversation with a handsome policeman from Nelson Island who had turned himself in to us after a four-day binge. He was en route to Sitka for additional police training at the end of the month. He had had to fly out of Nelson early before his village froze in, and it was hard to kill time in Bethel.

Some policemen friends of his came by looking for the firebath builder on behalf of the Recreation Department but stayed to lecture their fellow officer.

"If you can't lick 'em, join 'em!" he told them defiantly, although he didn't sound too proud of himself. "If I find a man with a bottle on Nelson Island, I take it away from him and dump it. A bottle costs $40 there but that doesn't stop 'em. Well, if you can't lick 'em, join 'em!"

I walked into the lean-to just in time to catch Harold sneaking along on his hands and knees on his way to the girls' dorm. I gave him a stern lecture and he wedged himself in behind the oil heater.

"I give you twenty dollars," he suggested hopefully.

I shook my head, no.

"Twenty-five dollars?" he asked.

"No," I said, trying not to giggle.

"Well, why *not?*"

The policeman was studying our calendar, counting the days he had to kill before going to Sitka. Four days. How could he ever stay sober four days in Bethel without being bored to death?

"Maybe you could go to the public library instead of the bar," I suggested.

"Yes," he said, giving Anna a good smile. Later I found him patiently discussing religion with Harold. Everything was quiet. Tom Michael said he'd keep watch. He needed only three hours sleep a night. So I went to bed.

The long-awaited snow finally arrived, glamorizing the garbage and all the odds-and-ends houses with clinging crystals. Bethel looked better. The air was crisp and invigorating. But I felt like hell.

It was so darned hard to sleep at the hotel. More drunks there, it seemed, than at Ekayurvik. Briefly I considered joining Bubbles sleeping in the office chairs, but I hated to sleep with my clothes on.

Feeling sorry for myself, I hauled on my boots and slogged to Joe's Bar, recently renamed the "Wild Goose," to interview the management. The Nelson Island policeman was standing in the entryway, eating popcorn. Mortified to see me, he looked around for a place to hide. Finding none, he stood his ground.

"If you can't lick 'em, join 'em," I said gloomily. And walked on in.

Manager Wayne Bruha said the Wild Goose had been purchased the previous fall by a Fairbanks group which was very optimistic about the development of this area. On a good night the Goose was grossing $1,200. Bruha had made about the same in a Fairbanks bar selling eight cases of beer a night and the rest in hard liquor. Here he did it with thirty cases of beer.

He was also amazed at the taxi business. Fairbanks had a population of 15,000 and Bethel 2,500 and yet they had the same size taxi fleet. Drivers here told him the people sometimes walked farther to phone for a cab than they were driven when they got in the cab.

Bruha brightened the interview by treating me to four bloody marys in addition to the one I'd bought myself.

"Well, old Bethel doesn't look so bad, after all," I decided, emerging in a mellow mood. I did have second thoughts about going to work with liquor on my breath, but who'd smell it at the center?

I arrived back at the center early, to find one of the counselors besieged by an ex-husband. She was a placid girl wear-

ing square glasses and she listened unruffled while the man
complained of child-support payments. Also in attendance
was a ragged little Eskimo named Mr. Sugar, who seemed to
have moved in. He was stationed on a couch reading a large
complicated book on psychology.

Anna arrived dragging her compact, dark-complexioned
father, with her diminutive mother pushing from behind. The
old man had been picking on the younger children, they
complained, and they were leaving him here until he sobered up. Helen Andrew was on duty as counselor. Originally
she had been a patient, then married another patient, and
now they both counseled. She was young, with a strange raspy
voice, but she inspired the same kind of trust as Freddy and
was good at the job.

The old man was worried about a younger daughter who
hadn't come home in a week. So, I knew, was Anna, for she
had asked the Nelson Island policeman about her. The girl
had just run off and nobody knew where. Helen suggested
that maybe she hadn't come home because the old man had
been drinking and everybody in Bethel knew he was mean
when he drank. Weakly he protested, but she left him to give
the matter thought.

Otherwise it was a slow night.

The next evening, Saturday, Eskimos crowded the river
landing, hurrying into town in spite of the threat of a freeze-up.
I headed for the Kashime Room, the town's other bar, where
Wally Wallace was bartender and manager.

"I'm so sick of drunks I'm going to move to Kwinhagak.
That's a Moravian village where drinking is not allowed," he
began. "When I took the bar a year ago, a good night was
$600. Now a good night is $1,000 and when I drop below $800
they say, 'What happened? Where did everybody go?'

"Most of our business is in vodka. The problem is they
drink straight alcohol with a straw. I got swizzle sticks and
everybody said, 'What's the matter? No hole in these.' When

you drink straight alcohol with a straw, the fumes hit the back of the roof of your mouth and you get drunk really quickly."

You could get bombed on an eyedropper full of whiskey, he added gloomily. Well, he was married to a wonderful Eskimo girl and they had a new baby and Kwinhagak was definitely the place to be.

I went to the center before my shift, to find Bubbles really low. She was supposed to meet a girl friend at the Wild Goose but had lost courage. I volunteered to accompany her, and no sooner had we found barstools than we were joined by another counselor who'd really gone off the wagon. He was a good man, but he had been taking codeine for a bad back and it didn't mix with bourbon. Some of the drunks he had counseled were giving it back to him in kind and eventually he suggested we evacuate to the pool hall where liquor wasn't served.

The hall was one of Bethel's oldest institutions, a moldy building with a snack bar and reasonably good coffee. The ancient pool tables listed and wobbled, but Bethel players weren't bothered by that. They listed and wobbled, too.

"Once this used to be the busiest place in town," the counselor recalled sadly. "Now it's pretty empty until the bars close and there's nowhere else to go."

Bubbles had mixed emotions when I got her back to the center. She had faced the bar without getting drunk, which pleased her. But a cousin had taken her aside while she was there and told her everybody thought she was a slut and worse. I tried to talk to the girl on why people said such cruel things. I had heard they were jealous of Bubbles' looks and ability to attract white admirers. Finally I wrote her a poem the language she knew best.

> People with minds like frozen tundra
> Criticize. Make you wonder
> What you're worth.

People, with dull imaginations and dull lives,
Criticize. Pass on lies—
Give them wide berth.
People . . . why let them bother you?
Who criticize? What, really, do they know?
Oh, why on earth let blind men judge your beauty?
Criticize? Go your blithe way unhindered—
And seek a little mirth.

Your friend.

She understood. Enthusiastically she showed me a poem she had just written on tolerance and decided to have it read over the radio. Her whole mood changed.

Saturday was the day that the federal funds stopped. Tom Anderson was out, but a note posted over the main desk told us all we needed to know:

"First the bad news: Bethel Social Services has received the termination papers today. And the good news, which all will be glad to hear: The Alcohol Program will continue."

"We opened without federal money," an Ekayurvik board member said unofficially. "The Title IV funds were too good to be true anyway. We knew they'd stop some day. Used them to buy equipment we could not have had otherwise. But we'll carry on somehow."

The first patient of the evening was a battered young woman with a split lip, in dirty jeans and jacket. She was so foul-mouthed that Nick left her to my mercy. I let her sit and swear for a while. Then she put her head on her arms and cried, "Glen, Glen, you motherfucker. You aren't mature, Glen. You never were. Oh, Glen, I love you."

"Men problems?" I said, feeling useless. "Maybe they'll look better in the morning."

"You don't know anything," she said, but she seemed grateful to be spoken to and she didn't swear at me. I let her cry a little more, then talked to her of unimportant things and we discovered to our mutual mirth that we shared the same last name.

In came an Eskimo from Legal Services with a huge, moose-like man he had found asleep on Mission Road, all covered with snow.

"I found him in front of my house," the Legal Services man said. "I tried to take him home but my wife won't have him."

Haggling followed on who had legal responsibility for the drunk. Meanwhile the subject of the debate blundered about, ricocheting off the close-set walls of the lean-to. Eventually I landed him on the couch. He said some uncomplimentary things to my namesake, who gave it back to him in kind, which seemed to increase his respect for her. Adding to the din was a fellow from Hooper Bay. His cherubic face was framed in swirls of black curls which made him look younger than his twenty-five years, but his tongue was wicked. Cheerfully he instigated a name-calling contest with the other two. The obscenities got so thick that they suddenly began to sound funny.

The Hooper Bay lad had a cup of coffee and then decided to go back to town to get a bit drunker. The big man sobered up enough to remember he was from Chevak and had eleven kids, but he couldn't remember his name.

"Never trust those up-river Indians," my namesake warned. It was a supreme insult and the Chevak Eskimo nearly gave her lip another split. More name calling.

"I never get drunk at home," the Chevak man said. "My wife won't let me. When I come to Bethel I go on a little party."

"This was damn near your last party," I told him. He could have frozen to death, but that didn't register. Finally we put him to bed.

Back came Hooper Bay, drunker yet, and homed in on my namesake. He informed her he was going to "stick" her.

"You don't mind if we get together?" he asked me. She watched anxiously, and finally what he was saying registered and she fled to the office.

"You'll have to talk to the management," I said. He followed the girl to the office in search of Nick.

"I don't want him in my pants," she howled. Nick refereed.

Then a long-haired Eskimo, who could have passed as a freak from San Francisco, burst in. He was from Marshall on the Yukon and had been working several weeks in Bethel building a new native co-operative store.

"It's a beautiful store," he announced proudly, handing out cigarettes all round. Then he requested coffee with salt, saying it would sober him. He had had a fight with his brother and two other guys and couldn't go home. That was why he had to sober up quickly. And he did, leaving us to ponder the powers of hot salt.

In came Levi Lot, a locally famous Eskimo radio announcer from KYUK, the educational station. He had been on the wagon for several months, but his reputation as a drinker was formidable. He had survived the last few months on Antabuse, a pill that made you sick when you combined it with alcohol, but he must have forgotten to renew his prescription. His fine brain was still working, but he was awesomely drunk.

His fans were driving him nuts, he confided. They were numerous and enthusiastic and some of the women pursued him to distraction. Also, his wife didn't understand him.

"I've got the same problems as the Rolling Stones," he lamented.

"And a few more to boot," I agreed.

"Nick, my unbeatable foe," he called warmly. But the counselor gave him no sympathy. Like most Bethel people, he was furious that Levi, the local hero, had fallen again. So Levi had a cup of coffee and staggered off uncounseled.

The Hooper Bay man began to entertain us with tales of his travels in California, Colorado, and Washington.

"I traveled all over and came home to be a drunk," he concluded. He bragged he had spent $100 that night and still had money at the hotel.

"I thought you were broke or I wouldn't have let you in

here," the counselor said unhappily. "I hate this. I'm tired of these drunks!"

"Do something else."

"I can't think of anything else. I *want* to do this," he said wearily. Then he brightened. "Maybe Louis will forget about daylight-saving time and come early." Louis had the morning shift.

A beautiful wisp of a girl rapped at the door.

"I'm too drunk to go home," she said, with a drunken slur in a baby voice that sounded unreal. "I walked a mile to get here. Did the police pick up my brother tonight?"

We didn't know. She had five brothers and three sisters. One brother was in jail for beating up her mother.

"A nice boy when he isn't drinking, though."

"Will your mother worry?" The girl was seventeen but looked fourteen and seemed quite fragile.

"No, she was drunk Friday and she knows I drink." She began sifting through her pockets for a cigarette. "I was in school in Oregon last year. Don't know why I came back here," she said. The search produced hairpins, a scarf, and assorted possessions that showed she had been living on the road. Finally she found a little watch which she cradled in her palm. Nick gave her a cigarette and after three puffs she fell asleep.

Tom Michael was cleaning up. He told us the big man from Chevak had propositioned him.

"The one with eleven kids?"

"Yes."

Nick suggested with a smile that maybe Tom should counsel him.

"No *thank* you," Tom said vehemently.

Luckily Louis did forget about daylight-saving time and relieved us an hour early. Everybody was exhausted.

On Sunday State Representative Joe McGill stopped by to give me additional insight into Bethel's progress with its drinking problems.

"A couple of years ago we had a statewide meeting on alcoholism with legislators, ministers, and the like in Fairbanks," he recalled. "Bethel sent two men. One never got out of Bethel and the other got to Fairbanks but was arrested twice in five days for being drunk in public and never did make it to the meeting. Naturally, we voted Bethel top priority in all state funding."

I told the story to Fred, who smiled sheepishly.

"I was the one who got to Fairbanks," he said.

On duty that afternoon a spooked Ekayurvik staff held down the desk. Tom had been working alone, heard someone come in, brush by his office door, and go into the middle dorm. While he was noting it in the log, he heard the sound of vomiting, but when he rushed to help, the room was empty. There was no exit except past the office door. About a month earlier he had been through the same experience and that time there'd been another counselor on duty to bear out the story.

"Well, at least drunken ghosts leave no mess to clean up," I observed. I hated to see Tom so down, for he was one of my favorites. He was always volunteering for the dirty work and he was also good with people, but when I asked him if he wanted to be a counselor, he was horror-stricken. Counselors earned $600 to $700 a month and he got paid nothing, but he didn't want the job officially.

"He knows people here find ways to cope," Anderson explained. "He's looking for ways to cope. A lot of people come here to get away from the pressure of the community to drink."

In search of statistics, I interviewed Captain Lorn Campbell, who with a two-man force represented the State Police in Bethel and fifty-seven small villages in a 93,000-square-mile territory.

"When these people are sober, they're worth their word. If we call a village and say to someone, 'You're under arrest. Get on the next mail plane and come to jail.' They'll come. In fact, there isn't even a lock on our jail door," he reported. But when they were drinking, they broke all records.

"Per capita we have the highest crime rate in Alaska. Per capita we have the highest suicide rate, the highest homicide rate, and a lot more wife beating than any place I've ever been.

"About 99 per cent of it is alcohol related. Most of the people I talk to tell me they drink to get drunk. You don't drink unless you're going to get drunk."

Liquor store sales were another eye opener. The gross for 1971, the year before, was $779,214, which was $130,916 more than it had been the year before. The store was owned by the city and Dave Swanson, who represented Bethel on the State Alcohol Control Board, gave me its history.

"In the late 1950s Bethel tried prohibition but it was a dismal failure. I was mayor at the time. Discovered if people were going to drink, they were going to drink, legal or not. I estimated in 1960 that $210,000 was being spent in bootlegging and the bootlegger called me and said, 'I think you're a little low.'

"At that time the city had a total income of $54,000 and we spent $33,000 of it on police protection. We decided if we couldn't stop the drinking, we could at least put some of the profit from liquor sales back into the community so we opened a liquor store."

The management plotted to discourage business, he added.

"That's why we don't open until afternoon. We figure if we wait maybe people will go to work sober."

That night before work I made the rounds to photograph the bars and was escorted back to the center by Sylvester Ayek, a King Island Eskimo I had known in Fairbanks. He had a job as a disk jockey at the Bethel radio station and was also pursuing a promising career as an artist. Ayek was a good drinker but in a bad mood because he had just had a fight with his girl. Maybe the center would cheer him up, he decided.

Mr. Sugar was still there, reading his psychology book. He was a special protégé of Simeon Arnakin's, I learned, and he had taken up residence.

"I always ask, 'Why do you drink?' and usually they say, 'To have fun.' Most of them don't think they have a problem," Simeon worried. "They drink a bottle a day and they don't think they have a problem."

Tom Anderson and Ayek got involved in a long discussion on how the whites had mistreated the Indians. Then Ayek got sentimental about King Island where he had been raised. It was a superbly beautiful place with all the houses built on stilts on the side of a rocky cliff. His people had been encouraged by government authorities to move away because the island was so remote, so the islanders had settled in Nome to be near city conveniences. Now many of them wanted to go home, he said. Their colony in Nome was a squalid slum and they had severe drinking problems.

"I'm going to go back. I won't need any alcohol . . . That's a white man's thing. No cigarettes. Just my art. And my friends can make appointments a year in advance to come out and see me."

After Ayek left, a cab driver entertained us. A recent fare—a young woman in town from an outlying village—had chartered his cab at 2 A.M. for $20 an hour. He tried to talk her out of it but she insisted. Although there wasn't much highway to cover, she rode around two hours picking up friends and stopping at the pool hall for coffee. She wanted to go another hour but he refused. He took her back to where she was staying and she packed her things and headed home, quite pleased with herself.

It had been a hard night, though, and he had stopped at the center to rest. One very drunk lady didn't want to leave his cab and he had had to lock all the doors to keep her from getting back in.

Nora Guinn, the Eskimo judge of the U. S. District Court in Bethel, had been a prime mover in establishing the sleep-off center, and an afternoon with her was enlightening. Her courtroom was scarcely larger than a country kitchen and doubled as an office for Mrs. Guinn and the local magistrate. During a

*Judge Nora Guinn ponders a case.*

long trial, witnesses from both sides, their lawyers, and the spectators were often forced to wait in a crowded corridor and the neighboring State Police office, but today's docket was light and I got a seat.

First up was an assault case—$500 and/or six months. The defendant, who looked like an Eskimo Clark Gable, had a black eye and a long history of beating up ladies who wouldn't say yes. He wanted to be released on bail because his son had just turned up sockless and dirty at the children's receiving home. Mrs. Guinn said he'd have to stay in jail three more days and that his son would be all right at the home until then. At that time he could get off on bail if he promised not to drink.

"Can you promise not to drink?" she asked gently.

"I'll try," he said, obviously under stress.

"No, trying is not enough," she said firmly. There was an anguished pause. Finally he promised.

"Then it will only be four days until the trial. That's not many days," she reassured him. "It's hard to think about not having a drink when you're still hung over," she said when he left. "But he'll be all right."

The next prisoner was a youth from up river, and she set the date for his robbery trial for some time in November. He was to go home until then.

"Can you promise me to behave good? Not drink much? A little bit?"

Slowly he translated the question in his mind and nodded. She spoke fluent Yupik, but she had asked him earlier if he spoke English and he said he was proud to be able to.

"Do you know what it means? Good behavior?" she asked patiently. He nodded. "I'm going to say limited drinking. That means if you want a beer you can have a beer but not get drunk."

She was a remarkable woman, the mother of eight, with one son recently dead in a snowmobile accident and three young ones still at home. Although mostly self-taught, she had the mind of a good lawyer and a long, fine record as a judge. She was also a community mover. Much to her credit was a pioneering day-care center, the receiving home for parentless children, and the creation of Bethel Social Services.

"But we needed a sleep-off center. Our 'drunk in public' arrests were out of reason and I estimated that maybe ninety-five per cent of my cases were alcohol related. Ekayurvik was our first attempt to face the problem head on. We didn't have the funding, so we started with what we had and made do with what we had."

For this reason, the recent cut in federal funding did not worry her and neither did the new law that prevented arrest for drunkenness.

"The sleep-off center is already established. People know it's a place to come for help. And our officers have been scouring the books and making some pretty creative arrests in cases of drunkenness where people won't get help voluntarily," she smiled. "I don't expect any deaths for not picking people up on the road."

Tom Dillon, the Bethel police chief, was less optimistic about the alcoholism program and bitter about the hardship the new law worked on his department.

"It's a confusing law and it should be reviewed," he maintained. "Before, we had the option of taking a person to the sleep-off center or to jail if he was going to be hostile. We had the option of protecting a violent person, a person who was violent to himself or someone else."

Wearily he went through his files.

"This man had frozen to death within fifteen feet of the door to the house where the party was in progress. We figure he got sick, went outside, and someone locked the door. Never heard him trying to get back in.

"One woman died in an abandoned house from exposure. She'd gone there, intoxicated, for the purpose of prostitution. Must have passed out. The customer left and she froze."

The year before the Bethel Police Department had fourteen similar reports to file under "Alcohol-related Deaths." This year there had been only four, but Dillon was quicker to give credit to his snowmobile patrol than the sleep-off center.

"The new law treats alcoholism as a disease and we all agree with the concept. But it presupposes there will be adequate place for rehabilitation and a competent counseling staff. The type of treatment they're doing now is nothing more or less than a sobering-up station."

I asked him about the rape rumors and he substantiated them. They had had five cases the month before and three the current month even though the weather was colder. And he produced a three-by-three board with a spike in it that the last victim had been threatened with.

"We're getting away from the village concept. We were a little, friendly town, but it's getting rough."

Ironically, it was to be Dillon's last interview. He was shot to death by a drunk two weeks later, and his murder was to be listed as the fifth alcohol-related tragedy of the season.

My last night in town I got a job as a barmaid at the Wild Goose to see how the other half lived. It was Halloween and the city fathers, with characteristic farsightedness, ordered the bars and liquor store closed until 8 P.M. so the drunk drivers wouldn't run over the young Eskimo trick-or-treaters. Business started slowly when we did open, but the bar rapidly became a mob scene. Besides beer, the favorite drink of the evening was a "harvey wallbanger"—equal parts Galliano, vodka, and orange juice. Excellent, I discovered, but it really put people under in a hurry.

Some of my customers were people I had counseled at the sleep-off center and they were confused by my presence. For a week I had been warning them about the evils of drink and now there I was, tray in hand, to take their orders. Some of them were so upset at the sight of me that they went home early while the rest got gloriously drunk.

I had been a barmaid one summer in a fisherman's bar on Cape Cod, but never had I seen so many people drink so much so rapidly as at the Wild Goose. The action was too fast for me and I had a terrible time with my bank. At one time I was $15 short. Then I must have shortchanged some poor soul be-

*The bar.*

cause I came out even. Wayne Bruha, the manager, gave me $15 for my work and said I had earned it and I agreed. It seemed fitting that I donate it to the Ekayurvik coffee fund.

After the bar closed I took my shift at the center as usual, but it was slow.

"I think you could have gotten us a little more business than this," Fred joked. "You must be a pretty bad barmaid."

At 5 A.M. it was so quiet I decided to check on the emergency ward at the hospital to see if it was as poorly run as people said. A delightful young nurse was on duty. She had just helped set a broken leg and deliver a new baby and now was monitoring a heart attack. I could understand why she didn't have time for drunks.

"I really believe alcoholism is a disease," she told me earnestly. "But if anyone wants medical advice and counseling, we just have to tell them to come back in the daytime during clinic hours."


The next morning was clear and it looked as if the planes would fly. But when I got to the airport the fog had come in and all planes were grounded. Larry Fulton, a newspaper editor, gave me a ride back to town where we had lunch.

Maybe Bethel looked a little grubby, Fulton conceded, but the place grew on you. He had been there a couple of years. He went outside occasionally, but he was always glad to come back to Bethel. It was like a family, he said.

Of course, in the outlying villages things could get rough. The previous spring a man had become angry with his wife and daughters and staked them outside with the dogs. The neighbors hadn't interfered and the family had remained chained for a month until a Catholic priest came through and made the man release them. Still, they were in fair shape, Fulton noted. They had been fed pretty well.

The fog lifted. I got a ride back to the airport with Fred. Thoughtfully, he looked at my plane.

"It's hard to take a vacation," he said. "I took nine days last year. Called the center every day to make sure everybody was all right but when I got back they said it seemed like I'd been gone forever."

Exhausted as I was, I hated to leave him. I even hated to leave Bethel. It was fascinating to watch the town fight against such heavy odds and I was coming to believe it would win.

Judge Nora Guinn had put it well.

"You just use good old common sense. Something we're long on here," she said. "We may fight among ourselves, sometimes, but when Bethel has a problem we always stick together. You know, people do care about one another out here."

*Main Street, Angoon.*

# Angoon Indian Village

## LOW ON THE POLITICAL TOTEM POLE

*The Tlingit Indians of southeastern Alaska were the fiercest and wealthiest of all Alaskan natives, and, even after some of their tribes had been defeated by warring Russian fur traders in the eighteenth century, they continued to annihilate the intruders and reap merciless revenge.*

*By the time the United States purchased their territory in 1867, the Indians—according to a government report—were "somewhat tamer but insolent and disrespectful," for their tribal system was still intact and through it they had power.*

*The Angoon Tlingits of Admiralty Island had never been defeated by the Russians and the new American overseers feared them enough to seek their destruction. In 1812 the U. S. Navy bombarded Angoon village after the Indians tried to avenge the accidental death of a member of their tribe who had been employed by an American trading company. Vengeance was very much in order under Tlingit law, since the Americans had refused to make settlement of the traditional workman's compensation of two hundred blankets. But the U. S. Government made it clear it honored no law but its own, destroying most of the settlement and Angoon's winter food supply.*

*The disaster caused the Tlingits to rethink their fighting strategy and it eventually served the Indians well. Unlike the majority of Alaskan natives, who were socialistic, the Tlingits understood capitalism because it was the root of their own social order. Now they determined to take advantage of the white man's system by working within it.*

From the beginning Tlingit leaders pursued the white man's education with considerable success, and when the Territory of Alaska passed legislation allowing municipal Indian self-government, the Tlingit people were ready.

About 1920 Angoon elected a town council, built a town hall, and installed street lights and electricity. Its citizens demanded and received their own school system under the charge of Katanook, an Angoon Tlingit. Their teacher also helped organize the Alaska Native Brotherhood (ANB) which led the Tlingit fight for equal rights and, in 1936, filed Alaska's first land claims suit against the U. S. Government for $80 million in lost timberlands.

But while outwardly the Tlingits came to live as white men, they warred inside the system. Presbyterian missionaries forbade the speaking of Tlingit in their school and forced the Indians to remove colorful tribal symbols painted on their houses. The awesome heraldic totem poles carved by Tlingit elders began to rot and villagers buried or destroyed them. Yet, secretly, the Tlingit tribal government remained strong and old ways prevailed.

The village of Angoon thrived on this double standard. Being remote, it managed to hold more closely to ancient Tlingit superstitions than other villages, but it also prospered under the white man's system. In 1950, negotiating a loan from the Bureau of Indian Affairs, residents bought a cannery at nearby Hood Bay, thus insuring their own employment. The cost was $226,000 and they managed to get half the loan paid off during the first year although fishing was poor.

The Angoons were well ahead of their time in the investment concept, but their cannery burned down mys-

*teriously about two years later and with it went expen-*
*sive fishing gear, which threw the Angoon fleet hope-*
*lessly in debt. Then, in 1957, the village came to near*
*hysteria when a young Tlingit girl declared herself a*
*shaman and began quite successfully to cast spells on*
*villagers. The public hearing and witch hunt that fol-*
*lowed made the headlines and hurt Angoon almost as*
*much as the cannery fire.*

*Because of the street lights and electricity and An-*
*goon's business acumen, government administrators*
*had been fooled into thinking that the village had for-*
*saken all Indian ways. Now they declared Angoon*
*hopelessly primitive and withdrew further funding for*
*investment. Even Tlingit leaders turned their backs on*
*Angoon. Soon, out of eighteen towns in the Tlingit re-*
*gional organization, Angoon ranked lowest, and al-*
*though it was situated in a resource-rich area where*
*poverty was generally not felt, Angoon reported the*
*lowest medium income for the entire state of Alaska in*
*the 1970 Census.*

I chose to live in Angoon because its residents had managed
to preserve more of their heritage than most Tlingit villages
and paid dearly for it. They didn't carry much weight with
their own native organizations and I wondered why.

Some outside observers believed there was a growing gap between native leaders and the disadvantaged villagers they
represented. The concern was not limited to the Tlingits, but
shared by widely varying groups of natives throughout the
state. Their leaders were sophisticated enough to push the
land claims settlement through Congress and to deal with the
complexities of the white power structure and win. But could
these same leaders remain in touch with the remote, backward
villages that were part of their power base and use these gains
for their good?

Angoon was an extreme case in point, for its downfall had
come at a time when neighboring Tlingit villages began to

prosper. After three decades of haggling, the U. S. Federal Court finally awarded the Tlingits $7.5 million in their land claims suit. That was less than 46.8 cents an acre for some of Alaska's choicest timberland, but Tlingit leaders decided to accept the money and successfully used it to further the state-wide land claims suit before Congress, which ultimately would bring them an estimated $83,160,000 to $144,760,000 and additional land.

Inspired, perhaps, by this new power thrust, Tlingit communities began to secure government funding for new docks, cold storage plants, airports, and city improvements, but Angoon's share was mostly just bad publicity.

At the top of the Tlingit political totem pole was John Borbridge, the first president of the Tlingit-Haida organization formed to administer the Tlingit court settlement, and then head of Sealaska, the Tlingit regional corporation formed to administer the statewide land claims settlement. Borbridge—urbane, well educated, city bred—seemed quite removed from Angoon, but he claimed he was not.

"It's easy for educated leaders to become satisfied with communicating only with each other," he admitted. "They forget about their constituency. One thing I did was get the support of the older people and a lot of that support came from Angoon. They chose to accept my leadership because some of them didn't have the education. But I listened to the elders' advice, and many of them have worked to teach me . . . still are. I think I really have a feeling for the land, the culture, and the way of life.

"There is a rising pride of culture in us. The knowledge of who we are as a people. The people who have fought hard to retain their land base are the people who still live on the land and use it."

And the Angoon people had fought hard, he pointed out. Residents had mustered early to push statewide land claims, staging bake-off and rummage sales to get their representatives to the meetings. Village elder Sam Johnson had spoken briefly but well at the first U. S. Senate hearing on the claims back in 1969.

"Our children growing up are forgetting the language," Johnson testified. "They are becoming more like the white man. They need the education. They need their homes in Angoon. They need support to help our people over there because the land we have we are losing . . ."

Borbridge himself had lost the language and become a white man.

"I like to think of myself as culturally disadvantaged," he said. "Although both my parents spoke Tlingit, I was brought up to speak only English. My father said he made a very determined choice. That it was a tough world and I was going to have to compete all the time, so he focused on formal education."

But formal education wasn't everything. Lydia George, an Angoon housewife and mother of eight children, had grown up impatient with the slowness of the land claims suit, and, with only a fifth-grade education, was elected to the Tlingit-Haida Central Council. She traveled widely and worked with her husband and the older people on land selection. In 1966, combining forces with Borbridge, she began mapping land selections for Angoon, something other villages only began to think about in 1971.

No, Angoon hadn't been forgotten, the Tlingit leader said. Of course, his job now was to oversee long-term investment of the land settlement for all the Tlingit people. But his recent election had been anything but a shoo-in and Borbridge was quick to proclaim awareness of the power his villagers held.

The only scheduled transportation to Angoon was by air. Two or three times weekly a little bush plane from Juneau braved the unpredictable winds of the Lynn Canal, topped the spruce-clad mountains of Douglas Island and coasted half an hour down the west side of Admiralty Island to Killisnoo Inlet where Angoon was sheltered. I arrived, inadvertently, with a team of advisers—Kai Dickey of the Office of Economic Opportunity Head Start program and Mary Zwiep, a VISTA volunteer from Worcester, Massachusetts, who had come on behalf of the Southeastern Alaska Community Action program to try and unscramble some of Angoon's administrative problems. Both girls were smart, young and enthusiastic. Kai was black, or at least tan. Mary, her roommate in Juneau, was a long-haired blonde whom the villagers confused with me and the food stamp lady, who was also on the pallid side.

Our plane docked at a float on Killisnoo Inlet where we were directed to the "airport limousine," a late model van. The town, located a mile away, was built in a U along the water on both sides of a narrow neck of land. Most of the buildings were frame—old, needing paint, with moss-covered shingles and weathered trim of an early 1900s vintage. Ravens, the sacred bird of Tlingit legend, inspected us from the telephone poles and flapped over our heads. Children stopped to stare and a Tlingit matron hurried past, carrying a beautifully decorated birthday cake.

Arrangements had been made for Mary Zwiep and me to stay with Cyril and Judy George, the mayor and village clerk, respectively. Their home was an old one featuring a new coat of bright red paint on three and a half sides and one of the eight bathtubs listed in the village census.

Cyril was a vitally handsome Tlingit who looked about twenty years younger than his age. He had been widowed four years earlier and only within the past year had remarried. His wife couldn't get away from her job as village clerk, he said, so he had come to welcome us. *Camelot* was playing on the stereo and he brewed us a pot of coffee.

The house was comfortably furnished with an upholstered couch and overstuffed chairs. There was a piano, lots of family photos, new wood paneling, and a glass-beaded curtain that separated the living room from the kitchen. Cyril had six children, all away—four in college and two attending high school—so there was plenty of room for us in his upstairs dorm.

Judy George was up to her elbows in paperwork at the tiny log cabin that served as the village hall. It was a new office and her job was new. Before it had been created the summer before through a state-funded public employment program, the mayor had been forced to carry on village business out of his own home and pocket. Records were scattered among village council members and there was little co-ordination of the village's activities.

Judy had been hired by the late mayor, Matthew Kookesh, and his choice had been a sound one. Before her marriage she had been one of the most respected executive secretaries in the state capital. She was a Juneau Indian and did not speak Tlingit, but she brought to Angoon a thorough knowledge of the workings of the state and federal government, quickly unscrambled the village correspondence, and, with Kookesh, began to investigate possible funding for village improvement.

They had already established a Youth Corps and adult education program and secured the promise of thirty low-income houses from the Tlingit-Haida Central Council when Kookesh died. Now, a month later, his job had been assumed by Cyril, who was on the village council, and the lights continued to burn late in the village office as the couple put together new grant proposals.

Judy had the rounded plumpness that Tlingit men admire and she radiated overpowering good nature. Nothing seemed to ruffle her. Not the fact that her pay check was usually delayed or that she had to take up collecting light bills to earn operating expenses for the town, nor the fact there was no plumbing in her office or that the nearest available rest room was a long sprint away.

The major village problem, she said, was welfare. Ninety-five per cent of the community of four hundred was on welfare, and the village was struggling to retain its dignity while on dole.

"There's a lot of people here that need the money but they'd rather work for it," explained Matthew Fred, Sr., the village social aide who shared the tiny city office. "In 1960 we started

*Judy and Cyril George on the village hall steps.*

negotiating with BIA, trying to get our general assistance money put into a work program. They were reluctant for a long time but, finally, we started in the fall of 1969."

Under the work program, welfare money was used for salaries in the enterprising village public works programs. The jobs were shared by the villagers who were paid according to their family needs. The program maintained water lines, buildings, and roads and helped care for the old people.

Also listed under village problems was the matter of an itinerant preacher, Brother Robert Walker of Arizona, whose visit to Angoon the previous summer had stirred the village almost as much as the old witchcraft scandal. He was a non-denominational preacher, with his own brand of religion, who had arrived pretty much out of the blue with a band of young rock musicians and started holding revival services in the town hall and mass baptisms on the beach. Attracted by the music or the novelty of his preaching or sincere religious fervor, the people of Angoon, especially the young people, flocked to attend.

"At first he told them he needed $9,000 for a boat to do the Lord's work and then, a week later, he amended it to $14,000," Cyril recalled. "Promised the size of the donation would get you into Heaven or Hell and that if people were withholding money he'd know it. We figure he left town with about $9,000 in collections. People were even pledging their wages which they needed to live on through the winter."

Concerned by the money siphoning out of their welfare-dependent settlement, the Angoon council voted to deny Walker use of village buildings and shut off electricity in the Salvation Army hall to which he adjourned with his parish. The village split over the move and those who backed Walker were furious with the council. Angoon officials were publicly cursed in traditional witchcraft style and icon burnings were held on the beach. Walker left shortly thereafter to spread his ministry to other villages, but he promised to return to Angoon soon and take up where he'd left off.

When Cyril and Judy were first married Cyril had stopped commercial fishing because his boat was in disrepair and they both worked full time on Angoon business. Cyril got no salary and Judy's pay check as clerk was being withheld because outside bureaucrats charged nepotism in her hiring in view of Cyril's council seat. No one in the village had her qualifications for the job and after several months her pay came through. They couldn't have survived without the venison that was the mainstay of the Angoon diet, she said. And they still liked it. That evening she quick-fried steaks for us and they were delicious. She served them along with pickled coho salmon hors d'oeuvres. When Tlingits lived off the land, it was gourmet style.

Mrs. Ramona Kookesh, the widow of the last mayor, appeared to be holding up well in the face of her husband's recent death. She was postmistress and currently in the midst of transferring the post office from her living room to a modern, prefabricated trailer nearby. She didn't have time for hysterics.

Originally from New Mexico, she had met Kookesh twenty-nine years before when he was in a sanitarium there with tuberculosis.

"People have changed a lot since I first came here," she volunteered. "More civilized. In the early days when you spoke to them, they'd just hang their heads."

She claimed it was the job as mayor that had killed her husband.

"All those people always at him, complaining. Never letting him alone. I tried to get him to quit. Almost had him talked into it, when he died."

He had left her with the post office, the local oil dealership, and six children. The youngest were twelve and thirteen but the older ones had rallied to help her. At mention of the children her self-possession seemed to waver, but she recovered it.

"My husband was a politician and it was hard on him. Would have killed me, too, all those people complaining," she said. "But his grave was covered with flowers. They came from everywhere. Everybody knew him."

Cyril insisted that for village history it was mandatory that I interview his uncle Robert Zuboff, and eventually I found him inching along on two canes toward the village store. He was a hulking old man with pure white hair and alert eyes.

"The only thing really wrong with me is my legs," he assured me. He was seventy-nine. His wife was hospitalized with cancer in Sitka and he got lonesome, Cyril had said. Introducing myself, I fell into a halting walk beside him, and a watchful raven who trailed along behind eyed me with suspicion. It probably served as Zuboff's winged watchdog.

"Once, thousands of years ago when the Angoon people lived way inland at Tetlin, they got very, very hungry," the elder began without preamble. "There were three brothers and the first went to seek food and never came back—that was in the days when people got so hungry they ate one another. Well, the second brother went out and didn't come back either. So finally the youngest, only seventeen, went out and after traveling a long time he saw a *savage* and got so scared he couldn't run at all."

The way Zuboff pronounced "savage" made me shiver. He was a dramatic storyteller, much on the order of the early days of radio.

"Well, that savage hit that boy with a club, trussed him up, and happily packed him back to his house. Then, leaving his club and knapsack outside the door, he went into his house.

"The young boy came to, cut his way out of the pack, and when that savage reappeared, he clubbed him and clubbed him and *clubbed* him!

"'I know that savage is dead and I did it,' the boy said to himself. 'But he killed my brothers, so what else can I do to hurt him?'

"He decided to burn him and cooked him down to fine white ashes but still he wasn't satisfied. Wanted to hurt him some more so he blew those ashes to the wind. . . . But then those ashes became mosquitoes and they have been *savage* ever since, taking big bites out of everybody!"

Well pleased with himself, he went on to talk about his adventures in Long Beach, California, where he had traveled with his wife some ten years earlier. He said all the girls there went just about naked and he had taken pictures of them to show the people of Angoon. However, his wife had wanted to go to an ice cream parlor and he had set the camera down for only ten minutes and when he got back it was "absent."

"I stood up and I told them, 'I come from Alaska and there, when anyone wants to steal something, they at least wait until after dark!'"

He was easily the finest storyteller I'd ever heard, and he was in rare humor that day.

"A white friend asked me how the Indians get the little worm out of the blueberries. You don't get out the little worm. That's the flavor," he chuckled.

And if I wanted to hear more stories, I was to visit him that evening. He would tell me the history of the world.

Zuboff turned off to do his shopping while the raven waited, and I continued along the wooded road to a small boat harbor. From a distance the fleet looked impressive—fourteen seiners and forty trollers—but close inspection proved it to be a miracle of floating dry rot, and the Angoon fishermen had no money to replace them. Their indebtedness; after the last two disastrous fishing seasons, was said to be in excess of $1.5 million.

While looking over the boats I encountered Frank Jack, the straight-backed, well-muscled owner of the *St. John*. When Angoon had owned the cannery, things had gone well, he told me. Many suspected the fire had been set by someone who didn't want to see the Indians succeed.

"The BIA said we'd be reimbursed for our lost gear but we never were, and we couldn't get them interested in helping with another cannery . . .

"My boat has a lot of dry rot. It will cost about $60,000 to

*Robert Zuboff tells school children a Tlingit legend.*

replace it and I don't know how . . . Seems like since the
Hood Bay fire we've just been drifting . . ."

Frank went to bail out the *St. John* and I walked home
along the shore admiring the tall green spruce and the lively
waters. Ducks and geese swam about, in a variety I had never
seen before. The tidal currents were strong with vicious whirlpools, but the violence of the water was fascinating.

In town I climbed the highest hill to inspect the Alaska Native Brotherhood Hall, built with $90,000 from a Kennedy ad-
ministration grant and $25,000 from the village. It was a fine
facility with kitchens and a beautiful gymnasium, but the kids
were playing basketball there without lights because the electric bill ran so high. Ironically, the hall had been built on the
site of Angoon's ancient tribal war house, but the hill was so
steep that many of the old people, who now largely made up
ANB membership, couldn't make the climb and often the
building sat idle.

For a better view of the town I walked the length of the village dock. Daylight was fading but my eyes were drawn to the
rotting belfry of the old Presbyterian church. Someone was up
there, watching. I blinked and looked again. Afternoon shadows can be deceiving, but I could have sworn someone was
there. I reported it to the Georges. The village was planning to
get a work crew up there to make repairs one of these days, but
nobody had been up this afternoon, they said. Ever since
Matthew Kookesh had died people were seeing him all over
town, but finally we decided the belfry of the Presbyterian
church would be the last place his ghost would want to be.

After a late supper of fried chicken, I took Mary Zwiep to
hear Zuboff tell the history of the world. He began in the Ice
Age with the Angoons trapped behind a glacier up Tetlin way,
but finally they had sent two expendable old women down
river under that glacier, and when they survived, the village
followed on rafts to the sea where salmon and game were plen-
tiful. The Angoons had traveled all over—from Whitewater
Bay to the land of the Chilkats in the north to the open Pacific
in the west—camping four or five hundred years in each loca-

tion until they got into battles and moved on. Zuboff gave a vivid, first-person account of the odyssey, reminding us from time to time that it had all happened thousands of years ago. Then he dug deeper into the past to tell how the Aleutians had been created when the raven tricked the loon out of the water he was hoarding on Hazey Island.

As Zuboff talked, engrossed in his good story, I studied him. He was the last of a line, chief of the Basket Bay people . . . with no direct heirs. His son had drowned. His brother had drowned. He wore his brother's valuable gold-nugget watch fob tucked into the pocket of his cotton work shirt, half hidden by broad suspenders. His house, crowded with modern furniture and heated by belching oil stoves, was the clan house of the Beaver tribe. One of his canes was beautifully carved with the beaver crest and that of the dog salmon who was also close to him.

In accordance with tradition he would pass all this on to his nephew, Cyril George, but relations between the uncle and nephew were strained and Zuboff was searching for another heir. Cyril complained the old man was always lending his tribal heirlooms to the women.

Another family had given Cyril their Tlingit hat, a magnificently carved coho salmon, so he would have something befitting his position to wear at ceremonial dances. It had been presented to him before the family died off, which was unusual but the family wanted to be sure he carried their symbol. Cyril was delighted with the gift but I sensed that he was hurt by his uncle's neglect. He said he didn't believe in a lot of the tribal stuff, that his own sons weren't interested. But as I listened to Zuboff, so proud and jealous of his rich heritage, I knew Cyril George could not ignore it.

Rain had been threatening for a week. Now it came in a steady drizzle but it didn't bother the Tlingits. Southeastern Alaska was technically a rain forest and, if business stopped for the rainy days, there would have been no business.

I struck out in search of the health aide, and Angela Willard

Detwiler, whom I'd met in the post office, volunteered to show me the way to the house. She was a fine-looking woman, back from eight years in Seattle. She had married and helped her husband through school there, had two kids, divorced, and re-married. Now she was home with her new husband, Gary, an ex-boxer. He couldn't find work in Angoon and he couldn't get welfare because he was white. They had moved into a village tribal house with her mother to save rent, but there were objections from the tribe. Her father had been in charge of the house but he had died and her mother, being of another tribe, was not welcome. For a while the Tlingits took it out on her husband, she said, but she didn't seem particularly upset about it. They were beginning to understand Gary. Maybe someone would let him work on a fishing boat the next summer, even though he was inexperienced. The last summer she had supported him by working in a cannery.

I knew Angela's brother, Bob Willard, a highly capable Tlingit who headed the state Human Rights Commission. She seemed every bit as sophisticated as he and volunteered to give me an assessment of Angoon. In the eight years she had been gone there had been no changes that she could notice except that there was now a general electric company and most people had given up their private generators.

We found Barbara Johnson, the health aide, in the midst of cleaning house for an eleven-o'clock patient and the impending visit of the food stamp representative from Juneau. She was a matter-of-fact woman who calmly managed her assignment as Angoon's major medical officer and local food stamp representative along with six children and a husband who served as Angoon's police force.

She had been up all night trying to deliver a baby which had arrived with the cord wrapped around its neck. The child had died. She had called a helicopter to take the mother to the Sitka hospital, but it had trouble landing because the tide was so high that there was no beach. Finally it had come down in an open space miraculously close to the patient's home and the rescue was made.

To add to Barbara's problems, it had just been learned there was diphtheria in the village of Hoonah to the north and that carriers of the disease had been staying in Angoon. She would be glad to give me an interview, she said, but perhaps I could come back a little later. Awed by the overpowering magnitude of her assignment I backed out the door, assuring her I was at her disposal.

That afternoon a meeting of the Community Action Committee was called and Judy lured the members into full attendance with the promise "the ladies will be there." That meant me and Mary and Kai. Apparently people wanted to have a look at us, for the village office had standing room only, and not much of that.

The order of the day was to set priorities of Angoon's needs. Number one was a breakwater to shield the town dock. The small boat harbor was around Danger Point on the other side of town. It could only be reached when the wind wasn't blowing from the north and on slack water, because the tide hit Killisnoo Inlet at twelve to thirteen knots, forming giant whirlpools that would swallow a boat. The run was so dangerous, even under good conditions, that it could only be made with a local pilot, and no boat insurance held past Danger Point.

The ten-year-old village dock was in good shape but unsafe in a blow. A breakwater would shelter it, provide safe anchorage, and encourage more freighters, tankers, and better shipping for the village. Building costs were estimated at about $1.5 million.

In addition, a cold-storage facility was needed so that the fishermen could hold their catch and insure a good price. There was much debate about Peter Pan Seafoods with whom the Angoon fleet had been forced to deal for lack of other interest since their cannery fire. Some of the fisherman wanted to abandon Peter Pan. The rest argued that that would be sure starvation. Either way, a cold storage would give them a new option.

The Angoons also wanted to be put on the state ferry run. Their only scheduled transportation was by air and a round-

trip ticket from Juneau was $42. In the neighboring village of
Hoonah you could make the trip by ferry for about a quarter
of the price. The boat was routed right by Angoon and it was a
major source of frustration that it wouldn't stop.

No one moved for action, though, in the hour I listened. The
Angoons talked in terms of writing resolutions as they had
done for fruitless decades of ANB conventions and of having
someone from the Office of Economic Opportunity—namely,
Mary Zwiep—draw up proposals. It was what the VISTA volunteer called the "Santa Claus syndrome" and privately she as-
sessed Angoon's major problem as a need for enterprise.

"What it boils down to is they're getting screwed by Peter
Pan," she said candidly. "And I don't know if there's anything
I can do about that."

I abandoned the meeting to hear Robert Zuboff address the
Angoon second- and third-grade classes. It took him so long to
walk to the school that the fourth-grader in escort feared the
class might recess before they arrived, but the students were
patient. Laboriously the old man hefted his huge bulk up the
school steps, recalling with frustration how he had once carried home two deer at a time weighing three hundred pounds.

After the session I lingered to talk with a teacher of many
years' Angoon experience. She liked the school and the Indians, she said, but, despite successive Head Start programs,
the children were backward. They didn't know their colors or
the general information most white kids just picked up on their
own, and they had very limited vocabularies despite the fact
they no longer spoke much Tlingit. There was a lot of drinking
and carrying on in the village, although she conceded, the
children were, for the most part, well fed and cared for.

"Inbred to low intelligence in many cases," she suggested.
And the witchcraft thing was far from dead. "I was in a home
the other night when a kid came in and said, 'A lot of witchcraft going on tonight!' It's there but they just don't like to talk
about it."

When I got to Zuboff's evening storytelling session, I found
him in the company of Albert Frank, seventy, who was local

*The boat harbor.*

president of Tlingit-Haida. Since Zuboff's direct bloodline had died out, he had "adopted" Albert as his brother and was passing on all the old stories to him. At this sitting we heard about the sea lion as big as an island and the Tlingits' strongest man who overcame ridicule to conquer the animal. Zuboff was disappointed that I hadn't brought a tape recorder, but I told him I'd take notes and that I was really here to work on contemporary problems. Albert told me briefly of the founding of ANB and how the organization had finally won full citizenship for the Tlingits. But the old stories interested the two old men most and I was happy to listen.

Later I was accosted by Mrs. Albert Frank who mistook me for the visiting food stamp lady and made an impassioned plea for more stamps. Fishing had been poor. Her husband was too old to work. Three of her children lived at home. One was only twelve and another had a new baby and the older son was out of work.

"I'm not the food stamp lady," I kept protesting. "No, I'm the newspaper reporter."

Either way, she said.

Zuboff summoned me at ten the next morning and, having been scolded for lateness on the previous occasion, I arrived promptly. He checked his watch and, satisfied, launched into a story of how the dog salmon got his beautiful markings from a tree shadow and red earth. They had been given to him by the bear as payment for the loss of his brothers and sisters which the bear had eaten, and, lucky for us, that bear didn't eat them all.

Then, for the first time, the old man talked of more current events. When his wife was first crippled with arthritis, he had taken her to California to see the faith healer Oral Roberts.

"But all those ministers ever want is money," he had decided. That's why he hadn't been fooled by the evangelist and the "jumping-up-and-down religion" that had hit Angoon the previous summer. He also spoke about his people's long fight for equal citizenship and for their land.

"The foreigners, the Russians, came and we licked them too, but then they turned around and sold this place to the United States." He shook his head, suddenly angry. "The white man is teaching us to forgive, forgive! That's one thing we haven't got, us Indians. Forgive your neighbor! Forgive your brother! Forgive your sister! *We don't do that!*"

It had never occurred to me, but when I recalled Tlingit history, it involved a repetition of revenge. I had been raised to believe that forgiveness was a virtue, but the Tlingits believed it a weakness. How differently the world must look to them.

Finally, Zuboff spoke of his Basket Bay people.

"When I was a boy there were lots of them. Now they are dying off, dying off." Almost desperately he began to recall individual members of the tribe who were still alive. There were two in Sitka, one working in Anchorage, another in Juneau . . .

"We still got a lot of them," he concluded with relief.

The visiting food stamp representative was at Barbara Johnson's and I stopped in to see if Mrs. Albert Frank had found her. Of course she had. Barbara was not particularly proud of Angoon's wholehearted participation in the stamp program and she wanted to know if I had heard of their work relief program.

"Some of us don't feel right to just get a check," she explained. "We worked out this program so we could work. We got us this social aide. If parents are drinking, the social aide is supposed to take over. When kids drop out of school, he's supposed to take over. It's worked out well going on three years."

Kai Dickey all this time had been meeting with Head Start mothers and teachers. I was impressed with the woman power, but she said she had had more trouble with them than any other group and she didn't know why. The whole place gave her "strange vibes," she said. Shortly after she had landed she complained to Mary that her tape recorder and radio refused to work and she felt really spooked. Kai knew nothing of Angoon's witchcraft incident, but I'd been impressed enough by reports of it to check with Mrs. Marie Day who had served as acting U. S. Commissioner at the time of the incident and had chaired the public hearings.

It had started when an imaginative sixteen-year-old Tlingit girl began holding nightly vigils during which dire pronouncements were made against "non-believers," Mrs. Day recalled. The girl had testified under oath that on several occasions she had turned into a cat when touched by a bone held by one of the witches during rites performed at the Indian cemetery. And several villagers backed her story, also under oath. The police chief reported becoming a believer after he saw a man turn into a bird and a fisherman had moved out of the village after his boat was cursed.

"I think it was just cabin fever," Mrs. Day maintained stoutly. "The girl had apparently hexed some children. There was a lot of measles and flu around that winter and this child had happened to die. It was weird. Nothing really made sense. They were burning fires at midnight . . . killing cats."

Villagers I queried on the subject said the sooner it was forgotten, the better. Most of the principals, including the girl and the police chief, had moved out of Angoon, but unfortunately some of the people who had been carried away by witchcraft had also become involved with the traveling preacher the summer before and the hysteria died hard.

At the suggestion of the Tlingit leader John Borbridge, I budgeted a good percentage of my time for interviews with Lydia George and I wasn't disappointed. At first she appeared overboastful but I soon decided it was simply from the frustration of not being recognized, for after she had completed her assignment of documenting Angoon's land selection she had been voted out of office on the grounds, she claimed, that she lacked education and was a woman.

"You rest and I'll take over where you left off," promised one of her sons who now studies law. And she was trying to stay out of things, but it wasn't easy. The conservative thinking of the majority of villagers really tried her patience.

ANB had that week passed a resolution chiding stateside Indians for vandalizing the Department of Interior Building in Washington, D.C. And, closer to home, the Angoons had recently voted against a high school, despite the fact their youngsters had to travel far from home to continue their educations and few ever returned. Lydia and the Cyril Georges had apparently been the minority in favor of the school. The official argument against it was that Angoon wouldn't be able to run anything but a second-rate facility. Unofficially, according to a survey Mary was making, the villagers didn't want to go to the expense of feeding their youngsters during the winter. Let BIA do it.

Yet Lydia didn't appear to harbor any bitterness about the local politics. She was an exuberant little woman, enthusiastic about her family and devoted to her husband although he was nearly forty years her senior. Her husband, Jimmie George, studied me without ever acknowledging my presence during the interview, but Lydia was outgoing and friendly and invited me back to use their fine collection of Tlingit history books.

That evening I went with Mary to visit Kai and the Assembly of God family with whom she was staying. Church was in session and we entered in mid-service to find eight adult Tlingits, two children, and the minister's wife in attendance. It was a conventional service until the close when the minister announced prayer and everyone crouched down low in the separate pews to pray aloud. Occasionally parishioners would peek over the top of their barricades, turning to see if everybody else was still praying and I found it unnerving. I had kept my seat in the back of the room, and the sight of those strange Indian faces popping up suddenly over the bench backs was too reminiscent of old Russian accounts of Tlingit attack. Had it been fifty years earlier, I would have departed long before the final "amen."

The Reverend Mr. Olson and his unusually pretty wife turned out to be charming people and long-time Alaskans. Their original ministry had been among the Athabascans of Minto on the Tanana River and I suspected that's where their hearts still were. But they said they enjoyed Angoon.

"It is just like civilization," Olson said with a smile.

Our close neighbors were the William Nelsons, and in passing their windows I had noticed a display of photos of military men. When I inquired, Mrs. Nelson invited me in to meet her husband, William Nelson, Sr., and inspect the collection. The photos were of their sons—one Marine wounded in Vietnam, another still there, and a third safely in and out of the Army.

Over coffee they learned that I was interested in Tlingit history and promptly produced a photograph of Katanook, the early Tlingit teacher, who had been their uncle. He had gone through the Russian seminary at Sitka, but the photo showed him resplendent in East Indian garb. It had been taken during his tour of New York, they explained.

Then William proudly brought out his Tlingit war hat, which was one of the finest I'd ever seen. It was cleverly carved in the form of a raven, with old Russian coins for eyes and an ermine skin dangling from its beak. Its wings were tufted with the hair of a Tlingit maiden and crowning it was a chestnut-haired scalp that was said to have belonged to an ancient witch doctor. Half jokingly they warned against touching the scalp and I readily complied. According to early explorers, Tlingits universally had blueish-black hair, so the raven's topknot might well have belonged to one of my seafaring ancestors.

Until recently the hat had never been shown to outsiders, Mrs. Nelson said. In fact, they hadn't known of its existence until the family that owned it died out and they found themselves in line to inherit it. It had cost them several thousand dollars to acquire. Under tribal law such heirlooms, as well as certain names and songs, were purchased, and in this case the Nelsons had had to meet expenses for four burials to take

custody. They were sure the hat was very old, though. Before
it had been repainted you could see dried blood on it.

Although I would have preferred to limit my inquiries in the
village to Tlingit history, eventually I found courage to interview the backers of Brother Walker, the itinerant preacher. The
mainstay of his ministry turned out to be Frank Jack, owner
of the *St. John,* and his wife Beth. I understood that Beth Jack
was particularly devout and so I directed my questions to her.
She was an enormous though well-proportioned woman, with
intense eyes and a wreath of wiry gray-black hair framing her
face. She said her husband knew much more about it than she
did, but she dominated the conversation and in the heat of her
fervor, I felt like a spot on the rug.

"Brother Walker, he gave us the hard meat of the Bible and
some of them couldn't take it," she declared And she dispelled
rumors that he would be back in December when the fishermen were due to collect their bonus checks.

"Brother Walker says he won't come back until the doors of
this town are open to him," she said firmly. He had been
treated shabbily and a few hearts would have to turn before he
would accept them.

We were joined by a young matron who was president of
the Head Start mothers. She, too, testified at length on the
wondrous powers of Brother Walker. It was the same spirit I
had seen among the "Jesus" movements in California and it
did not upset me.

The rain stopped briefly and I took advantage of the lull to
walk beyond the boat harbor to visit the Sam Johnsons. Millie,
a sprightly Tlingit grandmother, was the last traditional basket-
maker of Angoon and probably the entire tribe. Patiently she
explained how spruce roots were gathered, cut into fine weaving material, dyed, and worked to intricate patterns. She had
just acquired some new stock from a woman in Juneau who was
too sick to weave any more. I asked if she would teach the art
to a younger person to keep it alive.

"I might, but I don't think anyone is interested," she said evenly. "I wouldn't want to force it on anyone."

Sam Johnson, seventy-four, was painting a skiff. He still fished every season with his sons and the doctor told him to keep out in the fresh air.

"Like a motor, I've got to keep running."

He had been mayor of Angoon around 1915, then commissioner of the area. Under his administration the first church had been built as well as the Salvation Army hall and the village hall.

"We weren't allowed in the public schools," he recalled. "But we had white friends. They said, 'You must get your own to work among you.'"

I asked about the future.

"You and your white sisters, I hope you'll help us," he said.

"I think the Indians are strong enough to help themselves," I replied, not meaning to be unkind. But the answer bothered him and quickly he dismissed me.

Dissatisfied with the first interview I had had at the school, I returned to talk to another teacher and got a very different view of the Angoon youth.

"I think they all do just fine," she said, and she suggested perhaps Angoon children scored lower than average in placement tests because they came from large families and were used to dividing up the labor. The one who was good at math usually did everybody's figuring and the one who was good at writing wrote the letters.

With her husband the teacher had been adopted into the tribal system. The traditional Tlingit potlatches—pay-off parties—had been banned in the 1800s by American educators and missionaries who believed them to be a waste of the Indian's resources, but they were still popular in Angoon, she reported. There were several occasions for throwing them. For example, if a man died it was the duty of another clan to bury him, and then the clan of the deceased would pay the other

clan for their services. She had seen as many as forty-five people get paid $60 apiece for helping with a funeral. But since,
under tribal law, husband and wife had to be of different
clans, pay-offs generally stayed in the family.

William Nelson agreed to pose for photographs in his war
hat and we took advantage of the morning light. Majestically
he donned his button-trimmed ceremonial blanket, brushed his
hair, and set the hat on squarely. Then, when the film was shot,
the heirlooms were carefully packed away.

Would I care to hear a tape they'd recorded of the old people dancing and singing a few years ago in Sitka, the family
asked. The chantlike Tlingit melodies, accompanied by the
beat of a wooden drum, were great dance music, and Mrs.
Nelson, a plump woman (despite the fact she had just lost ten
pounds at Weight Watchers), swayed to the beat with considerable grace. I was so taken with her style, in fact, I didn't notice until practically the end that her head was encased in
blue plastic curlers.

Tribal affairs were still more important here than government business, William said. And much of the old culture remained. There were still the caves, one on the south side of
Whitewater Bay with the body of a long-dead witch doctor
covered with an animal skin. His hair was still there and his
toenails had grown enormously long; William had seen him
many times. There was a cave nearer the village too.

"Aren't you afraid to enter?"

"No," he said. "He is of our tribe and I tell him, 'I am of your
tribe, of your tribe.'"

I worried lest anthropologists disturb their witch doctors,
but the Nelsons said they were safe—Lydia George had marked
off a location for them in Angoon land selection. And indeed
she had. Proudly she showed me the maps and I was impressed
with the careful detail of her work. Every sacred place had
been marked—all the old village sites and burial places.

*William Nelson, Sr., in his war hat.*

Hesitantly, I then broached the subject of witchcraft with Lydia, pointing out that witchcraft cults were in vogue again in New York and California.

"It hurt Angoon. It blackened the face of our village," she insisted. "When Cyril George and I went to the AFN Convention they asked, 'Is the Angoon delegation here? If you don't see them here, you go down and look in the broom closet!' "

She and her husband, Jimmie, had been working outside of the village during the early witchcraft incident, but they'd been home to witness the coming of Brother Walker and people said there was much the same spell-binding element in his sessions.

"We do know the power of evil exists in the world. I, myself, have never seen this thing," she said carefully. "Maybe it's because I married a man who was very religious."

I pressed her. Who had been publicly cursed at Walker's sessions?

"They said the mayor would go crazy and that Matthew Fred would die and that Cyril George would die. They also spoke against my husband and my best friend. They said if either my best friend or I would die, the one that was left would go to Walker's church."

Matthew Fred hadn't known he was cursed until he woke that night and found that someone had turned up his stove until it was glowing red. He probably would have burned to death if he hadn't awakened when he did, she speculated. And his children were among Walker's congregation.

The full impact of these events was frightening, as the villagers described them. The mayor, Kookesh, was said to have taken to drink like a madman that summer and died shortly thereafter. Perhaps Mrs. Kookesh had been right when she charged that the people had killed him. And now Matthew Fred was going the same route. He roamed the streets at all hours like a ghost. He was an educated man, but he had been cursed and he must be frightened. If enough people believed something would happen, it would happen. Both Lydia's best friend and her husband had gotten sick after they were cursed. Only Cyril George, it seemed, had been able to shrug off dire predictions.

Luckily, Judy and Cyril intruded on my morbid speculation to provide a tour of the far end of Angoon, from which I could study Killisnoo Island. In the late 1800s Killisnoo had been the site of a fish-processing plant and a much larger settlement than Angoon. Before a devastating fire destroyed it in the thirties, it had grown to a formidable settlement with a lavishly decorated Russian Orthodox church and imposing waterfront. The Nelsons had photos of it in its heyday and I'd also heard of Killisnoo from the Aleuts of Atka who had been evacuated there during World War II. Half the population of Atka was buried in Killisnoo, but today it did not look sinister. Towering spruce had grown to shield the rotting old cannery buildings from the harsh winds of Chatham Strait.

The ladies of the Head Start program were holding a bake sale when I returned and I went to support it. Good news, announced Barbara Johnson. We had all been exposed to diphtheria for certain. Shots would start Monday if the plane got in with some vaccine.

Just what the hell exactly *was* diphtheria? I hurried home to look it up: "An acute contagious bacterial disease marked by fever and by coating of the air passages with a membrane that interferes with breathing." And my shots had expired a full year earlier.

Judy came home with the *Harvard·Lampoon* edition of *Cosmopolitan* Magazine and its nude center fold of Dr. Henry Kissinger, and if anything could have cheered me, that was it. But I remained upset and that night I was nervously roaming the streets in the wake of Matthew Fred. Not many were attending the Bingo game at the town hall, but lights in the ANB building were reassuring. Some philanthropist had at last turned on the electricity and just about every kid in town was over there, involved in a wild, free-form game of basketball. The teams had been picked with no regard for sex, size, age, or race, yet they were well matched. There were no supervising adults and no need for any. Kids who had been excluded from the lineup, cheered from the sidelines and the rest played fiercely.

There were three churches in Angoon besides Brother Walker's. The Russian church was closed because Jimmie George, Lydia's husband, hadn't been feeling well enough to lead services. I had already attended an Assembly of God gathering, so I decided to try the Presbyterian Sunday service. At 11 A.M. the bell pealed with an authority that belied the church's slim congregation of old-timers. Mary, the VISTA worker, and Judy were the youngest in attendance, with Cyril and me next.

Si Peck, a powerfully built Tlingit, who had trained for the ministry and quit just short of ordination, delivered the sermon. It was highly polished, in excellent English, and included a bilingual rendition of Psalm 145: ". . . One generation shall praise thy works to another and shall declare thy mighty acts." The theme was thanksgiving, and again and again Peck touched on the material things they were blessed with. Never had I heard such references in Eskimo or Athabascan country but the Tlingits had judged man's worth by material wealth long before the coming of the whites.

After the service Cyril's mother, Letty George, and her sister Emma Hamberg came back with the town's "most eligible bachelor," an old-timer named Charlie Joseph, and we breakfasted on waffles with canned wild berries. To make conversation I mentioned the basketball game I had seen the night before, but Charlie, an ANB member, complained about the electric bill and I found Mrs. Hamberg easier to talk with. She had studied at the Sheldon Jackson School, a missionary public school for natives in Sitka, and returned to Angoon a well-educated woman. Later she met and married a literate Swede, and they had helped bring Cyril up. That's why he spoke such fluent English, she explained.

Cyril's mother, a Sheldon Jackson drop-out, was the quieter of the two sisters. Good-naturedly she accepted kidding about her lack of scholastic prowess and her awkward first attempts at basketmaking. I knew her to be a handy woman, for she had skillfully sewn two pairs of bead-trimmed fur slippers for me a few days earlier.

Talk turned to the old ways and I mentioned the Tlingit war hat with the witch doctor scalp that I had photographed.

"That wasn't a witch doctor. You must have misunderstood," Mrs. Hamberg said sharply. "We didn't have *witch* doctors. Although there were Indian doctors."

I had read about Indian doctors, I told her. They had known much good medicine. In fact, Zuboff had said they had discovered an hallucinogenic like "Mary-wanna," although I didn't think I should mention that to her.

"They did have many cures," Mrs. Hamberg recalled. "But the young people make fun of us, saying it's old-fashioned to dig for the roots."

Monday was a good day, for Ramona Kookesh hoisted the American flag on the metal staff of the prefabricated post office and opened for business. It was a completely modern facility except for the postage scale. Her new one had broken in transit and she had unearthed a substitute that looked as if it belonged in a museum.

Matthew Fred had stopped drinking and was on his job too, and I interviewed him to find him such an articulate, reasonable man that I forgot all about curses and witchcraft.

At noontime I went to borrow one of Lydia's books and found her in the midst of cooking a double lunch. Her young son Garfield was having spaghetti and meatballs while she and her husband preferred the traditional dried fish. Old-timers recalled that before the coming of the whites the Tlingits never had bad teeth and when they first tasted sugar they had spit it out saying it was terrible. But you couldn't keep the modern generation from sweets and starches, and they kept the dentist busy.

Zuboff was being visited by Albert Frank when I arrived for the usual storytelling session, but the old storyteller had one ear glued to his radio. Three Tlingit hunters had drowned off

Sitka and the announcer said to stay tuned for identification. For once he let Albert do the talking and an astonishing monologue resulted. It was almost as though Albert had finally translated all the questions I had been fruitlessly asking all week and worked the answers back into English.

Originally the white man had not wanted the Indians to go to school, he said, but in the early 1900s a Presbyterian minister, Sheldon Jackson, had started classes for them and Albert had been lucky enough to attend.

"Everything was free in the first beginning. We ate good, too. And it was a good help to our people. Then the whites were going to kill Sheldon Jackson. Said he wasn't going to leave Sitka alive. So we Indians stole Sheldon Jackson. Hid him. Moses Jamestown led, singing 'We're Paddling Our Own Canoe.'

"We had to fight for our rights. Even though we were born and raised here we were not citizens. The ANB was started in 1912 but it was a long fight.

"About 1918 we decided, 'Let's start living like the white man!' We started the town council and improved our living conditions in Angoon. We built a path for our younger people.

"They passed a law the Indians were going to have local, municipal self-government. We can arrest each other but cannot arrest the white man. Can only complain to Juneau . . .

"Through the town council and the ANB we demand the school be given here. Put in coal-oil street lights. Think about electricity. Bought a little motor that throws a lot of light. Everybody happy. Later on people decided they wanted a bigger light plant. Raised the money in just one evening . . .

"In over fifty years from the time I can remember, I've seen a lot of change take place in Angoon, and all for the better!"

Zuboff sat unheeding, melancholy. The radio gave out the name of one hunter. Then the announcer reported the murder of Tom Dillon, the Bethel police chief I had interviewed only a few weeks earlier, and I became as melancholy as Zuboff. Thanking Albert for his concise summary of Angoon development, I left to walk a quiet path.

That afternoon I attended one of Art Demmert's Tlingit language classes and it was a welcome break. Demmert was a Tlingit, an affable bear of a man, totally enthusiastic about his job. This was the second year he had taught Tlingit in the school. He had three classes and they were doing well.

"If we don't pick it up now, the Tlingit language will be dead in a hundred years. Most of the parents speak it but none of the children."

It was a tough tongue but Demmert was a patient teacher. He had full teaching credentials and long experience, and he knew better than most instructors the limited attention span of his young charges. In mid-class, after a concentrated grammar session, they adjourned to the music room to entertain me with English renditions of "This Land Is Your Land" and "Spinning Wheels." Demmert played the piano like a talented madman and it was a good show. Then they returned to Tlingit with equal vigor.

After class I talked with a school administrator who confirmed the fact that Angoon youngsters scored below the rest of the state in academic testing and added that the school was not a good one. The state-operated school system was hopelessly bogged down in its own paperwork; it lacked funding and seemed completely unaware of the needs of remote communities.

"And although the Tlingits have long been exposed to white society, they violently resisted it," he observed. "Some of that resistance still remains."

A sign posted on the town bulletin board reported that no diphtheria vaccine had arrived but I found Barbara Johnson giving shots. She had located a small supply of vaccine which had been left in the school refrigerator by a traveling public health nurse. Since the children were 95 per cent up on their shots, she was using it for older people.

I had talked earlier to Kai Dickey, now back in Juneau, to learn she had been directly exposed to the Hoonah carrier and was not sure her shots were good. Barbara put out a call to the

*Angoon youngsters with Tlingit painting done in conjunction with their language class.*

Head Start mothers immediately and gave me a shot too. Whether it would do any good at this late date no one knew, but we could hope. Rumor had it that Hoonah was under quarantine with forty people sick and two dead. How horrible it must have been to sit out something like this a hundred years ago without vaccine or even a hazy notion of what precautions to take.

In past years Angoon town council meetings had apparently been fairly mysterious, usually held behind closed doors. Now Cyril George announced a public meeting and it was well attended. As the Community Action Committee had done earlier, the villagers discussed priorities.

"Twenty years have passed and we're no better off than we ever were," noted Danny Johnson, assistant social aide. "I think it's time we moved. If we can get this breakwater, I'm pretty sure we can develop some industry. Metlakatla has a two-million-dollar boat harbor. Hoonah is getting a two-million-dollar boat harbor. Yakutat has their million-dollar cold-storage plant . . ."

Cyril George agreed. "I'm beginning to see what Yakutat is getting . . . What Hoonah is getting, and we're getting nothing. I feel like Tennessee Ernie Ford—I owe my soul to the company store."

Peter Jack, top vote-getter on the council and one of Angoon's most successful fishermen, summed the problem up.

"I never made less than top ten [fishermen] for Peter Pan, yet I never made any headway on my bills. Who knows where we'd be if our cannery hadn't burned. If someone had been there to put the fire out. But unless we do something now, in twenty years Angoon is going to be the same. We don't have deep water. We don't have a harbor. We don't have nothing!"

Peter Jack had broken away from the Angoon fleet the year before and successfully fished for a cannery owned by the Metlakatla Indians. Now he urged other men to do the same. Peter Pan was refusing to insure some of the fleet and there was talk of sitting on the beach the next season rather than fishing for them. But there was opposition, too. Wisely, Cyril brought discussion back to priorities and there was argument over which was most important.

"We'll have ten number-one priorities," the mayor finally decided, and we adjourned so he could write up some more grant proposals.

It was a good meeting.

"Just in the last year I've seen a lot of enthusiasm," Peter Jack observed. "They never used to attend meetings on anything like that. They'd do all their talking after the meeting and we never did follow up. Mainly I think it's that they never had seen any results. I don't know if the land claims settlement had anything to do with it or not, but people are beginning to believe they might make things happen."

Opinion was divided on the effectiveness of the regional Tlingit organization. Many villagers were enthusiastic about John Borbridge because they liked him personally and had respected his father who was raised in Killisnoo. Some, like Lydia George, had watched him pioneer the land claims and admired his leadership ability.

"Nobody can fill his shoes. Not yet," she said thoughtfully. "And he still listens to us. With Borbridge I can actually call Washington and get something done. Before him we were not heard."

The opposition charged that Borbridge had become a "Godfather," misused his power, and, like many native leaders, overestimated his importance.

"Some of them think they're gods or something," fumed one Angoon politician. "We all came up from the same place about the same time. At a recent Tlingit-Haida meeting one of them had the nerve to tell us only he and John Borbridge were *qualified* to sit on the AFN board. Well, we've got some good people, too. And we haven't got twenty Angoon youngsters going to college for nothing!"

One afternoon I settled into the warmth of Lydia and Jimmie George's living room for a pleasant visit. For the first time Jimmie acknowledged my presence and even went so far as to allow me to photograph his handsome Tlingit ceremonial cape and killer whale war hat while Lydia unearthed a number of other precious artifacts. Their home was the tribal house of the killer whale. The old markings of their tribal crest had been painted over at the insistence of the missionaries, but the dim outlines still showed through. Proudly they spoke of it and of the traditions they hoped to preserve for their children.

During Alaska's centennial observance in 1967 the Angoon Tlingits had been invited to dance and celebrate in Sitka, Lydia recalled with a smile, but they turned down the invitation.

"We were the only Tlingits to do so, but we were never conquered by the Russians. Why should we celebrate being sold to the United States?"

There was talk Angoon might be quarantined and Mary Zwiep had been teasing me about spending Christmas and New Year's in the village. She could afford to be flip—her shots were still good. But I had assignments lined up that I didn't care to miss, and finally I phoned the hospital at Mount Edgecumbe to find out how the epidemic was faring. The original carrier had come to Hoonah from Seattle, according to a Mount Edgecumbe doctor, but luckily all the Hoonah children had been vaccinated and older villagers got shots immediately. Two cases of the rumored forty had ended up at Mount Edgecumbe hospital. No one had died and Hoonah wasn't quarantined. There had been no new cases in ten days.

His optimism was reassuring, but early next morning I was awakened by the roar of an unscheduled plane. During the night an Angoon resident had displayed all the symptoms of diphtheria and Barbara Johnson had chartered a flight to take him to the hospital. She had yet to receive any vaccine and, fearing quarantine might still be imminent, Mary and I made reservations on a bush flight that afternoon.

Luckily I had most of the interviews I needed and there was time for a leisurely round of good-bys. I found Robert Zuboff in good spirits again, enjoying a pinch of snuff. He had tried all sorts of things to keep the tobacco moist but the best was a drop or two of sweet wine, he confided.

Today the Metlakatla Indians were on the storytelling program. Had I heard how the minister Father Duncan had lead them from persecution in Canada to settle on Alaska's Annette Island?

"Those Indians took a lot from the Canadians, but what really made them move was the jail. The Canadians built this big jail. Painted one half white, one half black. Then they started buying frogs for fifty cents each and the Indians were glad to sell them for such a good price. But the Canadians filled the jail with those frogs and put the Indians in that jail naked and the frogs had suckers on them . . . and that's when the Metlakatlas took off.

"Father Duncan built a new village for them and installed a church bell and announced that Sunday was his day. The chief didn't agree for he was planning a big funeral party for his uncle on that day and when Father Duncan rang the church bell, the chief shot it . . ."

That reminded him of the funeral service that had been held the previous night for a stillborn baby. He asked anxiously if I had attended and I said I had not.

"I did not go either," he said. "A baby like that, the old-timers would have hidden it in a stump. No service. Not tell anybody. If they hold a service it will be very bad luck to that family."

I observed that perhaps they had already had bad luck. It was the third child they had lost. But the old storyteller just shook his head.

On the way home to pack I encountered Angela Detwiler's mother who answered the question that had been bothering me about bears. Although the grizzlies often attacked whites, I had never heard any reports of Tlingits coming to grief with them and I wondered why.

A long time ago, when she had been young, she recalled going berrypicking with her mother, grandmother, and husband.

She had been the last one dressed that morning and they had all gone ahead, leaving her to catch up alone.

"As I came over the hill there was a big bear and I said to him, 'Don't be afraid. We will not hurt you because we only come to get our living.' We talk to the bears in Tlingit and they understand."

On this, my last day, the sun finally honored Angoon and I arrived on a bluff overlooking town as light shot through the rain to create a vivid rainbow over the dock. Surely this is where the gold must lie in Angoon, I decided. And I went to get a final summary of its problems from the village office.

Point by point I went over my Borbridge interview with the Cyril Georges.

"We're pressed by short-term needs," Borbridge had said. "Better housing . . . better standard of living. But we've got to look beyond these needs. The initial steps will be profit seeking investment.

"Part of our money may have to go into areas of capitalization for native businesses. There's a lot of businesses we'd like to see get off the ground. We know that venture capital is hard for them to find. And if we don't provide it, they'll say, 'What's the difference between your organization and the bank? They both say no to us.'"

But generally Borbridge talked in terms of investment institutions, outside experts, statewide banking. Borbridge's salary as president of Sealaska was $35,000 a year which was fairly modest in view of what some other regional corporation directors were receiving but his views didn't differ much from most of theirs. Most of them dreaded the idea of dissipating their capital on social services and economic development in areas where the profit margin was doubtful.

But Borbridge's philosophy didn't generate too much enthusiasm in a village that couldn't afford to pay a mayor or business manager and had a median income of $2,154.

According to the congressional land claims settlement, Angoon was due for a share of royalty revenues received by its regional corporation but estimates on the amount of money were vague. To date, out of the $7.5 million court settlement the village had gotten $250 per capita grants for its older residents and $2,400 for village planning. Angoon had been promised but hadn't received $26,000 for village planning for the year and a housing project that was to be ready for occupancy by Thanksgiving (the next week) but hadn't even broken ground. And, understandably, the Georges and most knowing Angoon citizens were cynical about any bonanzas.

Barbara Johnson summed up their thinking when she was investigating funding for a much-needed alcoholism program for the village.

"Nobody's going to help us. We're going to have to help ourselves!" she said. But with that realization came a new and refreshing idea—that although Angoon was on the bottom of its political totem pole, the villagers might have some power to help with the carving. And as I took my leave of the Angoon town office, I definitely heard the sharpening of chisels.

# Living Off the Land

When explorers investigated Alaska in the mid-1700s, they found a population of tough, hardy natives living very well off nature. Even the Eskimos who dwelled in the extreme reaches of the Arctic made a fair living off the land, and the Indians who had settled along the coast and interior river systems where fish and game were abundant subsisted with enviable ease, enjoying an extraordinary amount of leisure time.

As the Alaskans became familiar with the white man's culture, they came to desire and then to depend on some of its manufactured goods, for the white man's iron and steel made better knives than native copper, his guns were surer and more deadly than any native weapon, and his sugar, flour, tea, and coffee added welcome variety to a wild-game diet. Yet the natives retained much that was good and useful of their early ways. For the most part, their villages were too isolated to work easily into the new cash economy and the goods of the whites were not easy to come by.

In the Canadian north the civilization of the whites made greater encroachment. Overhunted fur-bearing and game animals went into decline and the natives suffered extreme hardship, succumbing to disease and famine. By the 1950s their plight was so dire it became a cause célèbre, with Canadians, and a massive government program of relief and development was quickly instituted. The basic premise of the Canadian policy was the assumption that hunting and fishing could no

longer provide the natives with the minimal living re-
quirements acceptable either to the natives or to the
government and that therefore a welfare and wage
economy should be allowed to take over. By 1965 most
northern Canadian natives had moved into new, concentrated, government-staffed villages, and subsistence
hunting and fishing virtually disappeared as a way of
life.

Alaskan natives, too, endured disease and poverty,
but they benefited from the neglect of their government
to the extent that much of their culture remained intact.
Gradually their leaders acquired education and enough
understanding of the workings of politics to demand
increased benefits from white society, but even as they
pushed a monumental land claims settlement through
the United States Congress in 1971, over 70 per cent of
their people remained dependent on subsistence hunting and fishing.

The desire of the Alaskan natives to move further into
the cash economy was recognized with the billion-dol-
lar cash payment to settle their land claims, but law-
makers also recognized, respected, and attempted to
perpetuate the subsistence culture by granting the natives forty million acres of land.

Some predicted the two lifestyles—cash economy and
subsistence living—would become irreconcilable, that
industrial development by natives themselves would eat
into lands reserved for subsistence hunting. But natives
who successfully combined occasional seasonal employment with living off the land liked the lifestyle, and
there materialized a determined fight to preserve the
old way.

Never had I realized the wonderful freedom of living off the
land until I watched Alaskan natives heading into the wilds

with seeming casualness, armed with little more than a knife, a gun, ammunition, and a bit of salt. The land still provided! It was cruel, sometimes, but with cunning, man could make it his amenable host.

This worked best, it seemed to me, along the Yukon River, for the country was unusually rich and the Athabascan people managed a fine combination of two cultures there. Most of the Indians worked for wages part of the year but reserved the better half to pursue their hunting heritage. Whites tended to question the Indian's affinity for the land, for the Athabascans also enjoyed jet air travel and deep freezes and television. But the Indians' first love was the trackless wilderness that lay within easy access of their modern settlements.

When I decided to write about subsistence living, I chose to return to Galena for its residents had recently grown impatient with white outsiders who were invading their game preserves. The land claims settlement legislation hadn't been implemented to the point where they could legally protect their lands, so they had attempted to sink a six-passenger float plane moored by a party of outside hunters at the village. They had failed to destroy the craft completely, but they managed to ruin the pontoons, estimated by the pilot to be worth $9,600, and made their point. Outsiders moved to friendlier shores and the Indians again hunted in peace.

I chose Galena, also, for personal reasons for I had been very happy living among the Athabascans. Perhaps it had just been a moment in time. Perhaps it was something deeper. I wasn't sure why, but I very much wanted to return.

The summer following my first stay in Galena in 1972, I had toured the night spots in Fairbanks with Carlson Malemute and some of his friends who were in town for forest fire-fighter training under the Bureau of Land Management. In Galena I had seen Malemute at his best, ably handling a boat in deadly, drift-filled waters and picking hunting trails through the rough woods of the interior. In Fairbanks I saw him at his worst, drinking until he and his cronies ran through every dime they

*A winter morning on the Yukon at the Malemute fish camp.*

had earned or could borrow. He was a crew boss, however, and no matter how rough the party, he always managed to make it to work in fair shape next day. He was honest and he was fun. I thought him a good man, and I had asked him if he would take me on his trap line the next winter. He said he would and, with that in mind, he had spent $1,100 of his summer wages on a new snowmobile. Usually he partied away all his pay checks, he admitted. This was his first major investment.

I arrived in Galena in early December 1972 in a snowstorm. The jet was three hours late and since I hadn't heard from Carlson for a few weeks, I doubted he would meet me. The family was planning to go down river for some dog-sled races. But Carlson showed up, his long hair curling like a Viking's, covered with melting snowflakes, and proudly he escorted me to the new machine. It was a squarish blue Polaris with a heart-shaped sticker on the hood that read, "Polaris, I Love You!"

He had been up river on the trap line. That was why he hadn't written. Coming down to meet my plane, he had had to ride through water all the way and had gone through the ice once. The weather had been too warm and the river hadn't frozen solid.

Quickly he loaded my duffel onto a sled tied behind the Polaris. I kept my camera case, cushioning it on my knee as I straddled the seat behind him. The machines I was accustomed to had a metal handhold but there was none on the Polaris. Before I could find a grip, Carlson put the machine in gear and was roaring through the military base and up the dike to town. Miraculously I kept my balance. He was a good driver, but I was a bit nervous. My insurance company had written me a month earlier that my cameras weren't covered because I was "no longer in the United States"—and I was carrying well over $2,000 worth of gear.

Carlson's parents had moved up river to their trapping cabin, leaving Gail, his sixteen-year-old sister, to attend high school and mind the house. To surprise them she had taken money out of her summer earnings, bought paint, and completely redecorated the interior of their log cabin in light, cheerful blue.

Tonight she was at a basketball game, but she had left a good pork chop dinner simmering on the gas stove and a fire in the oil-barrel Yukon stove to keep the house warm for us. Over supper, Carlson asked where I was going to stay while we were in town.

"With you, if you'll have me."

He seemed surprised, but the Huntingtons, with whom I had stayed before, had trouble. Sidney's son Arnold had shot himself and lay near death and I didn't want to intrude. The Galena Lodge, the only village hotel, had burned to the ground a month before. Besides, whether I stayed with Carlson or not, people would talk when I went up on the trap line anyway, I reasoned. Carlson agreed and he was not displeased.

The next day was a lazy one. We began with beer for breakfast and then outfitted the expedition with $20 worth of fuel and spark plugs and $20 worth of groceries and no beer—the trap line was best run sober. From Anchorage I had brought a large ham, two frozen chickens, and a box of tangerines and apples. Now we rounded out the grocery list at Branum's general store.

Then I went to see Angela Huntington with whom I had lived the previous summer. It was a sad visit, for I liked Arnold, her seemingly easygoing, good-natured stepson, and it seemed there was no chance for him. He'd shot himself in the head. It was a cruel thing. He'd been a good hunter, but after he had gotten home from Vietnam he couldn't bear to point a gun at an animal, and what was an Indian if he couldn't hunt?

Angela's eyes were red with crying. We talked of small things. Sewing. Where was I staying, she finally asked? I told her, knowing it wouldn't go down well, but it upset her more than I'd expected. It wasn't a moral question now, but simply that she thought I was suicidal.

"Lots of luck," she said grimly.

Angela's reaction worried me. I knew she liked the Malemutes, but she shared the general opinion that Carlson was too wild. Also, a report had come from down river that three men

had fallen through the ice and one was dead. The only highway to the trap line, some twenty miles distant, was the river,
and that night I admitted to Carlson that I was worried about
our trip.

"I like you, Lael," he said simply. "I wouldn't do anything
to hurt you."

We set off next morning on Carlson's Polaris under a grayish-
white sky that looked like the bubbly top of a pot of sour
dough. About noon the sun turned it pink with a golden cast
and made the frosted willows sparkle along the riverbanks.
It was growing colder. The trail was smooth in the beginning,
but soon it ran out and we hit rough river ice that had worked,
broken, and refrozen. It was like running a mammoth strip of
sandpaper with jagged three- and four-foot ice chunks in place
of sand. Twice the sled we were pulling tipped over. Ahead I
sighted a puzzling hazy mist, but it didn't occur to me that it
was open water until we were already in trouble.

Suddenly the Polaris began to sink through the ice. I looked
to see which side Carlson jumped to and followed suit. There
was an ominous cracking as the whole surface threatened to
give way. The Polaris' motor was still running, but it had
settled to its nose in water and looked like a submarine.

Not understanding the working of the river, I was afraid we
would soon be over our heads. Actually, it was just an overflow.
The Yukon was deceptive, and even when it had been frozen
for a long time, it raced beneath the ice, bursting through to
form puddles and ponds. This overflow had pooled about three
feet deep to freeze again and we had simply gone through the
top crust. Not knowing what to do or where to step, I waited
to take orders. Carlson unhitched the sled and hauled it to
solid ice. Then he fished for the skis of the Polaris, tied a rope
to them, and, pulling with all our strength, we finally managed to haul the machine free. It fizzed and steamed but continued to run, and I looked at the "Polaris, I Love You!" decal
with new appreciation.

Carlson was wet to the knees and I had one soggy foot, but he said we'd make it. The temperature was only a little below freezing and we were half way to camp.

Cautiously we set off again, stopping often while he tested the dark, dangerous ice with his ax. Finally we were surrounded by floes on three sides. For fifteen minutes Carlson scouted for a frozen bridge. I waited by the Polaris, shivering violently, until I realized it was mostly fear that chilled me and I managed to get a grip on myself. Finally he returned, shaking his head. We could not get through to his folks' trapping cabin. Instead, we would go around the island in the middle of the river and then to the west bank of the Yukon where they had a fish camp. We could spend the night there and try to get to the trapping cabin from another direction next day.

Fifteen minutes later I spotted the fish camp nestling in birches under a bluff. I had been there in summer and loved it. Now it looked doubly welcome for I thought maybe my foot was freezing. We had forgotten to bring a door key, but we broke in easily and fired both the cook stove and the Yukon heater. Ice had formed on my sock but my foot was in good shape, and Carlson, who was much wetter than I, worked circulation back into his toes without complaint.

The cabin was as comfortable as the Malemute house in town, completely furnished with bedding, dishes, even a dining table and a library of leftover magazines and comic books (which doubled as toilet paper when we ran short). All that was needed to make the place livable was a pot of hot coffee and Carlson saw to that right away.

He said he was feeling "bum," but decided it was a hangover mostly, for we had celebrated our last night in civilization. After supper he brightened and we swapped all the jokes we had heard since last summer. Although his English was simplified, I was delighted to discover that he always understood the punch lines and had a fine sense of humor.

My host woke me about eight the next morning with a fresh
pot of coffee, and we breakfasted on chicken left over from
supper and bread I had baked the night before.

The first order of the day was to check the ice net he had
set a week earlier with the help of his brother. With a long stick
they had threaded a twenty-foot net under the ice where the
water eddied and anchored each end to forked sticks weighted
with rocks. The forks were supported by logs spanning a hole
at either end of the net. The Yukon had frozen around the
anchors, but Carlson quickly chopped them free with his ax
and ice chisel. Then, with his bare hands, he dipped a frozen
rope into the water, made it pliable, and tied it to one end of
the net. It was my job to play this line through the hole while
he pulled the net through another hole some twenty feet away.
If I lost my line, we would have a rough time getting the net
back, so I held on tight, intrigued by the ingenuity of this
Athabascan invention.

It was cold work but rewarding. Eventually we landed nine
large, flapping whitefish on the sled. They were dog food, but
we kept two for ourselves, just in case we weren't lucky enough
to shoot a moose. Carlson flipped them up on the cabin roof.
They were still lively and I was afraid they'd jump off, but the
cold finally immobilized them.

The morning was white, with traces of pink in the sky, and
on the point in the river the branches of the slender birches
curled with the weight of heavy frost until they looked like
giant ostrich plumes. I went to photograph them while Carlson
laid in a supply of firewood. Then, securing the fish to our sled
along with some chicken, half our ham, tangerines and a loaf
of new bread, we set out to visit his parents.

Again we headed up river, rounding the island on the far
end and turning back toward the east bank. There had been
a solid trail on our shore, but once around the island the ice
turned watery and black. Occasionally Carlson stopped the
Polaris and went ahead on foot to test it with his ax. Once he
sped the machine across an uncertain black span, ordering me

*Carlson Malemute taking whitefish from a winter net in the Yukon.*

to follow on foot if the bridge held. It was safe and finally we were in familiar territory, within sight of the trapping cabin. Sled dogs tethered along the bluff set up a howl and Mrs. Malemute came out of the cabin to see what the racket was about.

Carlson had crossed the river here only three days earlier, and it looked good so we shot across it unthinking. Then, without warning, the Polaris sank.

If there was a bottom where I landed I never found it. This I knew to be one of the deepest parts of the Yukon. Its depth had never been recorded, for it exceeded all the lead lines. And yet I was swimming there with no sensation of fear or cold. Swimming quite ably, too, despite my ungainly parka and oversized snowmobile boots, wondering what had happened to Carlson, who couldn't swim. Some ten feet distant I reached an ice ledge and hauled myself out, only to have it sink beneath me. I swam again, pulled myself out again—and again the ledge broke.

"Keep as flat as you can. Really flat!" Carlson ordered. He was somewhere behind me. I couldn't see him, but it was a relief to know he was still giving orders. I kept swimming, gained the ice a third time, and it held.

Still bereft of fear, I took stock. Carlson had stayed with the machine which rested on the illusive bottom of the floe with only two inches of the windshield above the water. By stretching he reached the hard ice and carefully pulled himself up. The whole surface shuddered but it held.

"Stay where you are," he warned. "Don't move."

Grimly I thought of the fish we'd caught that morning—they were all right as long as they stayed wet and kept flapping, but when they stopped, they froze like boards. I still wasn't frightened but as a matter of curiosity I wondered just how long we could last. It was about eight degrees below freezing.

Carlson's mother was peering over the bank in front of the cabin.

"Is that machine out of sight?" she called.

"It is," I answered.

"I thought so," she said sadly, and her diminutive silhouette seemed to slump.

My jeans were beginning to freeze. The camera, which I had been wearing under my parka, was probably ruined, I thought gloomily, and those bastards had refused to insure it. Then I grinned. No wonder they refused to insure it! Well, at least my down mittens were dry. I hadn't been wearing them for the swim but had them draped around my neck on a strap and they had floated on their furry backs without taking any water inside. I might turn into a solid pillar of ice but my hands would be saved.

Carlson, meanwhile, had managed to untie the sled and haul it to safety. After what seemed an interminable period he found a little ice bridge and cautiously picked his way toward shore, instructing me to follow at a safe distance. It grew more and more difficult to walk as my clothes froze but I made it, lumbering up the bank slowly to the warmth of the log trapping cabin.

Mrs. Malemute was a sensible woman of few words. She poured me a cup of tea, gave me a change of warm clothing, then turned her attention to her son. Jimmy, his father, had gone down river for groceries, she said. If the snowmobile was to be saved, it was up to Carlson, but she didn't say that. Carlson had paused only long enough to shed his frozen flight suit and, still in wet jeans, hurried to hitch up the dog team. Soon they were headed back to the river and I joined them after I got feeling back into my legs which had turned scarlet.

They had the team staked out and ready to pull when I got there, but every time Carlson tried to slide the Polaris out on two long poles, the ice broke under its weight. It looked pretty hopeless. His mother, who had been managing the dogs, went to help him wrestle the machine, but the ice gave way under her and she, too, fell in. When she retreated I tried the ice from another angle and took her place at Carlson's side. His face was grim and ashen. He'd been wet for about an hour, working barehanded in freezing clothing.

"I'm beginning to feel it," he admitted through clenched

teeth. But he was determined to salvage the machine. Finally in desperation he slid into the water beside it, dove for the skis and raised them. We got the haul line tied to them and finally got them pointed to solid ice. Then we gave a mighty pull. Mrs. Malemute pulled and the dog team mushed and out slid the gurgling Polaris. Half an hour later we had it up the bank and into the cabin. Carlson, still sheathed in ice, un-hitched the dogs. I heard him cough spasmodically and then throw up, but he was calm when he came in.

"Maybe you are bad luck," he said to me good-naturedly.

"If I was really bad luck, we would have gone in too far from camp to pull the Polaris out," I ventured. His mother nodded.

"If you had been a little further away, you never would have made it out alive," she told me later.

"But we could have built a fire . . . ," I argued.

"No, you would not have made it," she said with certainty.

We bailed and mopped the little trapping cabin all afternoon as the ice thawed and melted from the Polaris. Soggy as it was, it produced a spark at the first pull of the starter cord, and Carlson kept at it until well past midnight when it began to give a wet cough.

Next morning it started on the third pull. The family was always needling Carlson because he'd been to diesel mechanic's school in Chicago and they didn't consider him particularly mechanical, but this time he'd scored an unquestionable triumph. There were still some bugs in the Polaris to be worked out. When he first took the machine for a run, the throttle froze open and he had to drive it up the woodpile to stop, but generally it worked well.

Personally we had survived the venture with no damage. Mrs. Malemute said that when she was young it was considered bad luck for a woman to swim in the Yukon and this was the first time she had been in, but all she had gotten was wet. Carlson emerged without frostbite or a hint of a cold and was eating dry fish, rabbit stew, and pilot bread ravenously.

*The Malemute trapping cabin on the Yukon.*

I had lost my appetite, but it was only a mild case of delayed shock. I didn't develop so much as a sniffle and, what's more, my camera came through in functioning order. It must have been trapped in a pocket of air under my parka. When I took off the lens cap, it gave one little drip and that was it. It still worked in below-freezing weather so it couldn't have any water in it.

That afternoon Carlson took the Polaris for a long test run, partly to work the ice out and partly, I suspected, to get away from us women with whom he had been cooped up too long. I had known his mother only casually the summer before and had feared we might not get along in the isolation of the trap line. But having struggled with the Polaris and bailed side by side, it seemed we were old allies and I enjoyed being with her.

She was a stocky little trooper, strong despite numerous bouts with major surgery. There was youth in her carriage, too, rather like that of an insolent little boy. Her English was good, although she had been raised in the most traditional Athabascan manner and had not learned to speak English until her teens. She could recall going to school and not understanding a word the teacher spoke. Finally, when she was about thirteen, she had come to Galena where they were building the military base and gotten a job in a restaurant, first as a dishwasher and then as a cook, and she had picked up the language on her own.

She had been raised right here, on the site of this cabin, growing up the hard way. If they didn't shoot enough eider ducks in the fall, they had no mattresses in winter, she remembered, and had to sleep on their fur parkas. And dishes . . . she was so quick to wash them now because as a girl they had never had enough.

"I wish my mother was here to see all the extra things I have," she said wistfully. But her mother had died young. She had been orphaned, just as her husband, Jimmy, had been brought up lonesome.

When she spoke of Jimmy it was with considerable respect and love. He had become a heavy drinker in later years . . .

after he won the biggest dog-sled race in Alaska and then didn't win any more. She drank because it was the only way to get him to stop. He would have to stop to get her to quit. But it hadn't always been that way and it wasn't now. They had come up on the trap line this winter to celebrate their twenty-eighth wedding anniversary.

"We didn't want to drink and we knew if we stayed in town there'd be parties." Well, they had been up here for over a month and were obviously doing fine, with five good marten skins to show for their temperance. The skins would fetch about $30 apiece with the trader at Koyukuk.

"You can do pretty well living off the land," she observed with satisfaction. "Ten or twenty dollars goes a long way up here."

Carlson returned in the company of three more snowmobiles, a party from Ruby, east of us, heading to Galena. Ours was about the only occupied cabin en route and they welcomed an invitation for coffee and fish. When they left, Carlson took me with him to run the trap line. It was laid on a winding course through deep woods, with traps set to intercept heavily tracked areas.

To catch the marten, he explained, you built a little log shelter, setting a trap on the floor covered with dry grass and baited with a little dry fish.

"They look for a place to come in at night and get warm," he said. And the first one we found had done just that, digging a deep hole beside the trap that caught it in its last attempt to keep from freezing to death.

I studied the silk-furred little corpse with mixed feelings. Carlson was absolutely broke and I wanted him to be lucky in trapping, but the animal had died in agony. What about the "instant kill" traps, I asked? They were mentioned by the Animal Protection Institute of America in their "Grisly Death" advertising campaign against trapping, but the Athabascans had never heard of them. Finally I recalled with some relief that the marten, too, killed for a living and it killed quite without mercy.

*Carlson Malemute setting a trap for marten.*

We had caught two more marten but no mink for which traps were set in the old beaver houses. Still, it was a good day's work.

The trail was fair except for the thickly wooded edge of the lake and a frozen bog where I had to forsake my comfortable seat behind Carlson and help "pedal" the sled over the rough spots. Unfortunately, one of the back runners of the sled was broken, which left me only one to stand on—and I'd never pedaled a sled before. From watching, I knew you worked it the way a kid pedaled a scooter. I held my own on the first stretch and perhaps even fooled Carlson into thinking I had some experience, but on the run home I fell off, battering both knees. I was so exhausted that I thought of sleeping where I landed, but not wanting to work a hardship on the trapper, I struggled up and hobbled along until the going was smooth enough for me to ride again.

Jimmy was back with Carlson's youngest brother, Clyde, when we got in. We stopped to tell them of our mishaps and check trail conditions and then we set out for the fish camp, since the trapping cabin wasn't large enough for us all.

It was 3:30 and the sun was getting low when we turned down river just above the place we'd sunk the day before. Carlson stopped the machine and scouted ahead on foot. It was so dark when he returned I could barely make out his tracks with the anemic flashlight we carried, but he told me to head for the island while he zoomed the machine over. He figured that one man going at top speed had a fair chance of making it.

With considerable difficulty I found the way to the island and waited. I heard him try to start the machine but it didn't respond. I waited, growing cold and nervous. Finally I saw the light of Jimmy's machine approaching Carlson and, fifteen minutes later, the Polaris gave a welcome roar. Carlson headed it straight for the island at top speed and the ice held.

It was a marvelous night, clear and star-topped. Our cabin was cold, but the Yukon stove quickly made it comfortable and I cooked a huge supper of fried ham. After the meal Carlson read, slowly but stubbornly, through a pile of *Sports Illustrated* and men's magazines. I tried to start a book on a winter assault on Mount McKinley but the problems of the climbers were too close to what I had just encountered and I quickly gave up and fell asleep.

Dawn arrived under a frigid white haze. The sun poked up across the river about eleven, made a little U, and sank, discouraged, four hours later.

Carlson spent the day hauling wood. He picked up a nasty sliver in one finger but laid in a good supply of logs and I baked bread. His mother didn't have an oven in the trapping cabin and I wanted to take some loaves to her.

In the last light we had two visitors who were traveling from Ruby to Galena to buy a new snowmobile and a load of soda pop. Carlson offered them tea and "strips" (dried salmon) but didn't introduce me although they looked me over curiously. There were no real problems with overflows up river, they reported, but the wolves were out. They'd just come down river with a pack of them running right alongside, and Carlson wished the travelers luck.

Outside the temperature was dropping as rapidly as the sun had. The foam rubber inside of the seat of the Polaris had frozen solid and we brought the machine into the cabin to try and thaw it out.

Next morning it was 15° below zero and I awoke to find our fire gone out. I had established myself as a mere amateur fire builder so Carlson got it going and made coffee, to boot. A check of the fish net produced seven fat whitefish which we packed on the sled to take to the family. Once, en route to the trapping cabin, the Polaris spun completely around on the glare ice but there was no problem with overflows that morning. The river had finally settled down.

My knees got so cold riding that they grew numb and I wanted to wear my heavy down pants that day; Carlson wisely talked me out of it. I must learn to stave off the cold with my head as well as clothing. This was only the beginning of a cold spell and I had to get used to it or no amount of clothing would help when it really got bitter. On the other side of the river it was 28° below because the sun didn't hit there until late afternoon.

Clyde and Jimmy arrived at the trapping cabin about the same time we did, back from chasing a moose down river. The wolves were definitely after the moose, they reported, which made the game nervous.

Jimmy took his dog team for a workout and I enjoyed watching the former champ hook up. Most of his dogs were too old for racing but they were eager to hit the trail and left at a fast clip. Carlson and Clyde ran the trap line on the machine. Jimmy met them at the far end and they came home with two marten.

My assignment from here on in would be to stay home, as women were supposed to, and keep Mrs. Malemute company. She was sewing a pair of slippers and assigned me to embroider a flowery pair of mooseskin mittens. It was hard work as the hide was tough, but I enjoyed seeing the flowers grow and the day went fast. She didn't talk much but she was good company and we had a radio. Harry Truman was dying, it told us, and NASA was preparing for another moon shot.

When Carlson and I returned to fish camp that night the family gave us one of their dogs, Skooks, as company and a watchdog. She was a sorry-looking yellow animal, but willing and with the sharpest ears of any dog in their kennel. We also took along an old Coleman lantern that Carlson hoped to repair. We were getting tired of reading by our kerosene lamp, but the Coleman proved useless and we had to go back to it. By now I was halfway up McKinley (*McKinley at 40 Below* by Art Davidson) and Carlson was into something by Harold Robbins.

Jimmy Malemute had been complaining of a toothache and

*Jimmy Malemute and his wife hitching up the dog team.*

Carlson told him a dentist was visiting Galena. After some discussion the men decided to go back to town for the day to see about the tooth and pick up supplies.

First, Jimmy and his wife went to check the rabbit snares she had set on the island and then she took me on the little four-trap line she had around the cabin. She was a clever trapper and it tickled her that she could sometimes get as many pelts on her miniature line as the men did on the big run.

Carlson worried that his father would not want to ride to Galena with him because he drove so fast. Jimmy's machine was older and slower than the Polaris and he preferred it, but now he delighted Carlson by agreeing to ride with him. They gave Clyde Jimmy's machine and set off in high spirits.

Mrs. Malemute talked that day about raising her children. There had been seven but they had lost two daughters in the fire that destroyed their home when Carlson was little. She told of building the fish camp with the help of Carlson and Anthony when the boys were still small and Jimmy was away working in a cannery. She had kept Carlson out of school until he was nine and Anthony until he was seven because she thought it important that they learn the ways of the woods.

No wonder Carlson was a slow reader, but how come he didn't speak Athabascan, I wondered. He had told me he could say only "the good words."

In Athabascan he had stuttered, she explained. They couldn't break him of it, and when they discovered he had no stutter in English, they let him learn that instead.

Then, without embarrassment, she spoke about the family jail terms. While Jimmy had served his time, she had learned to run the snowmobile and had a good winter traveling the country with a woman friend her own age.

Jimmy had gone to jail for Carlson. Carlson had been home on leave from the Army at the time and "borrowed" some gasoline that hadn't been returned. They hadn't wanted to mess up his Army record so his father served the time. Then Carlson, in turn, served some time for a younger brother. There had been no thought of lawyers or of trying to beat the charges. The law in this country was something that just caught up with you eventually, like tuberculosis or the flu.

We dined on tender fresh-snared rabbit while the little house puppy growled and snapped at another luckless bunny that was waiting to be dressed.

"They're bringing back a hundred pounds of rocks," Mrs. Malemute mused.

"They are?" I asked incredulously.

"I don't know why. We have plenty of them here."

"They're bringing a hundred pounds of rocks? Jimmy and Carlson? From Galena?"

"No—the men from the moon," she laughed, relieved that it wasn't her lack of English that had fouled us up.

She expected our men for supper, but I was dubious.

"When Jimmy Malemute says he'll do something, he'll do it," she declared.

"Maybe Jimmy will but I'm not so sure Carlson won't want to stop in Hobo's Bar," I admitted.

"He won't stop there because of you," she said gently. "They'd be at him about it. He'd probably have to fight."

I was stunned. I had forgotten I was white because the family never made me feel any different. Now I wondered if they'd all have to fight because they'd taken me on as a guest, and I was doubly grateful for the kindness she was showing me.

As she predicted, the men arrived at 6:30, proud of having made good time. The dentist had left before they arrived but they had picked up some needed supplies. Mrs. Malemute went through the box quite pleased but asked why they had forgotten one staple. The men looked sheepish. The general store wouldn't give them any credit.

"He says, pay once a month," Carlson reported. "But them martens, they don't pay once a month."

When Carlson suggested I wear my down pants for the trek back to fish camp, I knew it must have gotten colder. He had frozen the inside of his nose coming up river and Jimmy's was chapped and bleeding. But we got home in good shape with

Skooks galloping along beside us. The northern lights played over the high bluff on the west bank and their colors were spectacular.

The sun rose red, a sure sign of a storm in my experience, but Carlson said there'd be no storm. He spent the morning reading while the weather blandly proved him right, and I cooked sour-dough bread and beans for lunch. Malemute declared the beans delicious, but we both decided soon after that they were not ideal camp fare for such a well-chinked cabin on a cold day.

In the afternoon we went out to find a birch tree we could use for making a basket sled. Five years earlier Carlson had built the one we now used. It was still strong but the missing back runner made it tippy and it was beginning to wear out.

First we headed up river where we climbed the face of an enormous bluff, not unlike what I had been reading about in the Mount McKinley book. My cumbersome snowmobile boots were a definite handicap and so was Skooks, who kept trying to get in my tracks before I made them. But by locating some fallen birch that had frozen to the bluff, I managed to pull myself up. On top was a good stand of birch and Carlson inspected it much as I would fabric for a new dress.

"I want a perfect one," he announced after he had turned down a dozen trees that looked perfectly all right to me. He lingered for some time by an unusually straight birch which was larger than the rest, but finally he shook his head. It had too many knots. Disappointed, we slid down the bluff and headed down river in back of the fish camp. The woods were much warmer than the open space of the river and overhead was an iridescent mixture of yellow, pink, and blue, as if someone had turned a crystal bowl over our section of the world. Slowly the clouds drifted into a mauve-blue layer and we were honored by a nearly full moon with a halo of pink.

Carlson chopped down one tree, only to find it rotten inside, but his second choice was sounder.

"It's too small, which means we'll have to have another one

for the runners, but it's very good wood," he said, so we hauled it home and let it season.

The thermometer registered only 15° below, still warm by Yukon standards but I couldn't convince my body. It was a new kind of damp cold that settled in your boots and ate away at you, and it put the Yukon in a deep freeze. Carlson had to chop through more than a foot of ice for the next hauling of the fish net.

We had five fish. Four were whitefish and the fifth, a lush, nearly put me in shock when I went to untangle it from the net. It looked like a cross between an eel and a catfish and was two feet long. I was afraid of it and Carlson said I had a right to be. It had sharp teeth and a vicious temperament.

Carlson found another birch for his sled and also took time out to show me how to make a rabbit snare. He used a little noose of soft picture wire hung from a limb that he slanted over the rabbit's path. Twigs and branches were planted either side of the path to keep the animal from detouring, but they had to be dry and uninteresting, he warned, or the rabbit would stop to eat them.

It was hard to find any tracks on which to set a snare around our camp. There had been fresh signs when we got there, but studying them later Carlson decided something—probably a marten—had eaten our rabbit. There wasn't nearly as much game on our side of the river as there was around the trapping cabin, anyway. Perhaps it was too close to the military base and town.

Jimmy and Clyde stopped for coffee about noon after chasing a moose all morning, and we took off on the Polaris when they left, going to the head of the island and following a slough to its interior. It was an exhilarating trip—roaring along, breaking fresh trail over the unmarred snow. The island willows turned a rich, rusty shade under a plum and blue sky but there were no new signs of moose. By the time we got to the trapping cabin, Carlson's mustache and hair were pure white with frost and he had frozen an ear. He took the brunt of the weather because the windshield of the Polaris was just a token

*A rabbit snare on the trap line.*

one and didn't stop the wind when he drove standing up, as he usually did.

Two travelers stopped en route to Galena. They had gone up to Ruby over the weekend for a wedding. One of them, John, from the Galena RurAL-CAP office, swore his traveling companion had intended to get married too . . . to make it a double service . . . but when they had arrived he found his girl's door locked and learned she had gone to Fairbanks. Now he was "lovesick."

"Lovesick" looked embarrassed and didn't say anything. He was wearing old mukluks crammed inside snowmobile boots and his feet were almost frozen. Carlson tried to talk him into giving his feet a little more room for circulation, but he didn't seem to understand and left as miserable as he had arrived.

It was a strike-out day. The men spent most of it being outrun by the moose and all the traps on the line were empty. Finally at dusk, Carlson heard a willow grouse chuckling down by the river and managed to shoot it in the dark.

Going back to the fish camp Skooks was reluctant for the first time. Her hair was short and I wondered if her feet were cold. Maybe we should let her ride, I suggested, thinking she might sit on the sled. Obligingly Carlson stopped the machine, scooped her up, and handed her to me to hold. She was a big dog and I had trouble enough keeping my own balance, but I managed her until we went over the island and the slapping willows made her nervous. Finally she jumped off and painfully followed us the rest of the way.

I didn't really like that dog and, to my surprise, I found out Carlson didn't like her either. Her hair was so short she seemed to have been designed for Africa. Every time we looked at her we felt sorry for her, but if we gave her a kind word or a pat she stuck to us like a dirty shirt. Still, she was a good watchdog and the wolves were ganging up.

Our food supplies were getting low. We had been eating the whitefish we had caught for the dogs, and willow grouse was a welcome departure. We made a fine supper on it and it put us in an expansive mood. I spoke of some of the things Carlson's mother had been telling me about living in the woods.

"If you take care of the wood and water, the food will take care of itself," she philosophized.

Carlson said his brother Clyde was getting a really good chance to learn from his father. He was just old enough to drop out of school and the old man wanted to teach him everything about trapping.

"It is a good thing," he decided. "He didn't do that with the rest of us. I wish I had had that chance."

With pride he recalled how his father had trained their dogs to win the North American racing championship in 1959. How he had brought home presents for the family and how the future had looked bright. But Jimmy had tried without success to buy some of the dogs he had borrowed for that race. One of the owners who refused to sell let the animals starve the following summer.

"He kept trying to win again but always with second-rate dogs. It broke his heart. Still he kept trying. Last year he trained the team up good for Anthony, but Anthony got drunk that race and the team got all turned around . . ."

He didn't think Jimmy would have any drinking problem if he had a good team to train, but most of his dogs would soon be too old to run. They had some good-looking pups now. He had some of his own, but he didn't really know enough about training. It would take time, too. At least three years to train them up.

We talked, also, about the Indochina war. Carlson had seen enough bloodshed, he said. Seen two of his buddies blown up while they were guarding an ammunition depot in Vietnam. But I noticed that Carlson had a new scar since I had seen him in the summer—a jagged five-inch gash over the stomach.

"Some guy made it with a broken beer bottle," he admitted. But he had almost killed the man who gave it to him.

"If you're so sick of bloodshed, why that?" I asked.

He shrugged. Barroom brawls were a way of life here.

The Malemutes were the finest of cabin builders, but their efforts fell woefully short in outhouse construction and I had to come to grips with the fact next morning. It was 30° below zero with a wind prevailing on the side of the facility where the slats were missing. Even a brief visit was a sure way to wake up in a hurry.

To add to my misery, Carlson and I were having a pitched battle over how to cook sour-dough hotcakes. He generally enjoyed my cooking but claimed my philosophy on sour doughs was all wrong. I liked small, thin pancakes—silver-dollar size, as they were described on discriminating menus. But he liked them the size of soup plates, and in defense of his position he captured my sour-dough pot that morning. Breakfast was a strained truce and we were both glad to head for his folks' cabin.

The cold made the Polaris cranky, and while Carlson tinkered with it, Skooks got so miserable that she lay down on the river ice on her back waving all four cold feet in the air. I took pity on her and carried her until we got to the island where she bounced off on her own accord and sprinted for her nest of straw by the trapping cabin. It was 40° below over there.

The men tracked moose unsuccessfully while Mrs. Malemute and I sewed the day away. She made a delicious rabbit stew, and when I ladled up the head by accident, Carlson congratulated me and told me it was the best part.

"Anthony and I always used to fight over the head when we were little," he added as I looked queasily at my prize. To my surprise, though, it was rich and tasty.

All the snares and traps were empty. Too cold for the animals to travel today, Mrs. Malemute said. Even Skooks wouldn't follow us home.

The moon was full and almost as bright as morning, and Carlson stopped the Polaris after we rounded the island to show me how strange it looked up river. Under the yellow gleam, the whole Yukon seemed wet again, shimmering off into a shadowy infinity of hills.

Jimmy and Clyde brought up another stove for us from Old Louden, and when we got back to camp we installed it in place of the big Yukon stove. This was an oil-drum conversion, too, but of a slightly better design and it worked more efficiently than the original. If only we could pipe some of that heat to the outhouse . . . but that was too much to ask.

Carlson was feeling spooky. There were wolves nearby that night—he could feel it. And after a while I sensed it too. It wasn't frightening, but just something you knew for sure and it made you restless. Like an animal, I thought: "I'm beginning to think like an animal. And I enjoy it. Enjoy the sharpening of my senses.

"Nonsense," I told myself. "Fall asleep!"

But Carlson prowled around long after I had settled down.

Through bursts of static on our battered transistor radio we learned that President Nixon had ordered the bombing of Hanoi and it put a heavy pall on the next day. Carlson followed the war news carefully and seemed to know the territory well, but both of us were at a loss to analyze this move.

I had been growing increasingly depressed, anyway, for there were times when I decided Carlson probably hated me. My inexperience in this kind of living was a real hindrance to him. I wasn't conditioned to take the long periods of sustained cold that he could. I lacked skill in untangling fish from the net, couldn't drive the snowmobile, pedal a sled, or build a decent fire. In short, I was dependent on him for my survival, and when I realized that he sometimes shortened a hunt or a wood-gathering excursion to keep me from freezing, I felt very guilty.

Yet I loved this life . . . the beauty of the country, the excitement of living on the edge, in danger . . . and staying alive. My admiration of Carlson continued to grow and I enjoyed the closeness of my relationship with the family.

But my time on the Yukon and in Alaska was getting short.

I was scheduled to go back to work in Los Angeles and I dreaded it. Now news of the outside world so thoroughly demoralized me that I couldn't eat breakfast, which was a real handicap. It was idiocy to start a day's work at 30° below zero on an empty stomach.

There was only six inches of ice to chop from the fish-net anchors this time but we hauled the net in for good. The mesh was getting dirty enough for the fish to spot it, and returns were decreasing. All we had was four fish that morning, two of them snarling lush that absolutely refused to die.

Crossing the island to the trapping cabin I got hit in the face by a large willow branch and it hurt so much I was surprised to find my nose wasn't broken. Carlson said nothing, but on the return trip he cut every willow within a quarter of a mile of the trail and it occurred to me perhaps he didn't hate me after all.

Settling in for a day of sewing with Mrs. Malemute also improved my spirits. I had never cared much for female companionship, but in this harsh, isolated country it was a comfort.

Jimmy had sighted a moose that morning but by the time he got his gun unstrapped from the sled behind the snowmobile, the animal had gone. Now the men went after it. Mrs. Malemute cooked one of the lush. I didn't care as much for it as for whitefish, though I did manage to eat a helping. There was an old Indian story about the lush head, she said. Each different bone in it represented something—a fish hook, a knife, and so on. The head was good eating, too, but there I drew the line. I couldn't stand the evil grin of that fish.

"I noticed someone ate the rabbit head yesterday," she observed.

"Yes. I did. Carlson said it was the best part."

She looked amused

"It is good. I always eat it. But Carlson hasn't eaten one since he was a little boy," she smiled.

It turned out that even she thought Carlson was unruly, and she worried about him—the way he drank and couldn't settle into anything and never saved any money.

"We couldn't believe he had bought that snow machine. I

asked him in the middle of the summer if he had saved anything and he hadn't. Had just gone through a thousand-dollar
check, drinking and chartering airplanes. Then this fall when
he said he'd bought it, we didn't believe him. He had had them
keep it so he wouldn't use it until it snowed and when he
showed it to us we were really surprised."

Doggedly I was still plugging away at the mooseskin mittens
and the design was turning out well.

"Who are they for?" I asked her.

"Carlson," she said. "It will give him something to remember
you by when you go."


Back at fish camp Carlson began making a trail with the
Polaris up the bluff behind the cabin so his father could drive
the dog team home that way if the river was bad. They were
all going to move back to town for the Christmas holidays, but
with the dogs and machines the exodus took a lot of planning.
I went with him for the final trail run and he revved the Polaris up to about fifty miles an hour and took off straight up
the hill. Not realizing how long and steep the trail was, I almost pedaled off the bottom of my boot and finally I dropped
off, hollering I'd rather walk. Later we found fresh rabbit tracks
and set some elaborate snares, but nothing much moved and
we were stuck with whitefish three meals a day. The moose
which had been so fat a week ago were now skin and bones
from running from the wolves and from us.

"But I'd like a bone anyway," Mrs. Malemute said wistfully
as we sat for whitefish fried in cornmeal. Then, ruefully, she
reminded Jimmy of last season when he'd had a clear shot at a
moose but decided to wait "for a fat one."

"We waited all winter," she chuckled. "But I'd sure hate to
go back to town and live off the store this year."

That day I volunteered to check some of her snares on the
island and found them empty. So were her four traps, although
a marten was just about to enter one of her little log houses
when she crept up on him.

"There was a squirrel chattering at him like a machine," she reported. "Told him people who enter that house, they never come back. The squirrel told him the facts."

Jimmy came in still laughing from an encounter he had had with a "cross" (black and dark gray) fox. The animal had never seen a snowmobile before and it just sat down and looked at it until he almost ran over it. He shot it, nicking it in the ear but his gun sight was off. Still no moose, either, although Carlson and Clyde brought in a beautiful marten.

Jimmy was in a storytelling mood and we lingered to hear how he had grown up in the woods, staying out there alone with his father, trapping and living off the land, until the old man died. Out there in the quiet of the woods, music meant a lot, he recalled. He had played the fiddle. He tried to get his sons interested in something like that but today it was all tapes and radio.

We went back to fish camp to disguise whitefish in Spanish rice, and after the meal I decided to go for a walk. Carlson, who was reading, told me to stay close to the cabin.

"The same thing that's been eating our rabbits might just as well eat you," he warned, but I didn't take him seriously.

The woods turned into a wonderful winter palace when the moon played through the arches of the white birch. It was still thirty below but I didn't mind the cold any more. I sought it, relished it, for it made me feel vital. This was my last night to sleep by the river and I wanted to remember it . . . to freeze it into my memory exactly as it was.

Carlson was pacing nervously around the cabin when I got back and I realized he hadn't been joking about the danger of the dark wood. We had a late cup of coffee and talked about the giant pizza I would make for us when we got back to Galena and of maybe having a fling at Hobo's Bar to make up for our temperance. We pretended we had a lot to look forward to and it was the first time, I think, that we'd ever lied to each other.

The radio was playing "Good-Time Charlie's Got the Blues."

"I guess that's my song," I said finally.

"I will never forget all our mishaps," Carlson said. "Usually I am out alone. You have spoiled me. Now it will be lonesome."

The next day was officially the first day of winter, which we found amusing. It was 30° below, as usual, and growing colder. There were still no rabbits in our snares but a yellow-orange sun winked at us as we headed across the island.

Mrs. Malemute said she felt rotten from eating so much fish. The men continued to play hide and seek with the moose and for the first time I heard Jimmy complain about the cold. He had come upon a cow moose and her calf in the slough but his gun had frozen.

"Damn it," Mrs. Malemute said.

"Damn it," I echoed.

Finally, with my stomach, I was beginning to understand the balance of nature. We were hungry, the moose were hungry, and I guess the wolves were the hungriest of all.

At 4:30 in the afternoon, Carlson and I prepared for the twenty-mile run back to Galena. The Malemutes were skeptical about my snowmobile boots, worried I might freeze my feet. I worried more about my nose, but there was little that could be done in either case.

Good-bys were tentative. The Malemutes might or might not make it back to Galena before my plane left. It depended on whether they got a moose.

"Come back with us when you get tired of the big city," Mrs. Malemute said.

It was dark when we set off except for a sliver of gray-pink on the horizon. Despite the 40-degree below zero temperature, I felt the Polaris twist into soft ice a little below where we had sunk on the first trip to the trapping cabin. Carlson didn't say anything at the time, just gunned the machine, and incredibly we escaped another overflow.

Twenty minutes out he stopped the machine, unstrapped his gun from the sled, and shoved it into a handy position under the Polaris hood.

"Why?"

"See the tracks?"

Five giant wolves were ranging just ahead of us in pursuit of a moose. Carlson turned down Bessie Slough and the wooded banks seemed to crowd us on both sides. Anxiously I watched the tracks. The Polaris hit a vaulted dome of ice and turned completely around. We had to push the machine. It kept slipping and making 180-degree turns. Finally we walked it over the hump. The wolf tracks stopped abruptly and detoured up the wooded bank. The pack had its moose at last, and they wouldn't threaten us any more.

Finally we were back on the broad river among the sandpaper ice chunks. I was cold all over. My left foot ached and I had to keep working my hands to find feeling in them. Both knees were in bad shape but I kept telling myself it was mental. I suspected the end of my nose was slightly frostbitten and I was right, but spotting a distant light from the military base outside of town made me feel warmer.

Carlson stopped from time to time to ask how I was doing and rub circulation back into his hands. His hair was all white again and I worried that his ears might freeze, but we were making good time.

In the sky over a high bluff, all at once, appeared a huge yellow man-in-the-moon face with a ruby in one eye. I blinked and looked again. The red light on the radio tower at the Campion Air Force base lined up perfectly to provide the moon with a monocle.

Then suddenly we could see the lights of Galena and lighted Christmas decorations. We raced across the river, up the familiar bank, and on to the main street where we had to stop for a car. It was a terrible shock. For two weeks the only human traces we had seen had been ours, and now all this . . .

But I felt warmer and it occurred to me that I was going to survive. I *had* survived out there where the living was roughest. Now I was being carried back to civilization . . . for whatever that was worth.

And we did have the fling—Carlson and I—and the pizza; and we kept avoiding any mention of the future until Carlson

*Author Lael Morgan overseeing a Yukon stove in a trapping cabin on the Yukon.*

finally said, "This is really it," and piled my duffel bag back on the sled and me on the Polaris and we hurried to a waiting jet plane.

He was going to continue to try and make a living off the land, he said, because it was a good way to live . . . although he intended to get all-out drunk for a few days and maybe even until beaver season in the spring. And we talked about sled dogs and joked with friends, who pretended that Carlson was going to get on that plane for Anchorage and then to New York City and that I was going to stay in Galena. But finally it was time.

Numbly I boarded the jet and it lifted and turned, and from behind the hills along the Yukon the moon rose, graceful and golden, and I thought about how it would glimmer on the sandpaper ice somewhere, thousands of feet below me. And I wished I could run it all again—run it even a little scared in the track of the wolves—with Carlson. For even with the over-flows and nothing but fish for supper when the snares hung empty, it was the best, the freshest, the most exhilarating life I'd ever known.

# Index

Adak, 151
*Aangus* (berries), 164
Admiralty Islands, 239, 243
AEC. *See* Atomic Energy Commission (AEC)
Ahgook, Charlie, 43
Ahgook, Elizabeth (Betty), 36, 37
Ahgook, Freddy, 27
Ahgook, Jack, 24
Ahgook, Lela, 8, 23, 38, 40–41
Ahgook, Minnie, 37
Ahgook, Nancy, 8
Ahgook, Noah, 41
Ahgook, Richard, 20
Ahgook, Robert, 18–19, 22, 25, 27
Akiak (village), 197
Alaska (*see also* specific organizations, people, places): alcoholism, ix, xxii (*see also* Alcoholism); culture and history, xv–xvi, 280–81 (*see also* specific aspects, people, places); health conditions, vii, xi (*see also* Disease; Health conditions); land claims and settlements, ix, x, xi, xii (*see also* Land claims and settlements); languages, xv, xvii (*see also* Languages); legends, xv (*see also* Legends); oil, x, xxv, 24–25; people, v–xiii, xv (*see also* Eskimos; Indians; specific people, places); population, xviii; purchase of, xxi–xxii; Statehood Act, xxv; subsistence hunting and fishing, v, vi, 280–316 (*see also* Fish[ing]; Hunting); and welfare programs, 280–81 (*see also* Welfare programs)
Alaska, University of, 208
Alaska Federation of Natives (AFN), xxvi, 132, 199, 200, 275
Alaska Native Brotherhood (ANB), 240, 252, 256, 258, 261, 268, 270; Hall (Angoon), 252, 268–69
Alcoholism (drinking, drunkenness), ix, xxii; Angoon Tlingits, 279; Atkans, 182–85; Bethel, 198, 200–37; Galena, 113–15, 135, 140; Point Hope, 46
*Aleutian Boy* (Oliver), 158
Aleut League, 156, 185–86, 187, 193, 194
Aleuts (Aleutians), vii, x, xvii, xviii, xxi, 147–95
Alexander, Chief, xxiii–xxiv
Alexander Lake, 103
Anaktuvuk Pass, settlement and Eskimo people of, xii, 1–44
Anchorage, v, vi
Anderson, Andy, 41
Anderson, Squeaky, 159
Anderson, Tom, 202, 203–4, 206, 210–12, 224, 228, 230
Andrew, Helen, 222
Angoon Tlingits, 239–79
Animal Protection Institute of America, 295